CONTENTS

INTRODUCTION

A note from the authors

Our work on *Solutions* began in the spring of 2005 with a research trip. We travelled from city to city with colleagues from Oxford University Press, visiting schools, watching lessons and talking to teachers and students. The information we gathered on that trip, and many subsequent trips across Central and Eastern Europe, gave us valuable insights into what secondary students and teachers want from a new book. These became our guiding principles while writing *Solutions*. Most people we spoke to asked for:

- a clear focus on exam topics and tasks
- easy-to-follow lessons which always have a clear outcome
- plenty of support for speaking and writing
- plenty of extra practice material

In response, we designed a book which has a crystal-clear structure: one lesson in the book = one lesson in the classroom. We included twenty pages of extra vocabulary and grammar practice within the Student's Book itself to provide more flexibility. We included ten specific lessons to prepare students for the school-leaving exam, and ensured that the book as a whole corresponds to the syllabus topics required in this exam. And we recognised the difficulties that students naturally have with speaking and writing, and therefore ensured that these activities are always well prepared and well supported. Achievable activities are essential for motivation!

Our research trips also taught us that no two schools or classes are identical. That is why *Solutions* is designed to be flexible. There are five levels (Elementary, Pre-intermediate, Intermediate, Upper-intermediate, Advanced) so that you can choose the one which best fit your students' needs.

Solutions has benefited from collaboration with teachers with extensive experience of teaching 14–19 year olds and of preparing students for their school-leaving exam. We would like to thank Anita Omelańczuck and Meredith Levy for sharing their expertise in writing the procedural notes in the Teacher's Book. Cultural and language notes as well as the photocopiable supplements in the Teacher's Book were provided by Caroline Krantz.

We are confident that *Solutions* will be easy to use, both for students and for teachers. We hope it will also be interesting, engaging and stimulating!

Tim Falla and Paul A Davies

The components of the course

The Student's Book with MultiROM

The Student's Book contains:

- 10 topic-based units, each covering 7 lessons
- 5 *Language Review/Skills Round-up* sections, providing a language test of the previous two units and a cumulative skills-based review
- 10 *Get ready for your exam* lessons providing typical tasks and preparation for the students' final exam
- 10 *Vocabulary Builders* with practice and extension options
- 10 *Grammar Builders* containing grammar reference and further exercises
- tip boxes throughout giving advice on specific skills and how best to approach different task types in all four main skills

You will find more details on pages 5–7 in the section 'A tour of the Student's Book'.

Two class audio CDs

The two audio CDs contain all the listening material from the Student's Book.

The Workbook

The Workbook mirrors and reinforces the content of the Student's Book. It offers:

- further practice, lesson-by-lesson of the material taught in class
- additional exam tasks with support for students and teachers
- *Challenge!* exercises to stretch stronger students
- writing guides to provide a clear structural framework for writing tasks
- regular *Self-checks* with *Can do* statements to promote conscious learner development
- cumulative reviews to develop students' awareness of their progress
- a *Functions Bank* and *Writing Bank* for reference
- an irregular verbs list
- a *Wordlist* which contains the vocabulary activated in the Student's Book units

Procedural notes, transcripts and keys for the Workbook can be found on the *Solutions* Teacher's Website at www.oup.com/elt/teacher/solutions.

The MultiROM

The MultiROM is an interactive self-study tool that has been designed to give guidance, practice, support and consolidation of the language and skills taught in the Student's Book. The MultiROM is divided into units and lessons corresponding with those of the Student's Book.

- every grammar lesson in the book is extensively practised and is accompanied by a simple explanation
- all target vocabulary is consolidated with crossword, word search, and gap-fill activities
- one exam-type listening activity per unit is included so that students are able to practise listening at their own pace
- speaking and writing sections help students improve these skills outside of the classroom
- an audio CD element is included, with all the exam listening tasks from the Workbook, which can be played on a CD player

The Teacher's Book

The Teacher's Book gives full procedural notes for the whole course, including ideas for tackling mixed ability teaching. In addition, it offers:

- optional activities throughout for greater flexibility
- structured speaking tasks to get students talking confidently
- useful tips and strategies to improve students' exam technique
- a teacher's guide to dyslexia in the classroom
- 20 photocopiable pages to recycle and activate the language of each unit in a fun, communicative context

Tests

A separate resource CD contains:

- unit tests
- mid-year and end-of-year progress tests
- short tests

Solutions

Pre-Intermediate Teacher's Book

Anita Omelańczuk, Caroline Krantz
Tim Falla, Paul A Davies

OXFORD
UNIVERSITY PRESS

OXFORD
UNIVERSITY PRESS

Great Clarendon Street, Oxford OX2 6DP

Oxford University Press is a department of the University of Oxford.
It furthers the University's objective of excellence in research, scholarship,
and education by publishing worldwide in

Oxford New York

Auckland Cape Town Dar es Salaam Hong Kong Karachi
Kuala Lumpur Madrid Melbourne Mexico City Nairobi
New Delhi Shanghai Taipei Toronto

With offices in

Argentina Austria Brazil Chile Czech Republic France Greece
Guatemala Hungary Italy Japan Poland Portugal Singapore
South Korea Switzerland Thailand Turkey Ukraine Vietnam

OXFORD and OXFORD ENGLISH are registered trade marks of
Oxford University Press in the UK and in certain other countries

ISBN: 978 0 19 455177 9

Printed in China

ACKNOWLEDGEMENTS

*The publisher and authors are very grateful to the many teachers and students who
read and piloted the materials, and provided invaluable feedback. With special thanks
to:* Kati Elekes, Hana Musílková, Zsuzsanna Nyirő, Eva Paulerová, Zoltán
Rézmüves, Ela Rudniak, Dagmar Škorpíková

*The publisher and authors would like to extend their special thanks to Meredith Levy,
for the part she played in developing the material.*

The publisher and the authors would like to thank the author of Dyslexia: a guide for
teachers: Katarzyna Bogdanowicz

Illustrations by: Jean-Luc Guèrin/Agent 002 p128; Rebecca Halls p137; David
Oakley/Arnos Design Ltd p125; Dylan Teague p124

The publisher would like to thank the following for their permission to use photographs:
Empics p127 (NG Han Guan/AP)

This book is printed on paper from certified and well-managed sources.

Solutions and the exam

Solutions Pre-Intermediate is intended to bring students up to a B1 level. Typical exam requirements are reflected throughout the course in the choice of topics, task-types, texts and grammar structures. In addition to this, *Solutions* offers a comprehensive range of exam support:

Student's Book

The Student's Book includes ten exam-specific lessons designed to familiarise students with the task-types and requirements of their final exam. The lessons provide strategies and exam techniques as well as the language needed for students to be able to tackle exam tasks with confidence.

Workbook

The Workbook provides further practice for both the oral and the written exam. Work in class can be followed up with Workbook tasks done as homework.
The listening material for the Workbook listening tasks is available on the MultiROM.

Teacher's Book

The exam lessons in the Student's Book are accompanied by full procedural notes with advice and tips for exam preparation.

A tour of the Student's Book

There are ten units in the Student's Book. Each unit has seven lessons (A–G). Each lesson provides material for one classroom lesson of approximately 45 minutes.

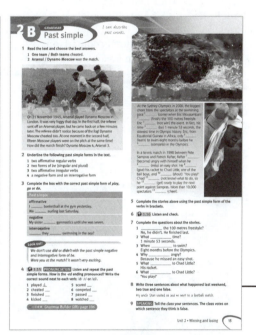

Lesson A – Vocabulary and listening

* The unit menu states the main language and skills to be taught.
* Every lesson has an explicit learning objective, beginning 'I can ...'.
* Lesson A introduces the topic of the unit, presents the main vocabulary set, and practises it through listening and other activities.
* This lesson links to the *Vocabulary Builder* at the back of the book, which provides extra practice and extension.

Lesson B – Grammar

* Lesson B presents and practises the first main grammar point of the unit.
* The new language is presented in a short text or other meaningful context.
* There are clear grammar tables.
* *Look out!* boxes appear wherever necessary and help students to avoid common errors.
* This lesson links to the *Grammar Builder* at the back of the book which provides extra practice and grammar reference.

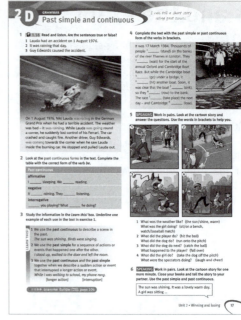

Lesson C – Culture

- Lesson C has a reading text which provides cultural information about Britain, the USA or other English-speaking countries.
- Students are encouraged to make cultural comparisons.
- New vocabulary is clearly presented in boxes wherever it is needed.

Lesson D – Grammar

- Lesson D presents and practises the second main grammar point of the unit.
- The grammar presentation is interactive: students often have to complete tables and rules, helping them focus on the structures.
- *Learn this!* boxes present key information in a clear and concise form.
- This lesson links to the *Grammar Builder* at the back of the book which provides extra practice and grammar reference notes.
- A final speaking activity allows students to personalise the new language.

Lesson E – Reading

- Lesson E contains the main reading text of the unit.
- It occupies two pages though it is still designed for one lesson in class.
- The text is always interesting and relevant to the students, and links with the topic of the unit.
- The text recycles the main grammar points from lessons B and D.
- Important new vocabulary is highlighted in the text and practised in a follow-up activity and in the Workbook.

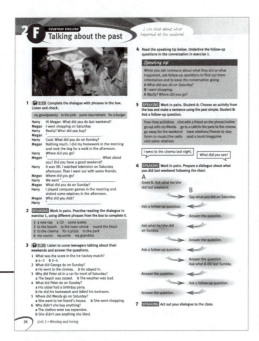

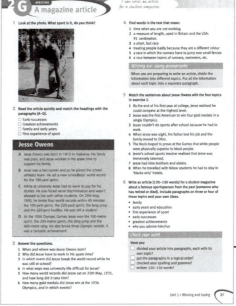

Lesson F – Everyday English

- Lesson F presents a functional dialogue.
- The lesson always includes listening practice.
- Extra vocabulary is presented, if necessary.
- Students follow a clear guide when they produce their own dialogue.
- Useful functional phrases are taught and practised.
- The step-by-step approach of 'presentation, practice and production' is suitable for mixed-ability classes and offers achievable goals.

Lesson G – Writing

- Lesson G focuses on writing and normally involves one of the text types required for the students' final exam.
- The lesson always begins by looking at a model text or texts and studying the structure and format.
- Students learn and practise useful phrases.
- There is a clear writing guide for the students to produce their own text.
- This supported approach to writing increases students' linguistic confidence.

Get ready for your exam

- There are ten *Get ready for your exam* lessons (two after units 1, 3, 5, 7 and 9) which focus on exam skills and preparation.
- The lessons include exam tasks for reading, speaking and listening.
- Each lesson includes activities to prepare students for the exam tasks and provide them with the language and skills they need to do them successfully.
- These lessons also recycle the language from the previous two units and link with the topics.

Language Review/Skills Round-up

- There are five two-page reviews (after units 2, 4, 6, 8 and 10).
- The first lesson of each review is a *Language Review* of the preceding two units.
- There are exercises focusing on vocabulary, grammar and functions.
- The marks always total 50, so it is easy to monitor progress through the book.
- The second lesson of each review is a *Skills Round-up* which covers all the preceding units of the book.
- The lesson includes practice of all four skills: listening, reading, writing and speaking.
- The material is centred around a Polish girl called Joanna, who is living and working as an *au pair* in Britain.

Tips and ideas

Teaching vocabulary

Vocabulary notebooks

Encourage your students to record new words in a notebook. They can group words according to the topic or by part of speech. Tell them to write a translation and an example sentence that shows the word in context.

Vocabulary doesn't just appear on Vocabulary pages. You can ask students to make a list of all the verbs that appear in a Grammar section, or to choose five useful words from a reading text and learn them.

Learning phrases

We often learn words in isolation, but a vocabulary item can be more than one word, e.g. *surf the Internet, have a shower*. Make students aware of this and encourage them to record phrases as well as individual words.

Revision

Regularly revise previously learned sets of vocabulary. Here are two games you could try in class:
- **Odd one out**. Give four words, either orally or written on the board. Students say which is the odd one out. You can choose three words from one vocabulary set and one word from a different set (a relatively easy task) or four words from the same set, e.g. *kind, confident, rude, friendly*, where *rude* is the odd one out as it's the only word with negative connotations.
- **Word tennis**. This game can be played to revise word sets. Call out words in the set, and nominate a student to answer. The student must respond with another word in the set. Continue round the class.
  Students must not repeat any previous words. For example, with shops:
  T: bookshop
  S1:   supermarket
  T: jeweller's
  S2:   electrical store

Teaching grammar

Concept checking

The concept is important. Do not rush from the presentation to the practice before the students have fully absorbed the meaning of the new language. You can check that they truly understand a new structure by:
- asking them to translate examples into their own language.
- talking about the practice activities as you do them, asking students to explain their answers.
- looking beyond incorrect answers: they may be careless errors or they may be the result of a misunderstanding.
- contrasting new structures with forms that they already know in English and in their own language.

Practice

Practice makes perfect. Learning a new structure is not easy, and students need plenty of practice. Use the extra activities in the *Grammar Builders* and on the MultiROM.

Progression

Mechanical practice should come before personalised practice. This allows students to master the basic form and use first, without having to think about what they are trying to express at the same time.

Teaching reading

Predicting content

Before reading the text, ask students to look at the picture and tell you what they can see or what is happening. You can also discuss the title and topic with them.

Dealing with difficult vocabulary

Here are some ideas:
- Pre-teach vocabulary. Anticipate which words students will have difficulty with. Put them on the board before you read the text with the class and pre-teach them. You can combine this with a prediction activity by putting a list of words on the board and asking students to guess which ones will not appear in the text. For example, for the text about Bethany Hamilton on page 18 of the Student's Book, list these words:
  surfing   surfboard   motorway   waves   beach   mountain   water
  Ask students to look at the picture and tell you which two words they are not going to find in the text (*motorway* and *mountain*). At the same time, check that they understand the other five words.
- Having read through the text once, tell students to write down three or four words from the text that they don't understand. Then ask them to call out the words. You can then explain or translate them.
- Rather than immediately explaining difficult vocabulary, ask students to identify the part of speech of the word they don't know. Knowing the part of speech sometimes helps them to guess the meaning.
- After working on a text, ask students to choose four or five new words from the text that they would like to learn and to write them in their vocabulary notebooks.

Teaching listening

Pre-listening

This is an important stage. Listening to something 'cold' is not easy, so prepare the students well. Focus on teaching rather than on testing. Here are some things you can do:
- Tell the students in broad terms what they are going to hear (e.g. a boy and girl making arrangements to go out).
- Predict the content. If there's a picture, ask students to look at the picture and tell you what they can see or what is happening.
- Pre-teach vocabulary. Put new vocabulary on the board and pre-teach it. Translating the words is perfectly acceptable.
- Read through the exercise carefully and slowly before the students listen. Ensure that the students understand both the task and all the vocabulary in the exercise. (You can check that they understand the task by asking a student to explain it in their own language.)

Familiar procedure

It isn't easy to listen, read the exercise and write the answers all at the same time. Take some pressure off the students by telling them you'll play the recording a number of times, and that they shouldn't worry if they don't get the answers immediately. Tell students not to write anything the first time they listen.

Monitor

While the students are listening, stand at the back of the class and check that they can all hear.

Teaching writing

Use a model

Ensure that the students understand that the text in Lesson G serves as a model for their own writing.

Preparation

Encourage your students to brainstorm ideas and make notes, either alone or in pairs, before they attempt to write a composition.

Draft

Tell them to prepare a rough draft of the composition before they write out the final version.

Checking

Encourage them to read through their composition carefully and check it for spelling mistakes and grammatical errors.

Correction

Establish a set of marks that you use to correct students' written work. For example:

sp	indicates a spelling mistake.
w	indicates a missing word
gr	indicates a grammatical error
v	indicates a lexical error
wo	indicates incorrect word order

Self correction

Consider indicating but not correcting mistakes, and asking students to try to correct them.

Teaching speaking

Confidence building

Be aware that speaking is a challenge for most students. Build their confidence and they will speak more; undermine it and they will be silent. This means:

- encourage and praise your students when they speak.
- do not over-correct or interrupt.
- ask other students to be quiet and attentive while a classmate speaks.
- listen and react when a student speaks, with phrases like 'Really?' or 'That's interesting'.

Preparation

Allow students time to prepare their ideas before asking them to speak. This means they will not have to search for ideas at the same time as trying to express them.

Support

Help students to prepare their ideas: make suggestions and provide useful words. Allow them to work in pairs, if appropriate.

Choral drilling

Listen and repeat activities, which the class does together, can help to build confidence because the students feel less exposed. They are also a good chance to practise word stress and intonation.

Teaching mixed ability classes

Teaching mixed ability classes is demanding and can be very frustrating. There are no easy solutions, but here are some ideas that may help.

Preparation

Try to anticipate problems and prepare in advance. Draw up a list of the five strongest students in the class and the five weakest. Think about how they will cope in the next lesson. Which group is likely to pose more of a problem – the stronger students because they'll finish quickly and get bored, or the slower students because they won't be able to keep up? Think how you will attempt to deal with this. The Teacher's Book includes ideas and suggestions for activities and fillers for different abilities.

Independent learning

There is the temptation in class to give most of your attention to the higher-level students as they are more responsive and they keep the lesson moving. But which of your students can best work on their own or in pairs? It's often the stronger ones, so consider spending more time in class with the weaker ones, and finding things to keep the fast-finishers occupied while the others catch up.

Peer support

If you are doing pairwork, consider pairing stronger students with weaker students.

Project work

Provide on-going work for stronger students. You can give your stronger students extended tasks that they do alone in spare moments. For example, you could give them readers, ask them to keep a diary in English or work on a project. They can turn to these whenever they are waiting for the rest of the class to finish an activity.

Correcting mistakes

How much we correct should depend on the purpose of the activity. The key question is: is the activity designed to improve accuracy or fluency?

Accuracy

With controlled grammar and vocabulary activities, where the emphasis is on the accurate production of a particular language point, it's best to correct all mistakes, and to do so immediately you hear them. You want your students to master the forms now and not repeat the mistake in later work.

Fluency

With activities such as role-play or freer grammar exercises it may be better not to interrupt and correct every mistake you hear. The important mistakes to correct in these cases are those that cause a breakdown in communication. We shouldn't show interest only in the language; we should also be asking ourselves, 'How well did the students communicate?'. During the activity, you can make a note of any serious grammatical and lexical errors and put them on the board at the end of the activity. You can then go through them with the whole class.

Self correction

Give students a chance to correct themselves before you supply the correct version.

Modelling

When you correct an individual student always have him or her repeat the answer after you correctly.

Peer correction

You can involve the rest of the class in the process of correction. Ask: *Is that answer correct?* You can do this when the student has given a correct answer as well as when the answer is incorrect.

THIS UNIT INCLUDES ●●●○

Vocabulary • personality adjectives • negative prefixes: *un-*, *im-* / *in-* and *dis-* • hobbies and interests • time phrases
Grammar • present simple and continuous • verbs not used in continuous tenses • verb + infinitive or *-ing* form
Speaking • talking about personality • expressing likes and dislikes
Writing • personal profile
WORKBOOK   pages 4–10 • Self check 1 page 11

A VOCABULARY AND LISTENING
Personalities

LESSON SUMMARY ●●●○○

Vocabulary: personality adjectives, negative prefixes
Listening: dialogues; listening for specific information
Speaking: talking about personalities of friends and relatives
Topic: personal identity

SHORTCUT *To do the lesson in 30 minutes, skip the Lead-in and set Vocabulary Builder (part 1) as homework. Do not spend more than 3–4 minutes on exercises 1 and 6.*

➡ Lead-in 2 minutes

• Inform the class of the lesson objectives.
• Put students in pairs. Ask them to work individually first. Students note down two adjectives which describe their own personality and two adjectives about their partner's personality. In a **weaker class**, let students use the adjectives on the Student's Book page. In a **stronger class**, students work with books closed. Allow a minute. Then ask students to compare their notes in pairs.
• Share answers as a class. Put the adjectives on the board.

Exercise 1 page 4

• Focus students on the photographs. Elicit what students know about the films or characters. Ask different students to describe the characters using the prompts. In a **stronger class**, encourage them to use other adjectives too.

KEY

1 Trinity: serious, hard-working
2 Blofeld: unkind, mean
3 Garfield: lazy, funny
4 Yoda: kind, serious
5 Cruella de Vil: unkind, mean

CULTURE NOTE

Trinity, from the *Matrix* films: the first officer of the hovercraft ship Nebuchadnezzar. She is a legendary computer hacker with super-human combat skills.

Blofeld, from the *James Bond* films: a villain who plots to take over the world.

Garfield, originally a newspaper cartoon: a fat, lazy cat who makes humorous observations about human behaviour.

Yoda, from the *Star Wars* films: a 900-year-old and 66 cm tall wise master and trainer of the Jedi Knights.

Cruella de Vil, the villain in the Disney film *101 Dalmatians*. She kidnaps Dalmatian dogs with a plan to kill them for their fur.

Exercise 2 page 4

• Students can work in pairs. Set a time limit of 1 minute.

Exercise 3 page 4   🎧 1.01

• Play the recording once. Students check their answers.

• Play the recording again stopping after each pair of adjectives for students to repeat chorally and individually.
• In a **weaker class**, if students need further practice, play the recording once more. Stop after each adjective and elicit its opposite from different students.
• Check understanding by asking: *Does a mean/generous person give expensive presents? Who tells jokes – a serious person or a funny person?* etc.

Transcript 1.01

kind, unkind   confident, shy   polite, rude
funny, serious   talkative, quiet   patient, impatient
optimistic, pessimistic   lazy, hard-working   friendly, unfriendly
generous, mean

For further practice on the adjectives, go to:

Vocabulary Builder (part 1): Student's Book page 124

KEY

1 a talkative   d lazy   g kind
    b friendly   e rude   h funny
    c shy   f hard-working

2 1 unkind   3 patient   5 generous
    2 pessimistic   4 funny

3 1 He's kind. He always helps people.
    2 He's optimistic. He always thinks good things are going to happen.
    3 She's impatient. She doesn't like waiting.
    4 He's serious. He never tells jokes.
    5 She's mean. She never spends money on other people.

Exercise 4 page 4   🎧 1.02

• Focus students on the instructions and the chart. Check understanding of the task by asking: *How many adjectives are there?* (6) *How many people are you going to hear about?* (4) *How many adjectives will you need?* (4)
• In a **stronger class**, play the recording once. Check as a class. To get more feedback, play the recording again. Stop after each dialogue and ask further questions, for example: *Why is Martin pessimistic?*
• In a **weaker class**, play the recording twice. Let students compare their answers before checking as a class.

KEY

1 Martin – pessimistic   3 Terry – impatient
2 Julie – generous   4 Emma – shy

Transcript 1.02

1
Girl   Hi, Martin. What are you doing?
Martin   I'm revising for my History exam.
Girl   How's it going?
Martin   Oh, you know – badly.
Girl   Why? What's wrong?
Martin   Nothing's wrong. It's just that I know I'm going to fail.
Girl   What? Oh, don't say that!

Martin	It's a really important exam and I'm going to fail it. That's just me. Things always go wrong.
Girl	Oh Martin! Come on, let's go and watch TV.
Martin	OK, but there won't be anything good on.

2

Julie	Happy birthday!
Boy	Thanks, Julie.
Julie	I've got a present for you.
Boy	Really? That's very nice of you.
Julie	Oh, it's nothing really. Here you are. I hope you like it.
Boy	Wow! A CD – no, three CDs!
Julie	Yes. And I got you this, too.
Boy	But …
Julie	It's only a little present.
Boy	A T-shirt! That's lovely. Thanks, Julie!
Julie	Come on, I'll buy you lunch in a café.

3

Girl	Hi, Terry.
Terry	Hello. Are we ready to go?
Girl	No, not yet. We're waiting for Sue.
Terry	Where is she?
Girl	I don't know. But she'll be here in a moment, I'm sure.
Terry	Can you phone her?
Girl	Why?
Terry	Tell her to hurry up.
Girl	It's only two minutes past eight, Let's wait for a few minutes before we call her.
Terry	OK. (PAUSE) Let's call her now.
Girl	No! Let's wait!

4

Boy	Hello, Emma. How are you?
Emma	All right, thank you.
Boy	Having a good time?
Emma	Yes, thank you.
Boy	Do you know where … oh … sorry … sorry.
Emma	Have you got something to … oh … sorry … no, you, please.
Boy	Do you know where my sister is?
Emma	Yes.
Boy	Where is she?
Emma	Oh, sorry. She's over there.
Boy	Oh yes.
Emma	Bye then.
Boy	I'm not going. I just wanted to know.
Emma	Oh. Sorry.

Exercise 5 page 4

- Ask students to choose three people they know well and make notes about their personalities. Explain that they should not write full sentences.
- When students are working, go round monitoring and helping. When they are ready, ask them to practise saying their descriptions in pairs. Remind them to talk about the reasons.
- **Fast finishers** can be asked to prepare a short description of one of their classmates without saying their name. It should include some of the person's typical behaviour so that the rest of the class can guess who it is. Collect the descriptions and read them out to the class at the end of the lesson or next time for revision. Students guess who has been described.

Exercise 6 page 4

- Bring the class together again. Ask students to tell the class about one of their friends or relatives.

In this section students learn about the negative prefixes:

Vocabulary Builder (part 2): Student's Book page 124

- Read the *Look out!* box with the class. Check understanding by asking: *What is the most popular negative prefix in English? What other negative prefixes can you use? If you don't know the prefix, which should you try first?*

KEY

5 1 A dishonest person doesn't tell / never tells the truth.
    2 An unambitious person doesn't try to be successful.
    3 An impolite person is (often) rude.
    4 An untidy person doesn't put / never puts things away.
    5 A disloyal person isn't your friend for a long time / is your friend for a short time.
    6 An intolerant person doesn't listen to other people's opinions.
    7 An inactive person doesn't get a lot of exercise.
    8 An unlucky person doesn't usually have good luck.

6 1 attractive   3 uncomfortable   5 unbelievable
    2 fit   4 grateful   6 certain

➡ Lesson outcome

Ask students: *What have you learned today? What can you do now?* and elicit answers: *I can describe someone's personality. I can talk about my friends and relatives.*

1B GRAMMAR
Present simple and continuous

LESSON SUMMARY ●●○○○

Grammar: present simple and present continuous
Vocabulary: verbs not used in continuous tenses
Speaking: talking about habits, current activities and plans
Listening: a dialogue at a party

SHORTCUT *To do the lesson in 30 minutes, skip the Lead-in and do exercise 1 as a class. In a **weaker class**, skip exercises 5 and 6. In a **stronger class**, set the Grammar Builder for homework.*

➡ Lead-in 3–4 minutes

- Inform the class of the lesson objectives.
- Introduce the topic of clothes by asking students: *What are you wearing at the moment? What clothes do you wear for parties, for example, a wedding reception or a party with friends?*
- Focus students on the picture. What other clothes can they see?

Exercise 1 page 5

- Ask a student to read the list of verbs to the class. Model and drill pronunciation and explain any new words.
- Put students in pairs to describe the people in the picture and guess who is being described. Allow enough time for students to take a few turns. While they are working, go round monitoring and helping.
- Ask individual students to say sentences about the picture in front of the class.
- If necessary, refer students to Grammar Reference 1.5 and run through the spelling rules for the present continuous.

Exercise 2 page 5

- Ask two stronger students to read the text messages out to the class.
- Ask: *What does Ed think of the wedding? Why is Ed texting Cath?* and elicit as many answers as possible (e.g. He hates the wedding. He's bored. He doesn't know anybody there. etc.)

Exercise 3 page 5

- Read the table as a class. Elicit the differences in the formation of the tenses by asking: *Which tense puts 's' at the end of the verb in third person singular? Which tense changes the order of words to form a question? Which tense uses 'do' and 'does' to form questions?* etc.
- Students can work in pairs for a minute. Check as a class.

KEY

present simple affirmative: I need a laugh. They're so boring. My grandad always falls asleep. He's got the right idea.
present simple negative: I don't know many people here. You never wear ties.
present simple interrogative: Do you like weddings?
present continuous affirmative: I'm wearing a stupid tie. I'm going to my cousin's wedding next weekend.
present continuous negative: I'm not talking to anyone.
present continuous interrogative: Are you having a good time?

Exercise 4 page 5

- Students complete the rules in the *Learn this!* box in the same pairs. Check as a class.
- If necessary, drill the present continuous as a class using different prompts.

KEY

1 present simple	4 present continuous
2 present continuous	5 present continuous
3 present simple	

For further practice of the present continuous and present simple, go to:

Grammar Builder 1B: Student's Book page 104

KEY

1
1 I don't wear a suit at school.
2 He likes weddings.
3 She doesn't play volleyball after school.
4 We don't live in London.
5 My uncle doesn't work in a factory.
6 I don't want a sandwich.

2
1 What does she wear at school?
2 Where does he go swimming?
3 Why do they play computer games?
4 When does he get up in the morning?
5 How does he go to work?

3
1 They're / They are wearing tracksuits.
2 She's / She is chatting to her friend.
3 I'm not / I am not having a shower.
4 We're not / We are not winning the match.
5 He's / He is dancing really badly.
6 You aren't / You are not listening to me.

4
1 Is he wearing a hat? No, he isn't.
2 Are they standing up? No, they aren't.
3 Is he smiling? Yes, he is.
4 Are they eating a pizza? Yes, they are.
5 Is she wearing jeans? Yes, she is.
6 Is she holding a mobile phone? No, she isn't.

5
1	a wears	b 'm/am wearing
2	a 're/are going	b go
3	a love	b 'm/am enjoying
4	a travels	b 's/is travelling
5	a sings	b 's/is singing
6	a don't believe	b 's/is not telling

Exercise 5 page 5

- Remind students that Ed is at the wedding reception and he doesn't like it.
- Students work in pairs to complete the dialogue. Allow 3 minutes.
- **Fast finishers** can write more lines to continue the dialogue between Ed and Naomi.

KEY

1	Are you enjoying	5	's playing	9	Wear
2	prefer	6	don't know	10	are you doing
3	aren't playing	7	like	11	'm visiting
4	are dancing	8	Do you wear		

Exercise 6 page 5 🎧 1.03

- Play the recording for students to check, pausing if necessary for students to make corrections.

Exercise 7 page 5

- Ask students to draw lines to link the verbs and the nouns. Check as a class.
- Elicit which time phrases in the right-hand column are used with the present continuous or with the present simple. Ask students to make notes.
- While students are working in pairs, go round and help with problems.
- Ask pairs to read out their sentences. The class listens and assesses accuracy. If there is a mistake, prompt the pair or class to correct it.

➔ Lesson outcome

Ask students: *What have you learned today? What can you do now?* and elicit answers: *I can say what I usually do and what I'm doing now. I have learned how to use two present tenses.*

Notes for Photocopiable activity 1.1

Spot the difference
Pairwork
Language: present continuous, clothes vocabulary
Materials: one copy of the worksheet per pair of students (Teacher's Book page 124)

- Divide students into pairs and give out the worksheets. Tell students that they must not look at their partner's picture. Explain that they both have a picture of the same scene but there are eight differences.
- Students describe their pictures and ask questions about their partner's picture in order to find the differences. When they find a difference, they mark it with a cross.
- Demonstrate the activity with a student first to find the first difference. Make it clear that students must describe the actions in the picture and the clothes that the people are wearing.
- The activity continues until most pairs have found the eight differences.
- Elicit the differences from the class.

KEY

Picture B:
The two teenagers sitting on the floor are watching TV, not playing a computer game. The boy isn't wearing a hat. The boy in the corner is listening to music, not playing the guitar. The girl on the left on the bed is wearing a dress. Both girls are holding drinks. The girl standing up is texting someone, not taking a photograph. There is no dog. The boy in the doorway is wearing a coat.

1C CULTURE Free time

LESSON SUMMARY ●●●○○

Reading: an article about teenage leisure: scanning, detailed reading
Listening: conversations about free-time activities; matching
Speaking: talking about free time activities
Pronunciation: question intonation
Topic: leisure activities

SHORTCUT *To do the lesson in 30 minutes, skip the second stage of the Lead-in and do exercises 1 and 2 quickly as a class. Change the procedure for exercises 4 and 5. Students read both tasks. Play the recording twice. Check both exercises as a class. Keep a fast pace while working on intonation in exercise 7.*

➡ Lead-in 2–4 minutes
- Inform the class of the lesson objectives.
- Write *free time* on the board and ask students to brainstorm free-time activities. Put all their ideas on the board.
- Establish which activities are the most/least popular in the class by asking: *Who … every day?* and *Who never …?* about each activity. Students raise hands. Count the votes and write the numbers with the +/– symbols next to the activities on the board.

Exercise 1 page 6
- Focus students on the photos. Elicit what the teenagers in the photos are doing. Make sure students are using the present continuous and correct their mistakes.
- Ask: *Which of the activities do you do in your free time?* and elicit answers: *I watch TV. I don't play computer games.* etc. Make sure students are using the present simple and correct their mistakes.

Exercise 2 page 6
- Focus students on the title of the article and explain that *leisure* means *free time.*
- Elicit what the article is about.
- Ask students to read the text and find what the numbers refer to. Explain that they should not try to understand everything but only look for the information. This first reading should only take a minute or two.
- Make sure students can say the numbers correctly. 85% is *eighty-five percent* and £1,152 million is *one thousand, one hundred and fifty-two million pounds.*

KEY

1 85% of teenagers in the UK prefer playing computer games on their own to playing games outside with their friends.
2 £1,152 million is the total sum of money spent in British shops on computer games in 2003.
3 More than 75% of British teenagers played team sports in the 1970s.

OPTIONAL ACTIVITY

Write the following numbers on the board:

50%   1960s   2006   1,745 million   3.5

Ask individual students to read the numbers. If students make mistakes, write more numbers in the problematic categories and continue until they gain confidence.

Write the following expressions on the board in two columns:

half   more than half   less than half   a third

60%   33.3%   50%   45%

Elicit from students which expressions match which numbers and draw the lines on the board.

Exercise 3 page 6
- Ask different students to read the questions out to the class. Check understanding.
- Ask students to read the text again carefully and find answers to the questions. Allow enough time for everybody to do the task individually.
- In a **weaker class,** ask students to underline the answers in the text.
- In a **stronger class,** ask students to write full answers in their notebooks.
- Ask **fast finishers** to use the questions in 3 to write a few sentences about teenagers they know, e.g. *In my class boys are more interested in computers than girls. My friends watch less TV than teenagers in the UK.* etc.
- Let students compare their answers in pairs before checking as a class.
- Invite a short class discussion about teenage leisure by asking: *Do teenagers here and teenagers in Britain spend their free time in the same way?*

KEY

1 In the UK boys are more interested in computers than girls.
2 Teenagers in the UK watch more TV than teenagers in other European countries.
3 A third of children in the UK have a video recorder in their bedroom.
4 Less than half of teenagers in the UK play team sports.
5 Because they are too expensive.
6 Teenagers in the UK spend on average 2.5 hours a day watching TV.

Exercise 4 page 6 🎧 1.04
- Ask students to read the instructions and the task individually. Play the recording once. Stop after each conversation and elicit the answer.

KEY

1 d   2 c   3 b   4 a

Transcript 1.04

1

Interviewer	What do you do in your free time?
Duncan	I listen to music before school and after school.
Interviewer	Really? What kind of music do you listen to?
Duncan	Hip-hop, rap ... I mix CDs in my bedroom. I want to be a professional DJ one day.
Interviewer	Have you got any other hobbies?
Duncan	I sometimes go dancing. There are some great clubs near my house.
Interviewer	Do you go on your own?
Duncan	No, I go with my friends. It's more fun.

2

Interviewer	What do you do in your free time?
Shama	I've got lots of different hobbies. I like reading, for example – books or magazines. I also enjoy playing football and volleyball.
Interviewer	Do you watch a lot of TV?
Shama	Not really, but I love films. I watch DVDs or I go to the cinema with my friends.
Interviewer	Anything else?
Shama	I'm interested in photography. Oh, and I play chess. I go to a chess club on Thursday evenings.

3

Interviewer	What do you do in your free time?
Martin	I watch TV most evenings.
Interviewer	How much time do you spend watching TV?
Martin	Probably about two hours a day.
Interviewer	Have you got any other hobbies?
Martin	I'm interested in computers. I spend a lot of time surfing the Internet. And I love computer games!
Interviewer	Do you play computer games on your own or with friends?
Martin	I usually play on my own.
Interviewer	What about sport and exercise?
Martin	I like sport, but I don't actually do any sports. There isn't a park near my house, or a sports centre.

4

Interviewer	What do you do in your free time?
Karen	I go cycling. I love BMX bikes.
Interviewer	What else do you like doing?
Karen	I go swimming sometimes. I really like that.
Interviewer	How often do you watch TV?
Karen	Not very often. I prefer active hobbies – physical exercise. I go to an aerobics class twice a week too.
Interviewer	Where is it?
Karen	It's at the sports centre near my house.

Exercise 5 page 6

- Focus students on sentences 1–8. Check any vocabulary problems.
- Students individually complete the sentences with the names of the teenagers in exercise 4. Students should work from memory. Do not let students say their answers aloud at this stage.

Exercise 6 page 6 🎧 1.04

- Play the recording again so that students can check their answers. Check answers as a class.

KEY

1	Shama	**4**	Karen	**7**	Karen
2	Martin	**5**	Duncan	**8**	Martin
3	Duncan	**6**	Shama		

Exercise 7 page 6 1.05

- Explain to students that they are going to work on pronunciation and intonation. Play the recording. Pause after each question and ask a few students to repeat. If students find it hard to repeat the question, model it again. Correct mistakes.
- In a **weaker class**, make students repeat chunk by chunk starting at the end of the question, e.g. *free time?, in your free time?, do you do in your free time?, What do you do in your free time?*
- In a **stronger class**, ask students to close their books and repeat without looking at the questions.

PRONUNCIATION – INTONATION IN QUESTIONS

The general rule of intonation in questions is that the voice goes up at the end of *Yes/No* questions (questions which ask for *Yes* or *No* answers) and down at the end of *Wh-* questions (questions which contain a question word *What, Who, How*, etc.). To make the voice go down at the end of a *Wh-* question it helps to start the question with a high pitch. Students should be aware that if they don't use a range of pitch they will sound bored.

Exercise 8 page 6

- Ask students to prepare for an interview. They should choose the questions they want to use from exercise 7 or write their own.
- Allow a few minutes for students to prepare the questions. Encourage them to learn the questions by heart.
- Put students in pairs. Preferably, they should be paired with somebody they do not usually work with.
- Students take it in turns to do interviews. Get feedback by asking several students to report back on their partner's answers.

➡ Lesson outcome

Ask students: *What have you learned today? What can you do now?* and elicit answers: *I can talk about hobbies and interests. I have learned about teenagers in the UK and how they spend their leisure time.*

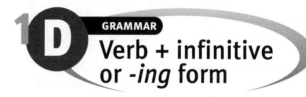

1D GRAMMAR
Verb + infinitive or *-ing* form

LESSON SUMMARY ●●●○○

Grammar: verb + infinitive or *-ing* form
Vocabulary: phrases for feelings and preferences
Reading: a questionnaire
Speaking: talking about feelings and preferences

SHORTCUT *To do the lesson in 30 minutes, briefly explain unknown vocabulary in the questionnaire to the class, then ask students to do exercises 1 and 2 individually. Set the Grammar Builder or exercise 5 for homework.*

➡ Lead-in 2–4 minutes

- Inform the class of the lesson objectives.
- Put the word *questionnaire* on the board. Point out that there is a part of the word that students know (*question*). Focus students on the text in exercise 1 and elicit the meaning of *questionnaire* (a written list of questions that are answered by a number of people, often so that information can be collected from the answers).
- Have a short brainstorming session on students' experience with completing questionnaires. Ask: *Have you ever completed a questionnaire in a magazine? What magazines print questionnaires? What are questionnaires about? Can you learn something about yourself from a questionnaire?*

Exercise 1 page 7

- If you think students are going to have pronunciation problems with some words in this speaking task, model the pronunciation for students to repeat.
- In a **stronger class**, don't explain the meaning of the words at this stage. Explain to students that they will have to use the context to understand the questions and answers.
- Focus students on the questionnaire. Allow a lot of time to work in pairs. Remind students to note down their answers.

Exercise 2 page 7

- Ask students to count their answers.
- If you have not explained yet, elicit what *fearless* and *phobic* mean. Do students agree with the results of the questionnaire?

Exercise 3 page 7

- Read the information in the *Learn this!* box as a class. Go over the questionnaire together.
- Ask individual students to read out the questions and point out the verbs followed by infinitive or *-ing* form.
- Students mark the verbs/expressions in their books. It would be convenient for students to underline the verbs in two different ways, e.g. with single and double lines. Make sure that students underline *spend time, can't help, don't mind, can't stand*, not *spend, help, mind, stand*. Remind them to learn them as whole expressions.

Exercise 4 page 7

- Students complete the table with the verbs from the questionnaire. Do the same on the board so that students can double-check their answers.

KEY

Verb + infinitive: want, decide, offer, hope, refuse, agree
Verb + *-ing* form: avoid, spend time, can't help, don't mind, can't stand, imagine, suggest

---

For further practice on the verb patterns, go to:

Grammar Builder 1D: Student's Book page 104

- Focus students on table 1.8.
- Go through all columns as a class. Students will find the verbs that do not appear in the questionnaire in lesson 1D. Elicit or explain the meaning of the verbs. Draw students' attention to the third column. Explain that after these verbs it is possible to use both infinitive and *-ing* form.
- **6–7** Ask students to work individually, referring to table 1.8 if necessary. Check as a class.

KEY

6 1 d   2 a   3 e   4 c   5 b

7 1 to be	5 to pass	9 playing
2 feeling	6 to watch	10 to tell
3 wearing	7 going	
4 eating	8 to have	

Exercise 5 page 7

- Go through the list of verbs and check understanding.
- Ask students to complete the sentences with the right forms of the verbs.
- In a **stronger class**, you can ask students to cover the table above and work from memory. In a **weaker class**, you can ask students to work on the sentences in pairs.
- Check as a class.

KEY

1 to help	4 to pay	7 chatting
2 to pass	5 studying	8 feeling
3 waiting	6 being	

Exercise 6 page 7

- Students complete the sentences about themselves. Remind them to use verbs, not nouns. While they are working, go round monitoring and helping with any problems. Allow enough time for everybody to finish the task.
- If there are **fast finishers**, ask them to develop their sentences by adding reasons, e.g. *I usually avoid going to discos because I hate crowds and noise.*

Exercise 7 page 7

- Ask students to read out their sentences. If there are mistakes, get the class to correct them. Have the most popular sentences written on the board.

OPTIONAL ACTIVITY

Students form pairs or small groups. Allocate a different topic to each pair or group, e.g. free time, music, telephoning, parties, friends, school, homework, etc. Ask students to complete the sentences in 6 starting with 'We ...' and using verbs from the lesson. By writing sentences on a given topic, students will create 'manifestos' expressing the attitudes of their group, their class or even their generation to particular things. Allow 5 minutes to do the task and help with vocabulary problems. Get feedback. If possible, ask students to write their manifestos on large sheets of paper. Hang them in different places all over classroom and read them out from there. Instruct students that manifestos should be read in a loud and decisive voice.

➡ Lesson outcome

Ask students: *What have you learned today? What can you do now?* and elicit answers: *I can identify and use different verb patterns. I have learned that I am phobic/fearless.*

1E READING Appearances

LESSON SUMMARY ●●●○○

Reading: an article about youth culture; multiple-choice questions
Listening: a song; identifying the gist
Speaking: expressing opinions on an article and song
Topic: fashion and youth culture

SHORTCUT *To do the lesson in 30 minutes, set exercises 4 and 6 for homework. Do not spend more than 12 minutes on the Lead-in and exercises 1 and 2.*

➡ **Lead-in** 3–5 minutes
- Inform the class of the lesson objectives.
- Introduce the topic of *appearance and fashion*. Elicit or explain the meaning of both words. Write the word *fashion* on the board with several expressions around it, for example, *things to do, places to meet, music bands, clothes, colours, cars, sports*. Ask students in pairs to think of two examples of items for each category – one which is fashionable and another one which is unfashionable. Share answers as a class.

Exercise 1 page 8
- Focus students on the photographs. As a class, brainstorm vocabulary useful for describing the teenagers. Put all the words on the board. Ask different students to say sentences about the teenagers in the photos and the fashions they represent.
- Elicit which fashions are current in the students' country. Are there any differences between these and British teenage fashions?

Exercise 2 page 8
- Focus the class on the instructions. If necessary, pre-teach *right, wrong, ban* and *hoodies* (hooded tops; young people wearing them). Try to avoid explaining vocabulary from the text at this stage.
- Read the exam tip with students and remind them that the first time they read, they should look for the main idea and not worry about unknown vocabulary.
- Ask students to read the text and find out where and why people ban hoodies. (People ban hoodies from shops and schools because they believe hoodies cause bad behaviour or problems.) Allow enough time for students to read the whole text. Share answers as a class. Ask: *Do you think people are right or wrong to ban hoodies? Do goodies wear hoodies?* Elicit answers.

Exercise 3 page 9
- Ask students to read the questions. If students have problems understanding the questions, explain new words and expressions.
- Ask students to read the text carefully and answer the questions. Students should underline the fragments of the text which contain the answers. Allow plenty of time for students to work individually, then let them compare their answers in pairs before checking as a class. While checking, students read a question, the answer and the relevant fragment of the text.

KEY

1 b   2 d   3 a   4 c   5 a

Exercise 4 page 9
- Go over the definitions with the whole class and check understanding. Encourage students to analyse the context of the words.

KEY

1	judge	4	trouble-makers	7	silly
2	agree	5	behaving	8	generation gap
3	for sale	6	banned		

CULTURE NOTE – AVRIL LAVIGNE

Avril Lavigne /ˈævrɪl ləˈviːn/ is a Canadian singer/songwriter now living in the USA. She became famous at the age of 17 when her album *Let Go* reached the US Top 10 in 2002. Her most famous songs are *Sk8er Boi* and *Complicated*. Her music can be described as a mixture of pop, rock and skater punk.

LANGUAGE NOTE – TXT

Sk8er Boi (Skater Boy) is an example of text messaging language. Further examples are: *B4* (before), *GR8* (great), *THNX* (thanks), *CUL8R* (see you later).

Exercise 5 page 9 🎧 1.06
- Focus students on the photo. Ask: *Who is in the photo? Can you describe her? What kind of person is she? What does she do? What is she doing?*
- Read the words in the box with the class and explain if necessary (e.g. *baggy* – loose-fitting, not tight).
- In a **stronger class**, ask students to read the lyrics and put in the missing words before listening. Play the recording so that students can check their answers.
- In a **weaker class**, play the recording straight through. Students listen and fill in the gaps.

KEY

1	girl	7	home	13	inside
2	punk	8	TV	14	skater
3	baggy	9	tickets	15	show
4	skater	10	skater	16	song
5	pretty	11	guitar		
6	earth	12	ends		

Exercise 6 page 9

- Students individually choose the best summary of the lyrics. Ask different students to give and justify their answers before telling the class the correct answer.

KEY

a

Exercise 7 page 9

- Write the following expressions on the board: *I think, I agree, I disagree* and elicit their meaning.
- Put students in pairs to discuss the message of the song. Go round monitoring and encouraging students to try to express their ideas. At the end have a short class discussion about the song. Ask: *Do you agree with the message of the song? Do you always tell your friends how you feel? Do you always do what your friends tell you?*

KEY

b

ADDITIONAL SPEAKING ACTIVITY

Look back at the photos of teenage fashions. Ask students' opinions of the fashions shown. Would they like to dress like this? Would they be friends with/go out with someone who dressed like this? Why?/Why not?

Ask: *Do you think fashion shows a person's personality?* As a class, use the personality adjectives from lesson 1A to brainstorm what the people in photos 1–3 might be like. Put the adjectives on the board. They may contrast, depending on students' opinions, but accept all suggestions for the moment.

Briefly contrast pictures 1 and 2 with picture 3. Ask why people dress differently from/the same as their friends. If necessary, teach *to stand out, to fit in.*

Put students in pairs and ask them to choose one photo and write 2–3 questions they would like to ask this person/these people. Remind them to use the present simple and elicit a

range of question words to list on the board. Allow 2 minutes for the writing. Share ideas as a class.

Correct any mistakes and put down at least nine different questions on the board. Make sure there are three questions to go with each photo.

Now ask students to imagine they are their chosen person or people from the photo and make notes of their answers. Refer them to the personality adjectives and tell them to choose the ones they think are the most suitable. If there are adjectives in the list that are unsuitable, encourage them to mention these and explain why they are wrong. For example: *Some people think I'm rude and unfriendly, but they don't know me.* Allow 3 minutes.

Put students in pairs again to ask and answer the questions.

If there is time, get a few pairs to act out their dialogues for the class. Encourage them to maintain eye contact and answer with feeling to make the conversations more realistic.

➔ Lesson outcome

Ask students: *What have you learned today? What can you do now?* and elicit answers: *I can understand an article and a song about youth culture. I have learned about teenage fashion in the UK. I have got to know a song by Avril Lavigne.*

LESSON SUMMARY ●●●○○

Functional English: expressing likes and dislikes
Vocabulary: hobbies and interests
Listening: dialogues about likes and dislikes; listening for specific information
Speaking: giving an opinion
Topic: leisure activities

SHORTCUT *To do the lesson in 30 minutes, skip the Lead-in or the first stage in exercise 1 (talking about the photo). Play recording 1.08 once. Stop after each conversation and elicit answers to exercises 3 and 4. Keep a fast pace.*

➔ Lead-in 5 minutes

- Inform the class of the lesson objectives.
- Ask students in pairs to write down the things and activities they like and dislike doing in two different lists. Set a time limit of 3 minutes. When the time is up, ask a few pairs to read one of their lists. The rest of the class guesses which list it is – likes or dislikes.

Exercise 1 page 10 🎧 1.07

- Focus students on the photograph. Ask the class to take turns to say one sentence about the people in the photo. Students should listen to each other in order not to repeat the same information. Prompt students who lack ideas saying, for example: *appearance, personality, age, nationality, likes, dislikes,* etc.
- Play the recording. Ask: *What do Alice and Jack like doing?* Elicit answers.
- Play the recording again. Students listen, read and underline the phrases which express likes, dislikes and preferences, then write them next to the expressions provided. Check answers as a class.
- Point out the difference between answers 1–3 and answer 4. (1–3 express general preferences whereas 4 refers to a particular situation.) Explain the difference between *What do you like doing?* and *Would you like to …?* If necessary, conduct a short drill to practise answering both questions.

KEY

1 I enjoy, I love	3 I'd rather
2 I can't stand	4 Do you fancy …?

Exercise 2 page 10

- Read out the list of activities and explain any new words.
- Focus students on the expressions in exercise 1 and point out what verb forms follow them (*like, enjoy, prefer, can't stand + -ing* form; *would rather* + infinitive without *to*; *would like* + full infinitive).
- Model the activity by reading out the dialogue with a strong student.
- Ask students to practise reading the dialogues in pairs.

Exercise 3 page 10 🎧 1.08

- Ask students to study the instructions and the table. Play the first dialogue and check understanding of the task by asking: *What do they both like? What does Fred prefer? What does Chloe prefer?*
- Play the rest of the recording. Students note down the answers. Check as a class.

KEY

Fred and Chloe – d	Kevin and Lucy – a
Simon and Tara – c	John and Pam – b

Transcript 1.08

1
Fred   What do you like doing in your free time?
Chloe   I enjoy watching sport on TV.
Fred   So do I. What's your favourite sport?
Chloe   Tennis. I love watching tennis.
Fred   Really? Tennis is OK, but I prefer watching football.
Chloe   I can't stand football. It's boring.

2
Simon   What do you enjoy doing at weekends?
Tara   I like shopping.
Simon   Me too. What's your favourite shop?
Tara   TopShop.
Simon   Really? That's a clothes shop, isn't it?
Tara   Yes, it is.
Simon   I hate clothes shops. I prefer buying books and CDs.

3
Lucy   What do you enjoy doing in your free time?
Kevin   I love listening to music.
Lucy   So do I. Who's your favourite singer?
Kevin   Eminem.
Lucy   That's interesting. I'm not really a fan.
Kevin   Who do you like, then?
Lucy   I really like Robbie Williams.
Kevin   Urgh! Robbie Williams is so arrogant!

4
John   What do you like doing?
Pam   I love eating out.
John   Me too. What's your favourite kind of food?
Pam   I love Indian food.
John   Do you? That's interesting. I don't really like Indian food.
Pam   What kind of food do you like?
John   I love Italian food. Pasta, pizzas … mm … delicious!

Exercise 4 page 10 🎧 1.08

- Play the recording again. Check answers after each dialogue.

KEY

1 tennis	3 Robbie Williams
2 clothes shops	4 Italian food

Exercise 5 page 10 🎧 1.09

- Read the speaking tip with the class.
- Elicit which expressions are used a) to show interest (*Do you? Really? That's interesting!*); b) to say that you feel the same (*Me too! So do I!*).
- Play the recording for students to repeat chorally and individually several times.

Transcript 1.09

Pam   I love Indian food.
John   Do you?

Chloe   I love watching tennis.
Fred   Really?

Pam   I love eating out.
John   Me too.

Kevin   I love listening to music.
Lucy   So do I. Who's your favourite singer?
Kevin   Eminem.
Lucy   That's interesting.

Exercise 6 page 10

- If students need more practice, ask them to change pairs and continue the activity.
- To add variety, you can ask the responding students to take the role of a parent, teacher, younger brother, etc.

Exercise 7 page 10

- Students write the dialogue in pairs. In a **weaker class**, ask them to write full dialogues. In a **stronger class**, it may be enough for students to make notes.
- When students are writing, go round helping and correcting mistakes.
- Remind students to follow the chart and use the expressions from the lesson.
- When they are ready, ask students to practise saying their dialogues in pairs. Encourage them to maintain eye contact while they are talking, react to what the other person is saying, and read as little as possible.

Exercise 8 page 10

- Encourage students to look at the chart rather than their notes.
- The chart makes it possible to ask students who have not worked together to act the dialogue out. Try it in a **stronger class**.

➡ Lesson outcome

Ask students: *What have you learned today? What can you do now?* and elicit answers: *I can express my likes and dislikes. I have learned how to react to what people say.*

1G WRITING A personal profile

LESSON SUMMARY ●●●○○
Reading: personal profiles for an Internet chatroom
Vocabulary: personality adjectives, modifying adverbs
Writing: a personal profile
Topic: personal information

SHORTCUT *To do the lesson in 30 minutes, skip the Lead-in and do exercises 3, 4 and 5 as a class.*

➡ Lead-in 2–3 minutes

- Inform the class of the lesson objectives.
- Focus students on the title of the lesson. Explain the meaning of *personal profile* (a short description giving some basic information about yourself).
- Elicit the meaning of *Internet chatroom* (an Internet site where people can type messages to each other, creating an on-line 'conversation'). Briefly brainstorm reasons why people use Internet chatrooms.

Exercise 1 page 11

- Read the writing task as a class.

- Put two lists of expressions on the board:
  A: *go, play, do, listen, get, be interested, be keen*
  B: *a job, sport, computer games, on sport, in photography, to university, to music*
- Students match As with Bs (*go to university, play computer games, do sport, listen to music, get a job, be interested in photography, be keen on sport*). Elicit the meanings.
- Students check the profiles with the task instructions.

KEY

Martin hasn't written about his family. Sarah hasn't written about her hometown and her profile is too short.

Exercise 2 page 11

- Give students time to read the profiles again and find the answers to the questions. Let them check in pairs.
- Elicit answers from different students. Ask them to read out the relevant fragments of the texts. Explain the meaning of new adjectives.

KEY

1 Martin is 16. Sarah is 17.
2 Martin is in Year 11. Sarah is in Year 12.
3 Martin likes swimming and karate. Sarah doesn't like sport (but she plays volleyball).
4 Martin: playing chess, computer games, photography
  Sarah: fashion, listening to music
5 Martin: ambitious, hard-working, impatient, intolerant
  Sarah: confident, kind, loyal

Exercise 3 page 11

- Read the writing tip as a class.
- Students find and underline the modifying adverbs. Work on the translations as a class. Explain that we often use *a bit* instead of *a little*, especially in conversation.
- Elicit which adverbs make the meaning of adjectives stronger (*really, very*) or weaker (*quite, slightly, a little*).
- Point out the spelling difference between the adjective *quiet* and the adverb *quite*.

LANGUAGE NOTE – MODIFYING ADVERBS

Slightly and *a little/a bit* are only used with adjectives with a negative meaning, e.g. *She's a little lazy.* It is not correct to say, *He's a little patient.* or *She is slightly polite.*

Really means the same as *very* but can only be used in informal language.

Quite can mean *completely* but it is more usually used (as here) to mean *a little/a bit.*

Exercise 4 page 11

- Allow enough time for students to work out the rules themselves or in pairs. Check as a class.

KEY

1 before   2 before

Exercise 5 page 11

- Students rewrite the sentences individually. Check as a class.

KEY

1 I'm slightly pessimistic.
2 My best friend is really confident.
3 He's not at all an impatient person.
4 I'm a student at quite a big school.
5 I find English quite difficult.
6 I'm sometimes a bit shy.

Exercise 6 page 11

- Students use the list in the writing task to make notes for their own personal profile. Point out that they will need to start a new paragraph for each part of the list.

Exercise 7 page 11

- Set a time limit of 10 minutes. Remind students to include all the information listed in the task. Ask them to use some personality adjectives and modifying adverbs.
- Go round to monitor and help students as they write.

Exercise 8 page 11

- Give students time to check their work, using the checklist, and to make changes if necessary.

OPTIONAL ACTIVITY

Ask students to erase their names from the profiles. Collect them and distribute them at random. Students read the profiles and guess who wrote them.

ALTERNATIVE WRITING TASK

Think of a character from a TV series that you watch. Write a profile for this character. Include the following information:

- name of programme, character's name, job, nationality
- where the character lives/works, what he/she does and who with
- a description of his/her personality

➡ Lesson outcome

Ask students: *What have you learned today? What can you do now?* and elicit answers: *I can write a personal profile. I can understand profiles for an Internet chatroom. I have learned new adjectives to describe personality.*

Notes for Photocopiable activity 1.2

Tell us about you ...

Board Game

Language: present simple and continuous, likes and dislikes, verb patterns
Materials: one copy of the board per group of two to four students (Teacher's Book page 125)

- Divide students into groups of two to four. Give out a game board and a set of dice and counters to each group. If dice are not available students can toss a coin to move around the board. (Heads = move one square, tails = move two squares.)
- Students take it in turns to throw the dice/toss a coin to move forward. When they land on a square they must talk for 30 seconds about the topic. The other student(s) ask a question about the topic.
- The game continues until a student lands on the *Finish* square.

Get ready for your EXAM 1

TOPIC ●●●○○
People and relationships

➡ Lead-in 3 minutes
- Inform the class of the lesson objectives.
- Ask students to turn back to the photos on page 9 and study them for 20 seconds. Then tell them to close their books.
- Invite students to make statements from memory describing the characters in the photos, e.g. *Trinity has short dark hair. She's wearing sunglasses. Blofeld is wearing a white shirt. Yoda is fighting. He has enormous ears.*

Exercise 1 page 12 3–4 minutes
- Focus on the photo on page 12 and use it to pre-teach *in the background* and *in the foreground*.
- Students can do the matching task individually or in pairs.

KEY
1 c 2 e 3 a 4 d 5 b

Exercise 2 page 12 🎧 1.10 6–8 minutes
- Explain to students that they are going to hear a boy giving his opinions about the photo in exercise 1.
- Read the sentences as a class.
- Play the recording twice. Students tick the sentences they hear.
- Focus on the structure *look* + adjective in sentence 6 and remind students that *look* means 'appear' in this context. Point out that *look* is normally used in the present simple, not the present continuous, when it has this meaning.
- Focus on the expressions in bold and ask students to repeat.
- Extract other useful phrases for the speaking task: *I can see …, The photo shows …*

KEY
1, 3, 4, 6, 7

Transcript 🎧 1.10
Well, I can see six young people and they are in a big garden or a park, perhaps. I think that they are about 14 or 15 years old. The photo shows them chatting and laughing. The girl on the right is holding some books. And the other people have got books too, so in my opinion they are studying something, perhaps English. Perhaps they are on a language course in Britain in the summer holidays. In my view they are friends because they look very relaxed and they are laughing. I'm not sure why they are so happy. Perhaps classes have just finished. Or maybe the boy on the left is saying something funny.

Exercise 3 page 12 5 minutes
- Focus on Peter's opinions in exercise 2 and give students a minute or so to think about what they want to say.
- Elicit students' views on each of Peter's opinions. Prompt a range of responses by asking, for example, *What do you think, Jan? Erika, what's your view? Why do you think that? Who's got a different opinion?* Encourage students to use all the expressions in bold in exercise 2 and to give reasons for their answers where possible.

Exercise 4 page 12 8–10 minutes
E Speaking: picture-based discussion
- Ask students to read the questions. Focus on question 4 and elicit some possible openings for a reply to it, e.g. *I feel happy when …, I like/love/really enjoy …* Give students a few minutes to plan their replies.
- Allow **weaker students** to jot down some key words to refer to if necessary when they are speaking. Ask **stronger students** to think of an extra question to ask their partner.
- Put students in pairs. Ask them to take it in turns to be the examiner, who asks the questions, and the examinee.

Exercise 5 page 12 🎧 1.11 10 minutes
E Listening: completing a table
- Ask students to study the table. Ask **weaker students** to give an example of the information needed for each column.
- Play the recording straight through. Students listen and complete the table. Check as a class.
- Play the recording again, pausing after each dialogue. Elicit what phrase is used to introduce oneself and what questions are used to ask about age, nationality and hobbies.

KEY

	Age	Country	Hobbies
Ralf	16	Germany	listening to music, surfing the Internet
Kate	16	England	dancing, listening to music
Marie	17	Belgium	shopping, reading
Marco	16	Spain	sport, going out with friends
Liam	18	Ireland	playing chess, chatting online
Laurent	16	France	playing chess, playing computer games

Transcript 🎧 1.11

Ralf	Hi. My name's Ralf.
Kate	Please to meet you Ralf. I'm Kate.
Ralf	Pleased to meet you too. Where are you from, Kate?
Kate	I'm from England. What about you?
Ralf	I'm from Germany.
Kate	Really? Where in Germany?
Ralf	Berlin. What are your hobbies, Kate?
Kate	I like dancing and listening to music.
Ralf	I like listening to music too, but I can't dance!
Kate	Do you have any other hobbies?
Ralf	Yes, I like surfing the Internet. I use my dad's computer now but I hope to get a PC for my birthday next month.
Kate	How old are you Ralf?
Ralf	16.
Kate	I'm 16 too.

Marie	Hello. I'm Marie. What's your name?
Marco	Marco. Pleased to meet you, Marie.
Marie	And you. Where are you from, Marco?
Marco	Spain. I live in San Sebastian. Where are you from?
Marie	I'm Belgian. I'm from Brussels.
Marco	Oh, that's interesting. I've never been there.
Marie	How old are you, Marco?
Marco	I'm 16. How old are you?
Marie	17. What are your hobbies?
Marco	I love sport. I play football. And I like going out with friends. What about you?
Marie	I like shopping. And I quite like reading.

Liam	Hi, my name's Liam.
Laurent	Hello, Liam. I'm Laurent. I'm from France.
Liam	I'm from Ireland.
Laurent	Where in England?
Liam	No, not England. Ireland. I'm from Dublin.
Laurent	Oh, I love Ireland. What do you like doing in your free time, Liam?
Liam	I like playing chess.
Laurent	Me too. What else do you like doing?
Liam	I like chatting online. Do you like chatting online?
Laurent	No, but I like playing computer games. How old are you, Liam?
Liam	18. How old are you?
Laurent	I'm 16.

Exercise 6   page 12   3–5 minutes

- Model the activity with a student.
- Students take it in turns to ask and answer the questions.
- Ask a few pairs to ask and answer in front of the class.

Exercise 7   page 12   5 minutes

E Use of English: word formation gapfill

- Write an example of the task type on the board: *Superman is a strong and … (FEAR) hero*. Elicit the answer (fearless).
- Pre-teach *tell (someone) off* and *criticism*.
- In a **weaker class**, read the text together before students complete the task. In a **stronger class**, students read the text themselves.

KEY

1	friendly	4	impatient
2	talkative	5	interested
3	funny		

Exercise 8   page 12   2 minutes

- Elicit the answer to the question, then read the tip with the class.

KEY

They are all adjectives.

➜ Lesson outcome

- Ask students: *What have you learned today? What can you do now?* and elicit answers: *I can express opinions. I have practised speaking about a picture. I have practised listening and filling in a table. I have practised a word formation task.*

TOPIC ●●○○
People and relationships

➜ Lead-in   3–4 minutes

- Inform the class of the lesson objectives.
- Brainstorm vocabulary connected with feelings and emotions with the class. Put the words on the board in two columns: adjectives (*sad*, *happy*, etc.) and nouns (*sadness*, *happiness*, etc.)
- Elicit what situations create particular feelings, for example, on birthdays children are happy as they get presents, but adults are sad as they feel old.

Exercise 1   page 13   2–3 minutes

- Read the instructions to the class. Encourage students to talk about different feelings and situations. Allow 2–3 minutes.
- To share ideas as a class, focus on positive feelings. Ask students: *When you are happy, who do you talk to? If you are proud of a success, who do you tell?*

Exercise 2   page 13   10–15 minutes

E Reading: matching headings with paragraphs; true/false/not known statements

- Read the exam task as a class. Ask students to say in their own words what they have to do and how/where they have to write their answers for each part of the task. They can explain this in their own language.
- Read the introduction (in bold) together and elicit what the text is about. In a **weaker class**, also read the topics (A–D) and the true/false statements (1–5) and explain any new vocabulary.
- Ask students to read the whole text through before they start answering the questions.
- Encourage students to underline the parts of the text that are relevant to the answers as they do the task.
- Check as a class. Get students to justify their answers by reading the relevant fragments of the text.

KEY

1 D   2 C   3 A
1 F   2 T   3 F   4 NK   5 T

Exercise 3   page 13   2–3 minutes

- Encourage students to talk about all the pieces of advice and say which of them are useful.
- Share ideas as a class.

Exercise 4   page 13   3–5 minutes

- In a **weaker class**, ask students to look back and study the table and *Learn this!* box in exercises 3 and 4 in lesson 1B.
- In a **stronger class**, use the rules in exercise 4, lesson 1B to elicit the differences between the present simple and the present continuous. For example, ask: *Which tense do we use for something that happens always or regularly?*
- Students work individually.
- Check as a class. Ask students to identify the rule from exercise 4, lesson 1B while reading their answers.

KEY

1	feel	5	are you wearing
2	never share	6	loves
3	doesn't think	7	is crying
4	are you laughing	8	Do you remember

Exercise 5 page 13 🎧 1.12 5–6 minutes

- Ask students to look at the list and number the items in order of importance for them. Ask them to compare answers in pairs.
- Read the instructions as a class.
- Play the recording through twice.

KEY

Kati: friends, family, sport, boyfriend, school
David: friends, sport, school

Transcript 🎧 1.12

David So, which do you think is more important – spending time with your friends, or spending time with your family?

Kati I think the most important thing is spending time with my friends. Well, they're both very important. But my family is always there. So I think that spending time with my friends is more important. What about you?

David Well, my family lives in Spain now, and I'm studying in London, so my friends are more important to me at the moment.

Kati Yes, I see. What about money? Do you think having lots of money is important?

David No, I don't think money is very important. It certainly isn't as important as being good at sport. I live for sport!

Kati Oh, me too. I love volleyball and tennis – and I want to be really good at them. And what about girlfriends? Is having a girlfriend more important than being good at sport, David?

David I don't really think that's very important. Personally, I think the second most important thing is doing well at school. I worry a lot if I don't do well, and I'm happy when I do well, so that's important to me.

Kati Yes, I agree with you about school. But having a boyfriend is important, too. Er, David, do you know Martin in our class?

Exercise 6 page 13 🎧 1.12 8–10 minutes

- Students read and complete the sentences. Ask **stronger students** to identify who the speaker is in each case.
- Play the recording again for students to check.
- Point out that the sentences are all stating or asking for opinions. Remind students of the language for expressing opinions in the previous lesson.
- Focus on sentence 6 and ask: *Why does David think this?* Elicit the reasons he gives in the recording to support his opinion. Invite students to suggest some possible reasons to support one or two of the other statements.
- Play the recording once more and pause to elicit expressions used to respond to an opinion (*Yes, I see. Me too! Yes, I agree with you, but …*) and to move the conversation on (*What about …?*).

KEY

1	most	2	both	3	more	4	as	5	than	6	second

Exercise 7 page 13 10 minutes

E Speaking: topic-based discussion

- Read the task instructions as a class. Explain to students that they are going to have a pair discussion that should last for 3–4 minutes.
- Point out that for the conversation to flow, both students will need to listen to what their partner is saying and respond to it, for example by showing interest, agreeing/disagreeing or asking a question. (Note that there is more structured practice on asking follow-up questions in 2F, Unit 2.)
- Give students 3 minutes to organise their ideas, making brief notes. Remind them to think about reasons/examples to support their opinions.
- Pairs discuss the topic for 3–4 minutes.
- Invite feedback on the activity by asking: *Did you both express opinions on two topics? Did you give reasons? Did one person speak a lot more than the other? Did the conversation stop too soon?* Discuss problem areas and ways in which they can be improved. If you have time, ask students to form new pairs and practise the task again.

➡ Lesson outcome

- Ask students: What have you learned today? What can you do now? and elicit answers: *I have practised matching and true/false reading tasks. I have practised discussing a topic.*

2 Winning and losing

THIS UNIT INCLUDES ●●●●
Vocabulary • sports • *play/go/do* + sport • collocations: sports and games • free-time activities
Grammar • past simple • contrast: past simple and past continuous
Speaking • talking about favourite sports • talking about the past • narrating a story
Writing • a magazine article
WORKBOOK pages 12–18 • Self check 2 page 19

A VOCABULARY AND LISTENING
A question of sport

LESSON SUMMARY ●●●●●
Vocabulary: sports, verb and noun collocations
Listening: sports commentaries; listening for gist
Reading: a questionnaire
Speaking: talking about sports
Topic: sport

SHORTCUT *To do the lesson in 30 minutes, ask students to do the questionnaire individually. Play recording 1.14 once, pausing after each commentary to elicit the answer. Set the Vocabulary Builders (parts 1 & 2) for homework.*

➡ Lead-in 4–5 minutes
• Inform the class of the lesson objectives.
• Brainstorm vocabulary connected with sports with the class.
• In a **stronger class**, put students in pairs and allocate different categories of sports to brainstorm, e.g. *individual, team, ball, summer, winter, indoor, outdoor, field, water, contact, Olympic,* etc. Allow 2 minutes. To share answers, students write their category and sports on the board.

Exercise 1   page 14
• Focus students on the title and the text. Elicit what type of text it is (a questionnaire). Students note down their partner's answers, then count the points and tell their partner their score.
• Ask: *Does your partner agree with the result of the questionnaire? Do you agree with your result?*

KEY

1 **a** Edwin van der Sar   **b** Tiger Woods   **c** Maria Sharapova
2 **c**

Exercise 2   page 14
• Allow a minute for individual work. Then let students compare their answers in pairs.

KEY

1 badminton	7 gymnastics	13 weightlifting
2 volleyball	8 judo	14 swimming
3 athletics	9 basketball	15 golf
4 cycling	10 karate	16 table tennis
5 tennis	11 surfing	17 ice hockey
6 football	12 baseball	18 rugby

Exercise 3   page 14   🎧 1.13
• Play the recording once. Students check their answers. Pause if necessary so that students can make corrections.
• Play the recording again. To practise pronunciation, stop after each sport for students to repeat chorally and individually.
• In a **weaker class**, if students need further practice, play the recording once more. Stop after every three sports. Students repeat the groups of words.

Exercise 4   page 14
• Students read the *Look out!* box on their own. Check understanding by asking: *What verb do we use with team sports and ball sports?/sports that end in -ing?/other sports?*
• Work as a class. Read out sports and elicit the collocating verbs from the class. Students note down the collocations.
• In a **stronger class**, ask students to add more sports to the three groups.

KEY

play – badminton, baseball, basketball, football, golf, ice hockey, rugby, table tennis, tennis, volleyball
go – cycling, surfing, swimming, weightlifting
do – athletics, gymnastics, judo, karate

LANGUAGE NOTE – SPORT
Point out that with the word *sport* we can say *play* or *do*. It isn't correct to say *practise* sport.

For further practice on the collocations and sports related vocabulary, go to:

Vocabulary Builder (part 1): Student's Book page 125

KEY

1 **b** He's playing baseball.
  c She's going cycling.
  d He's doing karate.
  e She's surfing.
  f He's playing table tennis.

2 **a** rugby
  b golf
  c badminton
  d weightlifting
  e ice hockey
  f basketball

3–4 Open answers

Exercise 5   page 14   🎧 1.14
• Students work in pairs for a minute. They choose a sport and note down key words connected with it. Ask a few pairs to read out their words.
• Explain to the class that they are going to listen to sports commentaries. Focusing on the sports vocabulary will help them identify the sport.
• Play the recording straight through twice.
• On the second listening, ask **fast finishers** to note down vocabulary connected with the sports from the recording. Check as a class.

KEY

1 football	4 ice hockey	7 weightlifting
2 athletics	5 golf	8 surfing
3 tennis	6 basketball	

Transcript 1.14

1 Commentator We're in the 19th minute of the World Cup Final. It's Italy nil, France 1. And Italy have a corner. Pirlo crosses the ball into the box to Materazzi – and he scores. What a goal! Italy have equalised!

2 Commentator And the 100 metre sprint is about to start. And they're off. Brown had a fantastic start ... Brown is in the lead ... Powell is just behind him ... And here comes Powell ... He's passing Brown ... Powell wins – it's a very fast time – 9.97 seconds.

3 Commentator What a great shot! The French girl is really hitting the ball hard today. Her opponent can't win a point!

4 Commentator And we're in the final minute of the match. It's five goals each. Here comes the Czech forward again – he shoots – but he misses the goal! The goalkeeper kicks it away with his skate. Who is going to win this match?

5 Commentator She's still about 150 metres from the hole, and this is her third shot. She's really having a bad day. The crowd becomes quiet as she prepares to hit the ball again – and it's a terrible shot. Oh dear. I think the ball is in the river this time.

6 Commentator Smith throws the ball to Jones. Jones runs forward and passes the ball back to Smith ... Smith shoots. Yes, it's in the basket! The score is 36 all.

7 Commentator And the Hungarian has asked for an extra 15 kilos on the bar. That's a very heavy weight indeed now – 165 kilos. Can he lift it? Let's see ... ah, no he can't. And I think he's in some pain now. But he's smiling – that's good to see.

8 Commentator Sandra Peters is lying on her board, about 100 metres from the beach. Here comes a big wave. She's riding the wave, she's standing up ...Oh, dear, she fell off her board. She's in the water ...

Exercise 6 page 14

- Encourage students to take notes by explaining that they will later present the information to the class. Set a time limit of 4 minutes to ask questions and note down answers. When the time is up, instruct students to change roles and work for another 4 minutes.

Exercise 7 page 14

- Allow a minute for students to read their notes and concentrate on what they will say.
- In a **weaker class**, let students rehearse in different pairs in a set time limit of 2 minutes per person.
- Ask different students to tell the class about their friends. Other students can listen and check if the talks include answers to all 5 questions.

For more collocations related to sports and games, go to:

> Vocabulary Builder (part 2): Student's Book page 125

KEY

5 lose/win a match
  lose/win a game
  lose/score/win a point
  miss/score a goal
  hit/kick/pass/throw a ball
6 b He's scoring a point.
  c He's passing the ball.
  d She's winning the race.
  e She's hitting the ball.
  f He's losing the match.

➡ Lesson outcome

Ask students: *What have you learned today? What can you do now?* and elicit answers: *I can talk about sports I like. I have learned words for different sports.*

2B GRAMMAR Past simple

LESSON SUMMARY ●●●●●

Grammar: past simple
Reading: short sports stories
Speaking: talking about a sports event

SHORTCUT *To do the lesson in 30 minutes, skip the Lead-in and set the Grammar Builder and exercise 7 for homework.*

➡ Lead-in 4–5 minutes

- Inform the class of the lesson objectives.
- Put students in pairs. Ask each pair to choose a sports person or team and write down four facts about them. Bring the class together and ask a few students to read their sentences out. The rest of the class guess the person/team and add more facts.

Exercise 1 page 15

- Explain *to cheat* (to do something wrong, dishonest or against the rules in order to win).
- Ask students to read the instruction. Elicit what sport the text refers to (football).
- Put the following two sets of words on the board: *fifteen, foggy, second, match, to send off, football* and *a player, pitch, day, half, referee, players.*
- Match as a class. (fifteen players, foggy day, second half, football pitch, to send off a player, match referee).
- In a **stronger class**, ask: *How did the players cheat?* and elicit students' ideas.
- Ask students to read the text, check their ideas and answer the questions.
- Check as a class.

KEY

1 Both teams 2 Dynamo Moscow

Exercise 2 page 15

- Ask: *When was the match? What is the grammatical tense in the text?*
- Work as a class to identify the past simple forms.

KEY

1 played, cheated
2 was, were
3 sent off, came back
4 didn't notice, How did the match finish?

Exercise 3 page 15

- Ask: *How do we form regular forms of the past simple?* (*cheat + ed = cheated*; *score + d = scored*) *How do we know irregular forms of the past simple?* (check them in a dictionary and memorise them) *What is the verb form in negative and interrogative forms?* (the infinitive without *to*) *What other word do we use in negative and interrogative forms?* (did)
- Students work individually. Check as a class.

KEY

affirmative: played, went
negative: didn't do
interrogative: Did they go ...?

- Read the *Look out!* box with the class. Put the past forms of *be* in all persons on the board and conduct a short drill, e.g. T: I, at the match   Ss: I was at the match.

Exercise 4 page 15   🎧 1.15

- Play the recording. Stop after each verb for students to repeat chorally and individually.
- Play the recording again. Stop after each verb for students to write down the sounds.
- Ask individual students to read out the verbs.

KEY

1 played /d/	5 scored /d/
2 cheated /ɪd/	6 competed /ɪd/
3 finished /t/	7 passed /t/
4 kicked /t/	8 watched /t/

PRONUNCIATION – -*ED* ENDINGS

The rules for the pronunciation of -*ed* endings are as follows:

1 If the verb ends in the sound /t/ or /d/ the pronunciation of -*ed* is /ɪd/, e.g. wanted /ˈwɒntɪd/.

2 If the verb ends in an unvoiced sound (a sound made without using the voice box): /p/ /k/ /s/ /f/ /tʃ/ /θ/ /ʃ/ the pronunciation of -*ed* is /t/, e.g. watched /ˈwɒtʃt/.

3 If the verb ends in a voiced sound (a sound made using the voice box): /b/ /g/ /v/ or a vowel the -*ed* ending is pronounced /d/, e.g. loved /lʌvd/, played /pleɪd/.

In reality, the difference between 2 and 3 is almost imperceptible and is unlikely to cause communication problems. The most important rule for students to be clear about is 1 as it involves the insertion of an extra syllable.

For further practice on the past simple, go to:

Grammar Builder 2B: Student's Book page 106

- Ask students to read the spelling rules in Grammar Reference 2.2.

KEY

1 1 competed	4 cheered	7 hated
2 finished	5 missed	8 stopped
3 chatted	6 carried	

---

2 1 knew		4 liked		7 enjoyed	
2 won		5 left		8 preferred	
3 scored		6 taught			

3 1 didn't know		4 didn't like		7 didn't enjoy	
2 didn't win		5 didn't leave		8 didn't prefer	
3 didn't score		6 didn't teach			

4 1 did you do		3 Did you enjoy		5 Did your sister go	
2 did you see		4 I did		6 she didn't	

5 1 weren't		3 was		5 was	
2 were		4 wasn't		6 was	

Exercise 5 page 15

- In a **weaker class**, pre-teach *cheer, spectators, freestyle, event, compete, become angry, miss a shot, ball boy, play against*. In a **stronger class**, elicit the meaning of the words after students have completed the task.
- Allow 4 minutes for students to work individually. Check as a class.

KEY

1 came	6 competed	11 didn't know
2 finished	7 became	12 got
3 didn't win	8 missed	13 cheered
4 was	9 gave	
5 learned	10 shouted	

Exercise 6 page 15   🎧 1.16

- Pause the recording after each story and repeat the forms so that students can make corrections. If necessary, write them on the board, eliciting the spelling from the class.

Exercise 7 page 15

- Students can work in pairs. Let them compare their answers with another pair before checking as a class.

KEY

1 Did Eric Moussambani win	4 did Patrick Rafter become
2 was his	5 did he give
3 did he learn	6 did he shout

Exercise 8 page 15

- Ask students to write the sentences about one particular event.
- Allow 3 minutes. Remind students to use the past simple and to include one false sentence. Go round and help with vocabulary problems.

Exercise 9 page 15

- Students vote by raising their hands. Ask two strong students to count the votes and put them on the board. Students reveal which sentence is wrong by reading it out in a negative form.

→ Lesson outcome

Ask students: *What have you learned today? What can you do now?* and elicit answers: *I can describe past events. I can ask about past events. I have learned to use the past simple.*

Notes for Photocopiable activity 2.1

Irregular verb bingo

Grammar game
Language: irregular past tenses
Materials: one copy of the worksheet per ten students
(Teacher's Book page 126)

- Give out one bingo card to each student. If there are more than ten students, give out extra cards. It doesn't matter if more than one student has the same card. Explain that they are going to play *Bingo*. Tell students that you are going to call out the infinitive form of an irregular verb and if they have the past form on their card they draw a line through it. Suggest that they use pencil so that the game can be repeated. When they have crossed out all the words on their card they shout 'Bingo!'
- Read out the verbs in the list below in any order. Each time you read one out put a tick against it.
- When a student shouts out 'Bingo' ask him or her to read out the six verbs in the infinitive and the past. Insist on correct pronunciation. If the student is correct he/she is the winner. If not, the game continues.
- If time allows, ask students to rub out the pencil marks and repeat the activity. This time pass the verb list to a student to read out, again in random order.

Verb list
be bring buy catch choose eat fall feel fight fly hear keep know leave put see sleep think throw wear

On the river

LESSON SUMMARY ●●●○○

Reading: an article about the Boat Race; skimming, detailed reading
Listening: a radio programme; matching
Speaking: talking about the history of a sporting event
Topic: sport

SHORTCUT *To do the lesson in 30 minutes, keep a fast pace and make sure you spend around 10 minutes for each of the three main parts: the reading, the listening and the speaking.*

➡ Lead-in 2–3 minutes
- Inform the class of the lesson objectives.
- Prepare students to describe the photo in exercise 1 by refreshing *there is/are*. Work as a class. Students take it in turns to say sentences about their surroundings, for example: *There is a board on the wall. There are fifteen desks in the classroom.*

Exercise 1 page 16
- Students work in pairs. Allow 5 minutes.
- In a **weaker class**, check the meanings with the students, then ask them to use the words to write down sentences about the photo.
- In a **stronger class**, students check the meanings in pairs, then take turns to say sentences.
- Remind students to use *there is/are* and the present continuous. Ask a student to describe the photo to the class.

Exercise 2 page 16
- Read the questions as a class.
- In a **weaker class**, to make sure students understand, paraphrase the questions (*When Is the race? – time, Where is the race? – place, Who is in the race? – people*).
- Allow 1 minute. Check as a class.

KEY
1 Every year in the spring.
2 Along the river Thames, in west London.
3 The Oxford team and the Cambridge team.

Exercise 3 page 16
- Students write down full answers in their notebooks. They should be able to do so without your help or further vocabulary explanations. Allow 5 minutes.
- Check as a class, then answer any vocabulary questions students have about the text.
- **Fast finishers** can draw simple mind maps around the word *rowing* to graphically represent vocabulary related to the sport, e.g. people (rowers, cox, spectators), places (river, course, bank), etc.

KEY
1 There are eight rowers in a team.
2 The cox is small so that the boat doesn't have to carry much extra weight.
3 The teams begin training in September.
4 There are practice races in December.
5 The race is 6,779 metres long.
6 About 250,000 people watch the race from the banks.

Exercise 4 page 16 🎧 1.17
- Pre-teach *dead heat* (a situation when two teams finish at exactly the same time), *female* (woman), *crash* (to hit something hard), *sink/sank* (to go/have gone down in water). Focus students on the pictures and prompts. Elicit what is happening in the pictures.
- Explain that students are going to hear about events in the order in which they happened – from the earliest to the most recent ones. Play the recording.
- In a **weaker class**, pause so that students have more time to make a decision. Check as a class.

KEY
1 a 2 f 3 c 4 b 5 d 6 e

Transcript 1.17

The idea for a boat race between the universities of Oxford and Cambridge started with two school friends, Charles Merivale and Charles Wordsworth. Merivale went from school to Cambridge University, and Wordsworth went to Oxford. On 12 March 1829, Cambridge sent a note to Oxford and challenged them to a boat race. The race took place a few weeks later on the river Thames (Oxford won it easily) and a tradition began. By 1856, the race was an annual event. In the 150 years since then, the boat race has provided lots of interesting and exciting moments.

1859 was a bad year for Cambridge. Their boat sank.

In 1877 nobody won or lost the race – the result was a dead heat – in other words, both boats finished the race at exactly the same time. However, Oxford believed that they won the race easily, but the referee was asleep and didn't see it!

In 1912, both boats sank. The race took place again the next day.

In 1938, the boat race was on television for the first time. Not many people watched it though, because only a few people had TV sets in their homes at that time.

1981 was an interesting year for the boat race, for this reason: Sue Brown became the first woman to take part. She was the cox for the Oxford team.

1984 was another bad year for Cambridge. Their boat crashed into another boat before the start of the race. The umpire had to abandon the race for that day while Cambridge prepared another boat. The race took place the next day, and Cambridge lost.

1998 was a more successful year for Cambridge. They won the race and set a new record for the course: 16 minutes and 19 seconds, the fastest time in history.

Exercise 5 page 16 🎧 1.17

- Briefly revise how to say dates in English. Write a few year dates on the board and ask different students to read them out (e.g. 1880, 1926, 2002, etc.)
- Play the recording straight through again. To check, elicit the years from students and write them on the board.
- In a **stronger class**, elicit what else students remember about the events from the recording.

KEY

picture	a	b	c	d	e	f
year	1877	1981	1938	1984	1998	1912

Exercise 6 page 16

- Tell students to use the pictures, dates and prompts for help. Encourage them to use different words/collocations and to ask at least one question about each picture.

OPTIONAL ACTIVITY

Students can work in pairs. Allow 5 minutes to prepare short presentations about the history of the Boat Race. Students practise in pairs before performing. Correct mistakes in the use of the past simple and collocations.

➡ Lesson outcome

Ask students: *What have you learned today? What can you do now?* and elicit answers: *I can understand information about a sporting event. I can ask and answer about the history of a sporting event. I have learned about the Boat Race.*

2D GRAMMAR
Past simple and continuous

LESSON SUMMARY ●●●○○

Grammar: past simple and past continuous
Reading: short sports stories
Speaking: narrating a story

SHORTCUT *To do the lesson in 30 minutes, skip the Lead-in focusing students on the picture and eliciting the sport instead. In a **stronger class**, set exercise 4 for homework. In a **weaker class**, set Grammar Builder exercise 7 for homework.*

➡ Lead-in 3–4 minutes

- Inform the class of the lesson objectives.
- Put students in pairs. Introduce the topic of sport. Model some past simple questions for students to repeat, for example: *What sports did you play/watch last week? What sporting events did you watch on TV/live last month? Did you win any matches/races last year?*
- When students are confident, instruct them to ask and answer the questions in pairs.

Exercise 1 page 17 🎧 1.18

- Pre-teach *cause an accident, go round a corner, lose control, catch fire, pull somebody out*. Elicit the past forms of the verbs (caused, went, lost, caught, pulled).
- Read the statements with the class.
- In a **stronger class**, ask students to cover the text while listening.
- Play the recording once.

KEY
1 T   2 T   3 F

CULTURE NOTE – NIKKI LAUDA

Born in Austria in 1949, Nikki Lauda was three times World Formula 1 Champion, in 1975, 1977 and 1984. He had a near fatal accident at the German Grand Prix but then won his second title in 1977 title. In 1979 he left the sport to set up his own airline, LaudaAir, but returned to racing in 1982 and won his third title two years later.

Exercise 2 page 17

- Students find examples of the past continuous in the text. Elicit the point that the tense consists of the past form of *be* and an *-ing* form.
- Students complete the table individually. Check as a class.

KEY
affirmative – was, were
negative – wasn't, weren't
interrogative – Were, was

Exercise 3 page 17

- Work as a class. Read out the rules in the *Learn this!* box and elicit examples from the class. Students note them down in their books.
- Elicit which two words are used to join the past simple and past continuous in one sentence (*when, while*).

KEY
1 It was raining.
2 The car crashed and caught fire. He stopped and pulled Lauda out.
3 While Lauda was going round the corner, he suddenly lost control of his Ferrari.
Another driver, Guy Edwards, was coming towards the corner when he saw Lauda inside the burning car.

LANGUAGE NOTE – VISUAL LEARNERS
Visual learners may benefit from seeing the following time line to contrast the uses of the past simple and past continuous, as exemplified in 3.

was walking

————————————————— X —————— | ——————————
                         my phone rang   Now

For further practice of the past simple and past continuous, go to:

Grammar Builder 2D: Student's Book page 106

- To check spelling of -*ing* forms and regular past simple forms, students go to Grammar Reference 1.5 and 2.2.
- To check irregular forms of the past simple, students go to the back of the Workbook.

KEY
6
1 was standing
2 was eating
3 wasn't listening
4 were dancing
5 was sitting
6 was holding
7 were shaking
8 wasn't crying
9 was laughing

7
1 were you doing
2 was watching
3 were you watching
4 wasn't paying
5 was wearing
6 wasn't raining

8
1 caught, threw
2 got, was watching
3 stopped, was snowing
4 put on, got on
5 broke, was skiing
6 scored, didn't win
7 wasn't raining, played
8 was surfing, saw

Exercise 4 page 17
- Focus students on the picture and elicit what it shows. Students should remember this from lesson 2C.
- Allow 4 minutes for students to work in pairs. Check as a class.

KEY
1 were standing
2 were waiting
3 was going
4 hit
5 was sinking
6 rowed
7 took place
8 lost

OPTIONAL ACTIVITY
Ask students to look at the verb forms in exercise 4 again and match them with the rules 1–3 in exercise 3.

1 were standing – 1
2 were waiting – 1
3 was going – 3
4 hit – 3
5 was sinking – 3
6 rowed – 3
7 took place – 2
8 lost – 2

Exercise 5 page 17
- Instruct students to answer in the tense in which the questions are asked. Do the first two with the class as an example.
- Allow 5 minutes for students to ask and answer in pairs and remind them to switch half way through.
- While students are working, go round and feed in useful words, e.g. *suddenly, at that moment, at the same time*, etc. Encourage students to add more details, for example, the people's reactions and feelings.

KEY
(Framework answer)
The sun was shining. A girl was sitting on a bench. She was watching a baseball match. One of the players hit the ball. Suddenly, her dog ran onto the pitch. The dog caught the ball and the player fell over. The girl took the dog off the pitch. The spectators were laughing and cheering.

Exercise 6 page 17
- Instruct students to speak slowly as it will help them control the structures. Encourage partners to listen carefully and point to mistakes so that they are instantly corrected.

OPTIONAL ACTIVITY
Tell the story as a class. Say the first sentence. One by one students add one sentence each to continue the story. Explain to students that they should keep their sentences short and add details so that there is enough of the story left for the last speakers.

➡ Lesson outcome
Ask students: *What have you learned today? What can you do now?* and elicit answers: *I can tell a short story using past tenses. I have learned to use the past continuous.*

Notes for Photocopiable activity 2.2
Roger Federer
Pairwork
Language: questions in the past simple, past continuous and present simple
Materials: one copy of the worksheet cut in half per pair of students (Teacher's Book page 127)
- Divide students into pairs and give out worksheets. Explain that students have a biography with some information missing. Tell them that their partner has the information that is missing.
- Students read through the biography and ask any vocabulary questions. Then they complete the questions under the text. Go round and check the questions as they write.
- Students take it in turns to ask each other the questions and complete their biographies.

QUESTIONS
Student A
1 When was he/Roger Federer born?
2 What is his mother's name?
3 What did he do at the age of eight?
4 Why did he leave school?
5 How old was he when he became professional?
6 What was he doing in Sydney in 2000?
7 What did he start in 2003?
8 Which language does he speak with his trainer?

Student B
1 Where was Roger Federer/he born?
2 What is his father's name?
3 Who was his idol when he was young?
4 When did he become professional?
5 When did he win Wimbledon for the first time?
6 Why did Miroslava stop playing tennis?
7 Which language does he speak with his girlfriend?
8 What does he enjoy doing in his free time?

2E READING
Surf's up

LESSON SUMMARY ●●●●●

Reading: a magazine article; making predictions, true/false questions
Vocabulary: irregular forms of the past simple
Speaking: acting out an interview
Topic: sport

SHORTCUT *To do the lesson in 30 minutes, skip the Lead-in and do exercises 5 and 6 as a class. Prepare the questions in exercice 7 as a class.*

➡ Lead-in 5 minutes
• Inform the class of the lesson objectives.
• Put students in small groups to list dangerous sports and reasons why they are dangerous. Allow 2 minutes.
• Ask each group to talk about two sports and why they think they are not safe.

Exercise 1 page 18
• Ask students to identify the sport in the photos and brainstorm related vocabulary. Students should say words like *board, sea, wave, wind, the sun, beach,* etc.
• Read the exam tip out to the class. Explain that making predictions about the text is a technique which helps you understand what you are reading.
• Ask different students to describe the photos and make predictions.

Exercise 2 page 18
• Allow a minute to read the two paragraphs. Elicit what happened to Bethany and her surfboard. In a **stronger class**, elicit more details. Prompt students by saying words like *time, weather, 300 metres, shark, arm, board, scream.*

KEY
A tiger shark attacked Bethany and bit her arm and her surfboard.

Exercise 3 page 18
• Ask students to read the task and try to predict the order of events before reading the rest of the text. Check as a class.

KEY
1 She decided to go surfing with some friends.
2 While she was waiting for a wave a shark attacked her.
3 The shark swam away.
4 She started to swim back to the beach.
5 Her friends saw the blood and came to help her.
6 Ten weeks later she took part in a surfing competition.

Exercise 4 page 19
• Allow 7 minutes for students to read the text and answer the questions.
• Ask students to underline the relevant sentences in the text.
• Check by having different students read their answers and lines of the text.

KEY
1 F 'The sky was clear, the sun was shining...'
2 T
3 F 'Luckily it attacked only once...'
4 F 'It happened so fast that Bethany didn't even scream.'
5 T
6 F '...only ten weeks after the accident she was surfing again in a competition.'
7 T

OPTIONAL ACTIVITY
For **fast finishers**, put the following numbers on the board: 31, 2003, 13, 300, 5, 1, 10. Ask them to check in the text what the numbers refer to.

When you have checked answers for exercise 4 with the class, students close their books.

Ask different students to say sentences about the numbers. Students who checked the numbers earlier should correct if necessary.

Exercise 5 page 19
• Set the activity as a contest among students. The one who finishes first reads out the verbs. Correct and model pronunciation for students to repeat chorally and individually.

KEY
1	bit	4	took	7	came
2	shook	5	thought	8	won
3	held	6	saw		

Exercise 6 page 19
• Allow a minute for students to work individually. Check as a class.

KEY
1	joking	5	world champion
2	incredible	6	a professional surfer
3	sponsors	7	eventually
4	scream	8	huge

Exercise 7 page 19
• Put students in pairs. Allow 3 minutes for preparation. While students are working, go round and help weaker students with the questions. Check as a class.

KEY

Questions:
1 What was the weather like on 31 October 2003?
2 What were you doing when the shark attacked?
3 What did your friends do?
4 How important was surfing in your life before the shark attack?
5 How important is surfing in your life now?

Exercise 8   page 19

- Make sure students understand the meaning of the questions. Put questions 2 and 3 on the board and contrast with the following pair: *What did you do when the shark attacked? What were your friends doing?*
- Elicit the difference (the question in the past continuous asks about actions happening at the same time, the question in the past simple asks about reactions to events).
- Ask students to act out their interviews in pairs.
- If there is time left, ask a strong pair to talk in front of the class and ask/answer the two additional questions as well.

➡ Lesson outcome

Ask students: *What have you learned today? What can you do now?* and elicit answers: *I can understand a magazine article. I have learned about Bethany Hamilton.*

EVERYDAY ENGLISH
Talking about the past

LESSON SUMMARY ●●●○○

Functional English: talking about last weekend
Vocabulary: free-time activities
Listening: dialogues between teenagers; multiple choice
Topic: leisure activities

SHORTCUT *To do the lesson in 30 minutes, do the Lead-in quickly as a class. Keep a fast pace in the first part of the lesson. Pause recording 1.20 after each dialogue and elicit answers. Save at least 10 minutes for the speaking.*

➡ Lead-in   5 minutes

- Inform the class of the lesson objectives.
- Ask students in pairs to tell each other what they did last weekend. Allow 2–3 minutes. Get feedback by asking different students a question and a follow-up question (see speaking tip). Elicit short answers and keep a fast pace.

Exercise 1   page 20   🎧 1.19

- Ask students to read and complete the dialogue individually. Play the recording to check.

KEY

1 Some new trainers	3 for a burger
2 To the park	4 My grandparents

OPTIONAL ACTIVITY

Explain that in exercise 2 students will read the dialogues in pairs and need to practise intonation. Play the recording again. Stop after each question for students to repeat chorally and individually.

Exercise 2   page 20

- Go over the expressions with the class. Explain or elicit the meaning of new words. Model the pronunciation for students to repeat.
- Read out the first lines of the dialogue, substituting the words as an example.
- Allow 4 minutes for pairwork. Remind students to switch roles halfway through.
- Encourage **fast finishers** to read the dialogue again, adding more details about what they did in the morning/afternoon/ evening and trying to use all the expressions.

Exercise 3   page 20   🎧 1.20

- Explain the task. Allow a minute to read the questions.
- Play the recording twice. On the second listening, stop after each dialogue to check answers.
- In a **stronger class**, elicit more details by asking questions, e.g. *Did George win the ice hockey match? What did he do after the match? What did he see?* etc.

KEY

1 a   2 b   3 b   4 b   5 b   6 a

Transcript   1.20

Natalie Hi George. What did you do at the weekend?
George I played ice hockey on Saturday afternoon. We won 4–3. And then I went to the cinema with some of the other guys from the team.
Natalie What did you see?
George *Troy*. It was really good.
Natalie What did you do on Sunday?
George I stayed in. I listened to music and read magazines.

Sarah Did you have a good weekend, Peter?
Peter No, not really.
Sarah Why? What did you do?
Peter It was my sister's birthday on Saturday so we went to the beach, but the weather was terrible and we sat in the car most of the time.
Sarah Oh dear. What did you do on Sunday?
Peter I had lots of homework to do. Then I tidied my bedroom.

David What did you do at the weekend, Wendy?
Wendy I went out with my friends on Saturday.
David Where did you go?
Wendy We went to town and went to some clothes shops.
David Did you buy anything?
Wendy No, I didn't have enough money.
David What about Sunday?
Wendy I went cycling with my brother. We took a picnic and went out into the country.

Exercise 4   page 20

- Read the speaking tip with the class and elicit the two follow-up questions.
- Put one of the questions on the board to highlight question formation in the past simple: question word + *did* + subject + bare infinitive + the rest. Conduct a drill and have a short practice:
  T: *where, go*   Ss: *Where did you go?*

Exercise 5   page 20

- Read the instructions as a class. Allow a moment to write sentences. Model the activity by eliciting sentences from students and responding with follow-up questions. Then reverse the procedure. Say past simple sentences and elicit follow-up questions. When students are confident, let them work in pairs for 3–4 minutes.

Exercise 6 page 20

- Allow 2 minutes for students to decide what they did last weekend and make notes. Go round and help with vocabulary problems.
- Instruct students to listen carefully to their partners and speak slowly as it will help them maintain a fluent conversation.

Exercise 7 page 20

- Put a simplified scenario of the dialogue on the board.
- In a **stronger class**, form new pairs and ask them to act out a dialogue to the class.
- Students can close their books and use the scenario on the board for help.

➡ Lesson outcome

Ask students: *What have you learned today? What can you do now?* and elicit answers: *I can chat about what happened at the weekend. I have learned how to ask follow-up questions.*

WRITING
A magazine article

LESSON SUMMARY ●●●●○

Reading: a biographical article about a sportsperson
Writing: a magazine article
Topic: sport

SHORTCUT *To do the lesson in 30 minutes, skip the Lead-in, do exercise 5 as a class, skip the class discussion in exercise 6.*

➡ Lead-in 5 minutes

- Inform the class of the lesson objectives.
- List four popular individual sports on the board. You could choose from the following: athletics, gymnastics, swimming, cycling, ice skating, weight-lifting.
- For each sport, ask: *Who are some of the great heroes of the past from our country? What did they do?* Write up the names and achievements that students suggest. Use this activity to introduce *achievement, Olympic Games, (gold) medal, break a record.*
- Have a class vote on the greatest sportsperson of those listed.

Exercise 1 page 21

- Students identify the sport (running). Ask them to guess when the photo was taken.

Exercise 2 page 21

- Remind students that they do not need to understand every word of the text to do this activity. Set a time limit of 3 minutes.

KEY

A Family and early years
B First experience of sport
C Early successes
D Greatest achievements

Exercise 3 page 21

- Elicit the difference between *break a record* and *set a record* (you <u>break</u> a previous record and you <u>set</u> a new one).
- Ask students to read the questions and underline the question words. Elicit the kind of information they will be looking for in each case.

- Students re-read the text to find the answers. **Weaker students** can work in pairs. **Fast finishers** can compare answers. If there are queries about new vocabulary, ask students to guess the meaning but do not confirm their answers yet.

KEY

1 In 1913, in Alabama.
2 Because his family was poor and he had to support them.
3 The 100-yard sprint.
4 He had to work to pay for his studies and he faced racial discrimination.
5 He broke four world records. It took him 45 minutes.
6 Four gold medals, for the 100-metre sprint, the 200-metre sprint, the long jump and the 400-metre relay.

Exercise 4 page 21

- Students find the words. Ask them to identfy clues that helped them to choose their answers.

KEY

| 1 spare time | 3 sprint | 5 hurdles |
| 2 yard | 4 racial discrimination | 6 relay |

Exercise 5 page 21

- Read the writing tip as a class.
- Read the sentences and explain/elicit the meaning of new words/expressions (e.g. *compete at the highest level, prove, physically superior, immensely talented, fellow students*).
- Explain to students that they need to match the sentences with the correct paragraph. Students work in pairs on this task.

KEY

1 C   2 D   3 A   4 A   5 D   6 B   7 A   8 C

Exercise 6 page 21

- Name the sportsperson that students voted for in the Lead-in. Brainstorm information about him/her for each of the six topics and write notes on the board.
- In small groups, students choose another famous sportsperson and share all the information they know about him/her. Tell them all to take notes.
- **Weaker students** can write about either of the two people they have discussed. Working individually, they select the topics they will use, plan their paragraphs and write a first draft. **Stronger students** may choose a different sportsperson to write about if they wish.
- Ask students to write a final version of their article at home. Encourage them to use the Internet to check and add to their information.
- Ask students to use the checklist to check their work.

ALTERNATIVE WRITING TASK

Write an article about an important historical figure or entertainer from the past. Write four paragraphs:

- Date and place of birth, family, early life
- Early successes
- Greatest achievements
- Why you admire him/her

➡ Lesson outcome

- Ask students: *What have you learned today? What can you do now?* and elicit answers: *I can write a biographical article for a student magazine. I can organise ideas in paragraphs.*

LANGUAGE REVIEW 1–2

1
1 optimistic	4 funny	7 generous
2 shy	5 quiet	
3 lazy	6 kind	

2
1 athletics	3 cycling	5 ice hockey
2 baseball	4 gymnastics	6 rugby

3 A **play:** baseball, ice hockey, rugby
B **do:** athletics, gymnastics
C **go:** cycling

4
1 eat	3 I'm wearing	5 isn't raining
2 often go	4 I'm visiting	6 I want

5
1 to be	4 doing	7 becoming
2 working	5 to be	
3 to appear	6 working	

6
1 played	3 didn't win	5 finished
2 scored	4 were	

7
1 met, was walking
2 finished, left
3 didn't hear, was listening
4 opened, looked, wasn't raining
5 got up, had
6 didn't see, wasn't looking

8 Girl c   Boy a   Girl e   Boy b   Girl d

9 1 went   2 see   3 about   4 OK   5 buy

SKILLS ROUND-UP 1–2

1 1 Sarah   2 Jim   3 Oliver   4 Ellie

2 b basic personal details
e personality
d hobbies and interests

3 1 On the AuPairNet website.
2 She's from Poznan in Poland.
3 She's seventeen.
4 She prefers looking after children.
5 Once a week.
6 She does gymnastics.

4 Open answers

Transcript 1.21

Narrator Joanna is in England. She's working as an au pair. She's living with Jim and Sarah Wood and their two children, Oliver and Ellie. It's Sunday afternoon. Joanna and the children are at home.
Joanna Hi, Oliver!
Oliver Hello.
Joanna What are you doing?
Oliver I'm watching TV. Do you like watching TV?
Joanna Yes, I do. But I prefer going to the cinema.
Oliver What else do you like doing?
Joanna I love playing volleyball.
Oliver So do I!
Joanna Do you fancy playing volleyball with me in the garden? It's a beautiful day.
Oliver OK!
Joanna Good. And Ellie can play, too.
Oliver Really? Oh. OK.
Joanna Come on. Let's go outside.

Ellie Yes! We won the point.
Oliver What's the score?
Joanna You're winning – eight points to six.
Oliver Come on, Ellie. Hit the ball.
Ellie OK, OK!
Joanna Oh! I missed it.
Ellie Wow! I hit the ball over the fence!
Oliver It's OK. Daniel's outside.
Joanna Who's Daniel?
Ellie He lives next door.
Oliver Daniel! Daniel!
Daniel Hi.
Oliver Can we have our ball, please?
Daniel Sure. Here you are.
Joanna Thanks.
Daniel Hello, I'm Daniel. Nice to meet you.
Joanna My name's Joanna. That's Joanna.
Daniel Are you … ?
Joanna I'm the new au pair.
Daniel Really? Where are you from?
Oliver It's our turn to start, Joanna.
Joanna I'm Polish.
Ellie Joanna. Can we have the ball, please?
Daniel When did you arrive in England?
Joanna Last week.
Oliver Joanna!
Joanna Sorry! OK. Let's play the next point …

Narrator It's Wednesday evening. Joanna is at her weekly English language class. She's talking to Maria, one of the other students in the class.
Joanna Hi, Maria. How are you?
Maria Fine, thanks. Did you have a good weekend?
Joanna Yes, it was OK. I went shopping on Saturday, but I didn't buy anything.
Maria What did you do on Sunday?
Joanna Nothing much. I played volleyball in the garden with the children.
Maria Oh, right.
Joanna And I met the next door neighbour – Daniel.
Maria What's he like?
Joanna He's really friendly.
Maria Really? And what does he look like?
Joanna He's really good-looking!

5
1 Joanna	4 Daniel
2 Oliver	5 Maria
3 Ellie	

6
1 going to the cinema	4 garden
2 loves	5 week
3 garden next door	6 and friendly

7 Open answers

EXAM For further exam tasks and practice, go to Workbook page 20. Procedural notes, transcripts and keys for the Workbook can be found on the *Solutions* Teacher's Website at www.oup.com/elt/teacher/solutions.

Town and country

THIS UNIT INCLUDES ●●●○○
Vocabulary • rural and urban landscapes • prepositions of movement • compound nouns • adjectives to describe places • prepositions of place • fillers • holiday activities
Grammar • *some, any, much, many, a lot of, a little* and *a few* • countable and uncountable nouns • articles
Speaking • describing places • giving directions
Writing • a tourist leaflet
WORKBOOK pages 22–28 • Self check 3 page 29

A VOCABULARY AND LISTENING
Landscapes

LESSON SUMMARY ●●○○○
Vocabulary: rural and urban landscapes; prepositions of movement, compound nouns
Listening: description of a route
Speaking: describing a route
Topic: home and environment

SHORTCUT *To do the lesson in 30 minutes, do exercise 2 and Vocabulary Builder (part 2) as a class. Set exercise 7 in the Vocabulary Builder as homework.*

➡ Lead-in 2–3 minutes
• Inform the class of the lesson objectives.
• Introduce the topic by asking: *Where do you live? What do you like most about this place/area/district? What don't you like about it?* Sharing your own experience with students is a good way to get students talking.

Exercise 1 page 24
• Students can work in pairs for 2 minutes. Share ideas as a class.
• Ask students who prefer the country to raise their hands. Elicit their reasons. Then ask students who prefer the town. Which group has more arguments?

Exercise 2 page 24 🎧 1.22
• Ask students in the same pairs to label the pictures. Allow a minute and check as a class. Play the recording once. Students listen and read.
• Play the recording again to repeat chorally and individually. Allow 2 minutes for students to look up the meaning of the other words. Check understanding by asking: *Which of these things don't belong to a rural landscape/urban landscape? Which can you see in both the city and the country?*

KEY
1 hill	8 hedge	15 pedestrian crossing
2 village	9 stream	16 pavement
3 wood	10 lane	17 traffic lights
4 cottage	11 advertisement	18 street lamp
5 field	12 road sign	19 roadworks
6 footpath	13 bus stop	20 rubbish bin
7 gate	14 postbox	

PRONUNCIATION – WORD STRESS
Focus on the word stress of the words in exercise 2 by reading them out and asking students to underline the stressed syllables.

Next write up the following two stress patterns on the board: ●• and ●••. Ask students to decide which of the words fit these two patterns. Tell them to consider the compound words (*road sign, rubbish bin, traffic jam,* etc. as one 'word'). Write the words on the board in two columns and then drill them. You could emphasise the stress by asking the students to clap or tap a pen to the rhythm.

Take this opportunity to point out that in compound nouns (nouns made of two shorter words) the stress is usually on the first word.

Key
●•
cottage, bus stop, footpath, pavement, postbox, road sign, roadworks, street lamp, village

●••
rubbish bin, traffic lights

OPTIONAL ACTIVITY
Students work in pairs for 2 minutes telling each other which of the things in exercise 2 they can see from the windows of their flat/house.

For more practice of landscape-related vocabulary, go to:

Vocabulary Builder (part 1): Student's Book page 126

KEY
1 1 rubbish bin		7 cottage
2 pavement		8 gate, field
3 traffic lights		9 pedestrian crossing
4 road sign		10 postbox
5 footpath / lane		11 village
6 street lamps		

2 a
3 Open answers

Exercise 3 page 24
• In a **stronger class**, students work in pairs for a minute. Check as a class.
• In a **weaker class**, work together. Feed in examples to help students, e.g. *go across the street, jump over the fence, drive past the cottage, walk through the door, go along the wall.*

KEY
1 across   2 past   3 through   4 along   5 over

Exercise 4 page 24 🎧 1.23
• Pre-teach *turn left/right*. Play the recording twice. Check by eliciting the route description from students. Use the transcript to prompt students with the nouns:
T: field   Ss: We walked across the field.

Transcript 1.23
We walked across the field to the gate.
We walked through the gate into the lane.
We turned left and walked along the lane.
We walked over a stream and past a cottage.
Then we went over the river.
We turned left onto a footpath.
We walked over the river again.

Then we walked along a footpath between two hedges. There was a small wood on our right.
We came to a beautiful lake. We walked along the edge of the lake and stayed there for the rest of the day.

Exercise 5 page 24

- Model the activity by telling the class that you have chosen a place in the picture for students to guess. Give directions. Students follow them and guess the place.
- Ask students to work in pairs in the same way for 3 minutes.

For more practice on formation, spelling and pronunciation of compound nouns, go to:

> **Vocabulary Builder (part 2):** Student's Book page 126

- Read the *Learn this!* box with the class. Check understanding by asking: *How many nouns are there in a compound noun? Are they written as one word or two words? How do we know how to write them?*

KEY

4 bus stop, footpath, pedestrian crossing, road sign, roadworks, rubbish bin, street lamps, traffic lights

5
1	h basketball	6	i
2	d	7	a
3	f weekend	8	j
4	b homework	9	g
5	e sweatshirt	10	c

6 Transcript 🎧 1.31
basketball, swimming pool, weekend, homework, sweatshirt, shopping centre, head teacher, pop music, computer game, table tennis.

7
1	shopping centre	6	sweatshirt
2	swimming pool	7	table tennis
3	head teacher	8	basketball
4	weekend	9	pop music
5	homework	10	computer game

➡ Lesson outcome

Ask students: *What have you learned today? What can you do now?* and elicit answers: *I can describe a place in the town or country. I have learned new words to talk about landscapes. I can describe a route.*

Notes for Photocopiable activity 3.1

Describe and draw

Pairwork
Language: prepositions of place and movement, rural and urban landscape vocabulary
Materials: one copy of the worksheet per pair of students (Teacher's Book page 128)

- Divide students into pairs and give out the worksheets. Explain that Student A and Student B have different pictures and that each student is going to describe their picture for their partner to draw in the blank section of the worksheet. Tell them that they need to use prepositions of place and movement to explain where things are.
- Students who are describing must not show their picture to their partner. Also, while they are describing they must not 'help' their partner by pointing at their partner's worksheet.
- When both students have finished describing their pictures they compare their pictures with the original.

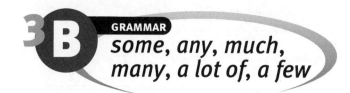

3B GRAMMAR
some, any, much, many, a lot of, a few

LESSON SUMMARY ●●●○○
Grammar: *some, any, much, many, a lot of, a few*
Reading: description of a city; matching
Speaking: describing an ideal town

> **SHORTCUT** *To do the lesson in 30 minutes, set the Grammar Builder for homework.*

➡ Lead-in 2–4 minutes

- Inform the class of the lesson objectives.
- Elicit from students what *SimCity* is (a computer game) and what its rules are. Ask: *What can you do in the game? What does not depend on you? What can go wrong? Why is the game so popular?*

> **CULTURE NOTE – *SIM CITY***
>
> *SimCity* is a highly popular computer simulation game which allows players to design and financially control their own city. It is not a competitive game that can be won or lost. Instead the enjoyment lies in creating and problem solving. The phenomenal success of *SimCity* has led to the publication of other simulation games such as *SimEarth*, *SimFarm*, *SimCopter*, *SimSafari* and *SimThemePark*. The game is now considered educationally useful and has been adopted for classroom use in many schools in the UK and USA.

Exercise 1 page 25

- Ask different students to say sentences about the picture.
- Allow 2 minutes for students to read and match. Let students compare their answers in pairs before checking as a class.

KEY

1 exciting   2 attractive   3 clean   4 friendly

Exercise 2 page 25

- Students can work in pairs to complete the rules in the *Learn this!* box.
- Check as a class. Ask students to read out examples which illustrate the rules.

KEY

1 some   2 any

Exercise 3 page 25

- In a **stronger class**, students work individually for a minute.
- In a **weaker class**, play the recording for students to listen and read. Instruct them to start filling the gaps in pairs after the listening finishes.

Exercise 4 page 25 🎧 1.24

- Play the recording for students to check.
- In a **weaker class**, choose two students to read the dialogue out. Work through any problems.

1 some	3 any	5 some	7 any
2 any	4 some	6 some	

Exercise 5 page 25

- Refresh the terms *countable/uncountable* by identifying example objects, for example: *rivers are countable, water is uncountable, shops are countable, money is uncountable*. Then ask and elicit answers from students: *Are books countable? Is homework countable?*
- Students note the words in two lists in their notebooks. Check as a class.

KEY

Plural countable nouns: cinemas, cafés, parks, discos, shops, buildings, accidents, people
Uncountable nouns: scenery, pollution, traffic, time

Exercise 6 page 25

- Students work in pairs. Check as a class.
- Read the *Look out!* box with the class. Check understanding by asking: *Do we use* much/many *in affirmative sentences? Do we use* a lot of *in negative sentences?*

KEY

Uncountable nouns: a lot of, much, a little
Plural countable nouns: a lot of, many, a few

LANGUAGE NOTE – QUANTIFIERS

The quantifiers *a few* and *a little* refer to a smaller quantity than *a lot, much* and *many*. However, they have a positive feeling. The sentence: *There are a few parks in the city.* focuses on the fact that they exist rather than on how few of them there are.

To express a lack of something it is usual to say: *There aren't many …* or to omit the indefinite article: *There are few …*

Lots of has the same meaning as *a lot of* but is more informal.

For more practice on quantifiers go to:

Grammar Builder 3B: Student's Book page 108

KEY

1	1 some	2 any	3 any	4 any	5 some	6 any

2	1 a little	3 a little	5 a few
	2 a few	4 a few	6 a little

3	1 many	2 much	3 many	4 much	5 much	6 many

4	1 a lot of money	4 a lot of old people
	2 a lot of traffic	5 a lot of countries
	3 a lot of goals	6 a lot of homework

Exercise 7 page 25

- Ask students to read the text and note down uncountable nouns in their notebooks. Elicit answers from the class (pollution, entertainment, scenery).
- Allow a minute for students to choose the words. Check as a class.

KEY

1 a lot of	3 a few	5 much
2 many	4 a little	6 a lot of

Exercise 8 page 25 🎧 1.25

- Play the recording so that students can check their answers.

Exercise 9 page 25

- Allow 5 minutes for students in pairs to discuss and agree on their ideal city. While students are writing, go round and help with vocabulary problems. Encourage students to use the vocabulary from lesson 3A.

OPTIONAL ACTIVITY

Put pairs in groups of four to compare their cities. What are the similarities/differences? Allow 2 minutes so that students can discuss and make changes or improvements to their original designs.

Exercise 10 page 25

- Give pairs a minute to prepare. Students decide who will say which three sentences and learn them.
- While students are talking, make notes of any language problems to go over with the class after the vote.
- Decide on the best design as a class. What are its most important features?

➡ Lesson outcome

Ask students: *What have you learned today? What can you do now?* and elicit answers: *I can talk about quantities. I have learned to describe a town.*

3C CULTURE In the country

LESSON SUMMARY ●●○○○

Reading: a guidebook article; matching, true/false questions
Listening: an interview with three Welsh people; listening for detail
Speaking: talking about your town/village/city
Topic: home

SHORTCUT *To do the lesson in 30 minutes, allow 10 minutes for the reading (exercises 2 and 3), 10 minutes for the listening (exercises 4 and 5) and 10 minutes for the speaking (exercises 1 and 6).*

➡ Lead-in 2–3 minutes

- Inform the class of the lesson objectives.
- Put the following groups of words on the board: *British Isles, Great Britain, United Kingdom; Ireland, Wales, England, Scotland, Northern Ireland; Cardiff, London, Edinburgh, Dublin, Belfast; the Welsh, the English, the Scottish, the Irish.*
- Elicit from students the relations between the terms: *The capital of England is London. The Welsh live in Wales.* etc.

Exercise 1 page 26

• As a class, brainstorm vocabulary related to the photo. Put the words on the board. In a **stronger class**, encourage students to suggest verbs, adjectives and adverbs as well as nouns.

• Ask individual student to describe the photo. In a **weaker class**, students take it in turns to say sentences about the photo.

Exercise 2 page 26

• Focus students on the headings and elicit/explain the meaning. Do not pre-teach any other vocabulary from the text at this stage.

• Instruct the class that their task is to match the headings and that they should not try to understand everything in the paragraphs. Allow a minute.

KEY

A introduction   B scenery   C language   D industry

Exercise 3 page 26

• In a **weaker class**, pre-teach *population*. Students should be able to answer all the questions without any further help.

• Instruct them to underline the relevant fragments in the text. Allow 5 minutes. Students can compare their answers and the underlined fragments in pairs. Check as a class.

KEY

1 F   2 F   3 F   4 T   5 T   6 F

Exercise 4 page 26   🎧 1.26

• Focus students on the photos. Elicit short descriptions of the teenagers.

• Focus students on the task. Elicit or explain the meaning of *leave* and *stay*, for example, by writing the phrases *continue to live* and *go away* on the board for students to match.

• Play the recording once. Check as a class.

KEY

1 Gareth   2 Bryn   3 Bethan

Transcript 1.26

Interviewer Good morning and welcome to the programme *Country Eye*. This week on the programme we are looking at the beautiful region of north Wales, and finding out about what life is like for the people who live there. First of all, we have three young people from north Wales here in the studio. Welcome to the programme, Bryn, Gareth and Bethan.

All Thanks!

Interviewer First of all we are going to hear from Bryn. Bryn – can you tell us a little about your life there?

Bryn Yes. Well, I was born on our farm in the village of Dolanog, a little village near Welshpool, and I've lived there all my life. My first language is Welsh – we speak it at home – but I learned English at school. My dad's a sheep farmer and I've helped him on the farm for as long as I can remember. I think the Welsh countryside is a wonderful place to grow up. As a kid, me and my brothers had a lot of freedom to run about. Everyone is very friendly, but life is difficult sometimes. There isn't much money in sheep-farming, and the winters can be hard.

Interviewer So, do you think you'll stay in North Wales, then?

Bryn Oh, yes. I wouldn't want to live anywhere else. When I finish school, I want to study agriculture at college. But then I'll come back to look after the farm with my dad.

Interviewer What about you, Gareth? Do you feel the same way?

Gareth Actually, no, not at all. I come from the small town of Llangollen. I've lived in Llangollen all my life and I can't wait to leave! I mean, Llangollen is beautiful. Quite a few tourists come in the summer to go walking in the hills or visit the famous music festival. It is a nice place, and I enjoyed living there when I was younger, but not any more. Nothing happens and there's nowhere to go! I want to meet new people and try new things. I'm interested in computers, so I'm planning to go to a university somewhere like London or Cardiff. I want to try city life!

Interviewer So Bethan, are you planning to leave the Welsh countryside as well?

Bethan Well, no, not really. I live in Caernarfon – it's a small town on the north coast. I've been there all my life, but I don't know if I can stay. You see, there aren't any jobs for people there, especially young people. A lot of young people are moving out of the area because of this. I love where I live. I think it's a beautiful place to live in, but I think that I'll never find a good job there. After I leave university, I'll probably have to live and work somewhere else, and I think that's sad.

Interviewer I'm sorry to hear that, Bethan. Well, you've heard the views of some young people from the region. What are your views? Call the programme now or send us an e-mail, and we'll read out your opinions at the end of the show. Meanwhile ...

Exercise 5 page 26   🎧 1.26

• Pre-teach *countryside*, *freedom*, *agriculture* and *region*. Model the pronunciation and repeat the words several times so that students can recognise them in the recording. Allow a minute for students to read the questions.

• Play the recording once, or twice if necessary.

• To check answers, play the recording again and pause it just before the answer appears. Elicit the answer from the class and then start the recording again.

KEY

1 Welsh
2 He's a sheep farmer.
3 There isn't much money and the winters can be hard.
4 To go walking in the hills or visit the famous music festival.
5 Nothing happens and there's nowhere to go.
6 Go to university.
7 On the north coast.
8 There aren't any jobs.
9 No, she isn't.

Exercise 6 page 26

- Read the questions as a class. Elicit the meaning of *advantages/disadvantages*.
- If necessary, point to question 3. Put the following two sentences on board: *Yes, I have lived in the country all my life. No, I lived in an apartment in the city when I was a child.*
- Elicit which one refers to an action that is finished, and which one refers to a situation that is still continuing in the present. Explain that students should use the present perfect to talk about a time up to now, and the past simple to talk about events or actions that are finished. If you think students will struggle with this, just tell them to use the past simple to answer about a specific period of time. For example: *Yes, my parents bought the house before I was born.* or *No, I lived in Prague for three years.*

➡ Lesson outcome

Ask students: *What have you learned today? What can you do now?* and elicit answers: *I can understand information in a guidebook. I have learned about north Wales.*

3D GRAMMAR Articles

LESSON SUMMARY ●●●○○

Grammar: articles: *a/an*, *the*, zero article
Speaking: expressing opinions

> **SHORTCUT** *To do the lesson in 30 minutes, skip the Lead-in and set the Grammar Builder for homework.*

➡ Lead-in 3–5 minutes

- Inform the class of the lesson objectives.
- Focus students on the photo. Revise *some, any, much, many, a lot of* and *a few* as a class by asking students to make sentences about the photo.

Exercise 1 page 27

- Students work in pairs for 2 minutes. Share ideas as a class.

Exercise 2 page 27

- Read the *Learn this!* box with the class. Students match the rules with the articles in the text on their own. Allow a minute. Check as a class.

KEY

a town – 1   The town – 2   a nice place – 3   the sea – 4

Exercise 3 page 27

- Ask students to underline all the articles in the text first, then match them to the rules. Check as a class.

KEY

the east coast – 4	a big boat – 1
a fisherman – 3	the boat – 2

Exercise 4 page 27

- Ask students briefly if they chat on the Internet, with whom, and how much time they spend doing it.
- In a **stronger class**, students work individually for 2 minutes. Read the answers out to the class. To check if they have learned how to use articles, elicit how many students have made four mistakes or fewer.
- In a **weaker class**, students can work in pairs. Allow 4 minutes. To check answers and see which rule is problematic, ask a pair to read an answer. The rest of the class vote on whether it is correct by raising hands. Give feedback by confirming the result of the voting or correcting it.

KEY

1 a – rule 1	6 a – rule 3	11 the – rule 2
2 the – rule 4	7 a – rule 3	12 a – rule 1
3 a – rule 3	8 the – rule 4	
4 the – rule 2	9 a – rule 1	
5 a – rule 3	10 a – rule 1	

For more practice on a/an *and* the, *go to:*

> **Grammar Builder 3D:** Student's Book page 108

KEY

5
1 a, a, The, the	5 a, a, The, the
2 a, a, The, the	6 a, a, the
3 a, The	7 a, a, The, the
4 a, a, the	

6
1	a a	b	the
2	a the	b	a
3	a the	b	a
4	a a	b	the
5	a a	b	The
6	a the	b	a

7
1 the President	5 the army
2 the world	6 the sea
3 the sun	7 The moon
4 the police	8 the capital

8
1 cold coffee	5 fashion
2 the coffee	6 football
3 cats	7 the CDs
4 the dogs	8 The water

PRONUNCIATION – HELPING YOUR STUDENTS WITH THE SOUNDS /ð/ AND /θ/

/ð/ and /θ/ are two of the most difficult sounds for students to produce correctly. To help your students to produce the sounds correctly demonstrate how the tongue sticks out beyond the upper teeth. Get them to practise the sound by putting their finger against their lips as if to say *Shh*. When they say the /ð/ and /θ/ sounds they should touch their finger with their tongue.

For extra practice dictate the following sentences and then ask students to repeat them several times in pairs.

1 Beth thought that the theatre was closed on Thursdays.
2 They lived with their grandfather in Denmark.
3 The footpath went through the field.
4 I think the meeting is at three-thirty on Tuesday.

Exercise 5 page 27
- Read the *Look out!* box with the class. Elicit which sentences are generalisations (the second one in each pair).
- In a **weaker class**, work together. If students have problems, remind them of rule 2 in exercise 2 (We use *the* when we both know the thing that we are talking about.)
- In a **stronger class**, students work individually. Allow 2 minutes. Check as a class. Encourage students to justify their answers.

KEY
1 Life (everybody's; not one person's life)
2 The weather (specifically the weather in Scotland last weekend)
3 bicycles, pedestrians (all or any of them)
4 Indian food (this type of food in general)
5 The fields (specifically the ones around the village)
6 advertisements (all or any of them)

Exercise 6 page 27 🎧 1.25
- Put two groups of letters (e.g. *a, e, o* and *b, c, s*) and two words (*vowels, consonants*) on the board. Elicit more examples from students.
- Point out that 'u' is a vowel but makes the sound /juː/ at the beginning of some words (e.g. *United States*).
- Read the instructions with the class. Play the recording and elicit the answer. Play the recording again for students to repeat chorally and individually.

Transcript 1.25
/ði/ advertisement /ðə/ cottage /ði/ east /ði/ end
/ði/ English /ðə/ gate /ði/ industry /ðə/ scenery
/ðə/ village /ðə/ west

Exercise 7 page 27
- In a **weaker class**, go over the table with students explaining the expressions and eliciting which ones are generalisations.
- In a **stronger class**, ask students to give reasons with their answers.

➡ Lesson outcome
Ask students: *What have you learned today? What can you do now?* and elicit answers: *I can correctly use 'a/an' and 'the' with nouns. I have learned to pronounce the 'the' sound.*

Notes for Photocopiable activity 3.2
Grammar lottery
Grammar game
Language: countable and uncountable nouns, *some* and *any*, *much, many* and *a lot of*, articles, prepositions of movement.
Materials: one copy of the worksheet per pair of students (Teacher's Book page 129)
- Divide students into pairs and hand out a copy of the worksheet to each pair. Ask them to decide whether each sentence is correct and put a tick in the *Correct* or *Incorrect* column accordingly.

- Explain to students that they are now going to put bets on their sentences depending on how sure they are that their answers are correct. Tell them that they must bet between £10 and £100 on each answer being correct. Set a time limit for them to place their bets, for example, 5 minutes. They write their bets in the *Bet* column.
- Go through the answers. If students are correct they win the amount that they bet on that answer and write the amount in the *Winnings* column. For example, if they bet £20 and they were correct, they write +20. If they don't have the correct answer, they lose the money they bet and mark it in the *Winnings* column with a minus sign, i.e. −20.
- If necessary, to avoid cheating, ask students to mark another pair's worksheet.
- At the end ask them to add up their total and find out who won the most money.
- Go through the incorrect sentences as a class and elicit corrections from the students.

KEY
1 incorrect	6 incorrect	11 incorrect
2 incorrect	7 correct	12 correct
3 correct	8 incorrect	13 incorrect
4 incorrect	9 correct	14 incorrect
5 incorrect	10 incorrect	15 correct

3E READING
Are you lonesome tonight?

LESSON SUMMARY ●●●●○
Reading: a newspaper article; true/false questions
Vocabulary: adjectives for describing places
Speaking: talking about where you live
Topic: home

SHORTCUT *To do the lesson in 30 minutes, do exercises 1, 4, 6 and 7 quickly as a class.*

➡ Lead-in 3–5 minutes
- Inform the class of the lesson objectives.
- Put *lonesome, lonely* and *alone* on the board. Elicit or explain the meaning (*lonesome, lonely* – feeling sad and unhappy because you have no friends to talk to; *alone* – without any other people).
- Ask students if they know any people who live alone. Ask: *are they happy about it? In what ways is life difficult/easy when you are alone? In what other situations can a person feel lonely?* Have a short class discussion.

Exercise 1 page 28
- Encourage students to share ideas by explaining that analysing the photos and the title will help them understand the text. While students are brainstorming, do not reveal which of their ideas match the text.

Exercise 2 page 28
- Read the instructions with the class. Check understanding by asking: *How many paragraphs are there in the text?* (5) *Why is it good to read sentence 1 in each paragraph?* (Because it gives you the general idea of what the paragraphs and the text are about.)
- Allow 2 minutes for students to match. Do not check yet.

Exercise 3 page 28

- In a **weaker class**, pre-teach *mayor, clerk, treasurer, librarian, railway, inhabitant, truck driver, surrounded by, filled with, compete with, industrialised, turn to dust, take care of.*
- Allow 4 minutes for students to read. Check answers.

KEY

1 Who is Elsie and what does she do? (topic 3)
2 A description of the town of Monowi (topic 1)
3 Monowi in the past (topic 4)
4 Finding work (topic 2)
5 What Elsie thinks of life in Monowi (topic 5)

CULTURE NOTE – JOBS

In the US the mayor /meə(r)/ is the head of the local government and is elected by the residents of the town. A mayor belongs to one of the two main political parties and often has a lot of political power. (In the UK the mayor does not have much political power.)

The town clerk /klɑːk/ is a person who keeps a town's records, for example: birth, marriage and death records, census information and voter registration.

The town treasurer /ˈtreʒərə(r)/ is the person who controls a town's finances.

Exercise 4 page 28

- In a **weaker class**, work together.
- In a **stronger class**, ask students in pairs to analyse the context on their own. Check as a class.

KEY

1 empty   4 rural   6 lonely
2 tiny   5 extraordinary 7 enormous
3 silent

Exercise 5 page 29

- Students read the instructions and do the task individually. Allow 5 minutes. Remind them to underline the relevant fragments of the text.
- Check by having different students read an answer and the text fragment.

KEY

1 T
2 T
3 T
4 F 'the farmers couldn't compete with the enormous industrialised farms. They left the town to look for other work.'
5 F 'Three years ago, the last inhabitant, apart from Elsie and her husband, moved away. Then Elsie's husband died.'
6 T
7 F '...as long as I can take care of myself, I'll stay here.'

Exercise 6 page 29

- Students can work in pairs. Explain that all adjectives refer to places, for example, a town. Check as a class. Model the pronunciation for students to repeat chorally and individually.

KEY

1 boring – **c** exciting   5 noisy – **g** quiet
2 clean – **a** polluted   6 pretty – **d** ugly
3 dangerous – **e** safe   7 relaxing – **b** stressful
4 modern – **f** old

Exercise 7 page 29

- Go over the questions with the class. Explain or elicit the meaning of *the best* and *the worst*. Check that students understand the second question (*What's it like?*) by writing two answers on the board (e.g. *I like it very much.* and *It's beautiful.*) and eliciting the correct one.
- Encourage students to write notes rather than full sentences as it saves time. Allow 3 minutes.

KEY

1 c   2 e   3 a   4 f   5 b   6 d

Exercise 8 page 29

- Put students in new pairs – the less they know each other, the better. Allow 4–6 minutes.
- Ask different students to report back on their partners. If they live in the same area, do they agree on their descriptions and evaluations?

ADDITIONAL SPEAKING ACTIVITY

Ask students: *If you were Elsie Eiler, would you stay in Monowi? Why/ Why not?*

Get students to look back through the text and find reasons why the other people left Monowi. Start a list on the board. Encourage them to add to it with their own ideas. Ask: *What shops and services do you need in a town? What do young families need? What do old people need?*

Now put students in pairs to think of reasons why people stay in a place. Allow a couple of minutes before sharing ideas as a class.

Divide students up into As and Bs. Explain to students that they are the residents of a town like Monowi. People have started moving away and the town is dying. Group A want to move away. Group B want to stay in their town.

Allow a couple of minutes for students to prepare their reasons for staying or going individually. Remind them of the quantifiers and adjectives to describe a town from lesson 3B and ask them to remember anything that they can from the interviews in 3C. Encourage them to make notes with key words rather than writing out whole sentences.

Put students in new A/B pairs. Tell them that they must discuss their situation and try to convince their partner to stay or go.

Allow 3–4 minutes for pairwork. Encourage students to respond to what their partner says and try to think of reasons why they are wrong.

Finally bring the class together again. Ask pairs who are leaving to raise their hands. Ask pairs who are staying to raise their hands. Briefly ask a few pairs to say why they made their decision.

→ Lesson outcome

Ask students: *What have you learned today? What can you do now?* and elicit answers: *I can understand a newspaper article. I have learned about Monowi. I can talk about where I live.*

3F EVERYDAY ENGLISH
Giving directions

LESSON SUMMARY ●●●○○

Functional English: understanding, asking for and giving directions
Vocabulary: shops and buildings; prepositions of place
Listening: a dialogue; following a route on the map
Speaking: asking for and giving directions
Topic: town life

SHORTCUT *To do the lesson in 30 minutes, skip the Lead-in and keep a fast pace. Do exercise 9 next time for revision.*

→ Lead-in 3–5 minutes
- Inform the class of the lesson objectives.
- Put students in small groups and explain that they are going to prepare a challenge for the other groups. To do so, they start by brainstorming and noting down vocabulary related to shops and buildings in town. Then they should make 'word links' in which the last letter of the first word is the first letter of the second word e.g. *shopostoffice* (shop + post office), *churchospital* (church + hospital). Allow 1–2 minutes.
- Explain that they will now write one of their 'word links' on the board but omit the first two and the last two letters; e.g. *opostoffi, urchospit*. The other groups try to guess the two words in the 'word link'. You can set it as a contest among groups. The group which has guessed the most words is the winner.

Exercise 1 page 30
- Focus students on the map. Ask different students to read out the names of the buildings. Check recall by asking: *What can you buy there? Why do you go there?* etc.
- Focus students on the prepositions. Illustrate the usage by saying sentences about the location of the buildings on the map.
- Allow 2 minutes for students to ask and answer. Check by eliciting answers from the class.

Exercise 2 page 30
- Students work individually, then compare their answers in pairs. Allow 2 minutes. Check as a class. If students have problems, draw the route on the board.

Exercise 3 page 30 🎧 1.28
- Play the recording, pausing for students to repeat chorally and individually.

Ask another student to come to the board and erase all of the articles. Practise the dialogue again. Continue with pronouns, then nouns. Finally, erase the remaining words and students should be able to say the dialogue with no prompts at all.

Exercise 4 page 30
- If students do not understand the sentences, ask them to look back at the dialogue and the map and work the meaning out from the context. Allow 2 minutes. Check as a class.

KEY
1 Go straight on.
2 Turn left at the traffic lights.
3 Go past the bus stop.
4 Take the first left.
5 Go to the end of the road.
6 Go along Queen Street.

Exercise 5 page 30 🎧 1.29
- Explain the task. Play the recording twice. On the second listening, stop after each dialogue to check answers.
- In a **stronger class**, ask a student to say the directions again.

Transcript and Key 1.29
1 Turn left into West Street. Take the second right and go to the end of the road. Turn left and it's, uh, let me see, on the corner, opposite the zoo. (= the music shop)
2 Go straight on. Take the third left. It's on the right, between the cinema and the swimming pool. (= the hotel)
3 Go straight on, take the first left and go to the end of the road. Turn left and it's at the end of the road. (= the station)
4 Go straight on. Take the first left, then the second right. It's on the right, between the police station and the supermarket. (= the clothes shop)
5 Go straight on. Take the fourth left, then the first right. It's on the right opposite the school. (= the church)

Exercise 6 page 30
- Read the speaking tip with the class. Conduct a drill to practise using fillers: T: *Where is the bar?* Ss: *Let me see, it's opposite the bank.*

Exercise 7 page 30
- In a **weaker class**, students write down the full dialogue. Allow 5 minutes.
- In a **stronger class**, students decide on the place and the route. Remind them to speak English when they are making decisions.
- Students practise their dialogues in pairs. Encourage them to use the map rather than their notes. Allow 2 minutes.

Exercise 8 page 30

- Encourage students to evaluate the dialogues they hear, e.g. by noting ticks or crosses in the following categories:
  - the student who asked for directions now knows how to get to the place
  - the student who answered gave full information
  - they were both polite
  - they used the language from the lesson (prepositions, fillers, etc.)
- Give feedback as a class.

Exercise 9 page 30

- In a **weaker class**, work together. Ask about different places and elicit answers.
- In a **stronger class**, students work in pairs.

➡ Lesson outcome

Ask students: *What have you learned today? What can you do now?* and elicit answers: *I can understand and give directions. I have learned to use prepositions and fillers.*

3G WRITING A leaflet

LESSON SUMMARY

Reading: tourist leaflets about places in Britain
Vocabulary: adjectives describing places
Writing: a tourist leaflet
Topic: travel and tourism

SHORTCUT *To do the lesson in 30 minutes, skip the Lead-in. Reduce discussion time in exercise 6 and get quickly into the writing.*

➡ Lead-in 2–3 minutes

- Inform the class of the lesson objectives.
- Ask: *Do you often get leaflets at home? Where do they come from? Do you read them? Where else can you find leaflets?*
- Focus on tourist leaflets and ask: *Why do tourist offices produce leaflets?* (To provide information about places/events and to persuade people to go to them.) *How is a tourist leaflet different from a tourist guide?* (A leaflet is short, it's quite cheap to produce and it's free.)

Exercise 1 page 31

- Write *Devon* and *York* on the board. Explain that Devon is a county (region) in England, while York is a city in the northern county of Yorkshire. Tell students that the Yorkshire Dales are an area of beautiful hills and valleys.
- Read the writing task as a class. Then allow 2–3 minutes for students to read the two leaflets.
- Elicit students' preferences and ask them to give reasons.
- Explain the meaning of *moorland, wander, don't miss, marvel, scenery,* but avoid explanation of the adjectives.
- Write the following two lists on the board. Students match to form collocations without looking at their book.
  A: *visit, relax, wander, climb, learn, marvel*
  B: *on the sand, at the scenery, about the history, through the streets, the museum, to the top*

Exercise 2 page 31

- Students should see that a bulleted list draws attention to each point separately and makes them easier to take in.

Exercise 3 page 31

- Before they work on leaflet A, ask students to say what each bullet point in B is about (1 walks in York, 2 York Minster, 3 Jorvik Museum, 4 Yorkshire Dales).

KEY
- There are miles … a good book.
- If you like walking … open moorland.
- Devon has got … castle at Totnes.

Exercise 4 page 31

- Note that not every bullet list uses imperatives. However, it is important to give the list a consistent structure. Imperatives are often useful for leaflets or other forms of advertisement because they address the reader very directly.

KEY
A verb in the imperative.

Exercise 5 page 31

- Students can work individually or in pairs. Ask **fast finishers** to find five more adjectives in the texts.
- Say the adjectives and get students to repeat.

KEY

1 vast	4 ancient	7 fascinating
2 historic	5 famous	8 stunning
3 atmospheric	6 wonderful	

Exercise 6 page 31

- Read the writing tip as a class.
- Ask students to consider their local region. Read the list with them and elicit one or two possibilities for each item. Ask them to suggest suitable adjectives.
- Students write notes to plan a leaflet on their country. **Weaker students** can get help by working in pairs or groups.
- Allow 15 minutes for writing. Go round and give help.
- Give students time to check their work, using the checklist.
- **Fast finishers** can form pairs and check each other's work. They then exchange comments, offering any suggestions that could improve their partner's work.

ALTERNATIVE WRITING TASK

Write a leaflet for parents, advertising your school (70–80 words). Include:

- general introduction – type of school, location and appearance, number of teachers/students
- facilities for learning
- sports and lunch-time/after-school activities

OPTIONAL ACTIVITY

Invite students to design their leaflet at home on the computer. Encourage them to create an interesting layout and to find suitable images to illustrate their text.

➡ Lesson outcome

- Ask students: *What have you learned today? What can you do now?* and elicit answers: *I can write a tourist leaflet. I have learned adjectives to describe places and buildings.*

Get ready for your EXAM 3

TOPIC ●●●●○
Sport

➡ Lead-in 4–5 minutes

- Inform the class of the lesson objectives.
- Write these two lists on the board:
  A: *win/lose compete in hit cross score kick*
  B: *a goal the line the ball a race a match a point*
- Set a time limit of 3 minutes. In pairs, students match A and B words to make as many possible collocations as they can and write an example of a sport for each one. Ask them to try not to use the same sport more than twice.
- The pair with the most correct answers is the winner. Answers:
  win/lose – the ball (e.g. football), a race (e.g. running), a match (e.g. baseball), a point (e.g. volleyball)
  compete in – a race (e.g. swimming), a match (e.g. tennis)
  hit – the ball (e.g. golf)
  cross – the ball (football), the line (e.g. cycling)
  score – a goal (e.g. hockey), a point (e.g. basketball)
  kick – a goal (e.g. football), the ball (e.g. rugby)

Exercise 1 page 32 3–4 minutes

- Go through the words and check that students understand them.
- Do the exercise as a class. To justify their answers, ask students to make sentences about the photos, using the words. They will need to change the form of the verbs. Remind them to use the present continuous as the main tense to describe what is happening in a photo.

KEY
Suggested answers:
Photo 1: happy, cyclist, individual determination, race, win
Photo 2: disappointed, lose, match, players, score, team spirit

Exercise 2 page 32 5–7 minutes

- Point out that when comparing photos, it is a good idea to start with what they have in common, and then move on to describe the differences.
- In pairs, students help each other to observe and describe similarities and differences.
- Ask some students to share their ideas with the class. Invite others to add their own observations or to express the comparison/contrast in a different way.
- As students speak, extract useful words and phrases for each photo and write them on the board, to add to those in exercise 1. In a **weaker class**, you can leave these on the board for students to refer to when they are doing exercise 3. In a **stronger class**, rub them off and ask students to cover the words in exercise 1.

Exercise 3 page 32 6–8 minutes
E Speaking: picture-based discussion

- Put students in different pairs for the exam task. Tell them they will need to speak for 1–2 minutes.
- In a **weaker class**, model the activity yourself.
- Allow 3 minutes for students to prepare, making brief notes. Advise them to plan how they will begin – it is good to establish confidence with a strong start.
- Students take it in turns to speak while their partner listens. They can offer comments to each other afterwards.

Exercise 4 page 32 10–15 minutes
E Reading: matching headings to paragraphs

- Read the exam task as a class.
- Students should understand that the exam is a challenge, so do not pre-teach any vocabulary. Explain that learning to deal with unknown words is a valuable part of exam training.
- Encourage students to try to infer the meaning of an unknown word from its context. Remind them to look at the words around it and decide whether it is a noun, verb, adjective, etc. It is often enough to have an idea of meaning. For example, the text mentions *competitive* and *sideline* cheerleading. It is not essential to know the words themselves but to understand that they describe two different types of cheerleading.
- Tell students to read the whole text first. Then they should read each paragraph carefully to understand its main idea. Often – but not always – this is expressed in the first sentence of the paragraph. The next step is to read the headings and try to find the matching paragraph. Finally they should make sure the remaining heading is useless. Tell them to read the remaining heading with each paragraph to make sure it doesn't fit anywhere.
- Students work individually. Check as a class.

KEY
1 F 2 D 3 B 4 C 5 A

OPTIONAL ACTIVITY
Put *compete against, competitive* and *competitor* on the board. Focus **fast finishers** on the last sentences in paragraphs 1, 4 and 5. Ask them to work out what part of speech the words are and their meaning from the context. Get feedback after checking the exam task.

Exercise 5 page 32 5 minutes

- Students look in detail at paragraph 4 and answer the questions in pairs.
- Check as a class and discuss question 3.

KEY
1 Their reasons are that cheerleading isn't a ball sport, cheerleaders do not score points, they do not win races and cheerleaders are entertainers, not competitors.
2 The writer points out that the first three reasons apply to many other sports, and the fourth is not correct as cheerleaders compete and train hard like other athletes.

➡ Lesson outcome

- Ask students: *What have you learned today? What can you do now?* and elicit answers: *I have compared and contrasted photos as a speaking task. I have practised matching headings to paragraphs in a text.*

Get ready for your **EXAM** (4)

➔ Lead-in 3–5 minutes
- Inform the class of the lesson objectives.
- Elicit the words for different rooms in a house/flat. Put the words on the board.
- Divide the class into as many groups as there are rooms. Allocate the rooms. Ask each group to put down as many words for furniture and utensils as they can in 2 minutes. Share answers as a class.

Exercise 1 page 33 4 minutes
- Get students to report on what their partners said.

Exercise 2 page 33 3–4 minutes
- Students work individually, then compare answers in pairs.

KEY

1 share	4 detached	7 rent
2 rent	5 neighbourhood	8 flatmates
3 furnished	6 neighbours	9 tube station

Exercise 3 page 33 🎧 1.30 10 minutes
E Listening: multiple-choice statements
- Read the task as a class. Explain that you will play the recording twice, with a pause in between. The information students need will be heard in the order of the questions.
- For the first listening students should focus on the questions, marking answers as they hear them. By the time they come to the second listening they should expect to be fairly definite about some answers, while others will still be unclear. In the second listening they should concentrate on confirming the answers they have and listening for the answers they still need.
- Allow 1 minute for students to read the questions. Play the recording twice with a 30-second pause in between.
- Check answers. Discuss students' experience of the task.

KEY
1 A 2 B 3 A 4 C 5 C 6 A

Transcript 🎧 1.30
Man Good morning, I'm looking for a house or flat to rent.
Woman OK. What exactly are you looking for?
Man Well, I want somewhere for me and two friends to share. We're students at City University, and we're going to be in London till the end of June. We need somewhere quite cheap – we can't afford to pay a lot of rent.
Woman I see. Are you interested in a furnished flat, or have you got your own furniture.
Man We want a furnished flat.
Woman Fine. Now, what parts of London are you interested in?
Man I suppose central London is very expensive.
Woman Very!
Man So somewhere in north London is fine. And near a tube station, if possible.
Woman Well, I think I've got just the thing for you and your friends: a three-bedroomed flat, furnished, not far from Finsbury Park tube station. The rent is £500 a week. Have a look at the photos.
Man Oh, it looks great.

Woman There's a pub within walking distance and a post office just across the street. Oh and there's an Internet café nearby too.
Man That's useful, because I haven't got a computer at home. When can we go and see it?
Woman How about Friday at 10.00 a.m. Does that suit you?
Man Fine. Where shall we meet?
Woman I'll give you the address and we can meet outside the house.
Man What's the neighbourhood like?
Woman It's really nice and quiet.
Man Oh, did you say 'quiet'?
Woman Yes, is that a problem?
Man Er, well, yes, perhaps. You see, we love having parties. And we like listening to music. One of my flatmates plays the electric guitar. So I don't think we'd be very popular with the neighbours – and we don't want to cause problems. Couldn't you find something in a different neighbourhood – somewhere ... exciting?
Woman Let me see. Well, what about this one: three furnished bedrooms in a big, detached house. Four students are already renting rooms there. They're looking for three more students to rent the other three rooms.
Man How much is the rent?
Woman Only £300 a week – £100 each.
Man Sounds great! It's a lot of people in one house, but we need somewhere cheap. When can we have a look at it?
Woman I'll have to call and make an appointment. Could you phone me tomorrow and we'll fix a time?
Man No problem. Thanks for your help.

Exercise 4 page 33 5–6 minutes
- Choose students to read out the words, and elicit translations. Practise the pronunciation where necessary.
- Students work on the photos in pairs. Ask **stronger students** to name other objects that are not in the list.

Exercise 5 page 33 3 minutes
- Do the exercise as a class. Some answers will vary according to students' tastes and preferences.

Exercise 6 page 33 5–6 minutes
- Students do the exercise individually. Explain that these sentences provide good models for making contrasts.
- Elicit other sentences contrasting the two photos.

KEY
1 difference 2 but 3 the other 4 However 5 Although

Exercise 7 page 33 8–10 minutes
E Speaking: picture-based discussion
- Give students 3 minutes to consider the questions and plan what they will say. Allow them to make brief notes.
- In pairs, students take it in turns to speak for 1–2 minutes. Their partner should only contribute by expressing interest or encouragement. They can comment at the end.
- Ask a strong student to describe the two photos in front of the class, and give feedback.
- Put students in new pairs to practise again.

➔ Lesson outcome
- Ask students: *What have you learned today? What can you do now?* and elicit answers: *I have learned words connected with renting a flat. I have practised a multiple-choice listening task. I have compared and contrasted photos as a speaking task.*

4 In the spotlight

THIS UNIT INCLUDES ●●●●
Vocabulary • types of film • adjectives to describe films
• -ed and -ing adjectives • types of TV programme
Grammar • comparatives and superlatives • (not) as ... as, too, enough
Speaking • talking about films and TV programmes • buying tickets
• giving opinions • checking understanding
Writing • a film review
WORKBOOK pages 30–36 • Self check 4 page 37

A VOCABULARY AND LISTENING
At the cinema

LESSON SUMMARY ●●●○○

Vocabulary: types of films, adjectives to describe films, -ed and -ing adjectives
Listening: film excerpts; matching
Speaking: talking about types of film/films you like and dislike
Topic: entertainment

SHORTCUT *To do the lesson in 30 minutes, set Vocabulary Builder parts 1 and 2 for homework. Skip the pre-listening activity in exercise 5. Play recording 1.31 once pausing after each item to elicit the answer. Or, if you want to do Vocabulary Builder part 2 in class, skip the Lead-in and the pre-listening activity in exercise 5.*

➡ Lead-in 3–5 minutes

• Inform the class of the lesson objectives.
• Focus students on the unit and lesson titles. Explain that *in the spotlight* is a phrase that comes from the theatre, but you are also in the spotlight if you attract a lot of attention from newspapers, television and the public. Elicit which film stars are in the spotlight at the moment and what films are on at the cinema.
• Brainstorm the names for types of films with the class. Put on the board all original titles in English that students can think of in the different categories. Keep the film titles on the board as students will need them later in the lesson.

Exercise 1 page 34

• Elicit what students know about the films and actors. Ask if students remember other films the actors played in. Add titles on the board.

KEY

1 *Mission Impossible 3*	5 *Chicago*
2 *Zathura: A Space Adventure*	6 *Hart's War*
3 *Along Came Polly*	7 *The Day After Tomorrow*
4 *Madagascar*	8 *Oliver*

Exercise 2 page 34

• Students can work in pairs for a minute.

KEY

1 action film	5 musical
2 science fiction film	6 war film
3 romantic comedy	7 disaster film
4 animated film	8 historical drama

Not illustrated: comedy, horror film, western

LANGUAGE NOTE – SCI-FI

Science fiction is often shortened to *sci-fi* (like hi-fi)
/saɪ faɪ/.

Exercise 3 page 34 🎧 1.32

• Play the recording for students to check. Play it again stopping after each item so that students can repeat chorally and individually.
• Elicit some titles of the film types that are not illustrated. Add titles on the board.

Exercise 4 page 34

• Focus students on the instructions and examples. In a **stronger class**, elicit other ways of expressing likes and dislikes (*I love, hate, can't stand, don't mind*, etc.). Remind students that they can use the titles from the board while they are speaking but they should focus on types of films. Allow 2 minutes to work in pairs. Elicit feedback from one pair.

LANGUAGE NOTE – *QUITE*

Quite has two meanings: *very* and *not completely*. The difference is expressed in the stress and intonation. In the context of exercise 4 the meaning is *not completely* and so it has strong stress and high intonation.

Exercise 5 page 34 🎧 1.33

• In a **stronger class**, brainstorm typical features of particular film types, for example: In action films there are a lot of special effects. In animated films the characters are often animals. In comedies people make a lot of mistakes. Play the recording once.
• In a **weaker class**, you can pre-teach *dead, one-eyed, galaxy, waitress, honour*. Play the recording twice if necessary.
• Check as a class.

KEY

1 horror film	4 comedy
2 western	5 historical drama
3 science fiction film	

Transcript 1.33

1
Girl Who is it? I said, who is it?
Man It's Tommy.
Girl But ... but you're dead!
Man I know.
Girl Where are you? I can't see you.
Man I'm right behind you.
Girl (SCREAMS)

2
Man Whisky. Where's One-Eyed Murray?
OEM Behind ya.
Man This town ain't big enough for the two of us. Get back on your horse and ride!
OEM I ain't going nowhere.
Man If you're not out of town by tomorrow, I'll kill you.

3

Captain   Ah, Jenson. Where are we?
Jenson   We're approaching a galaxy called Proteus 5, Sir.
Captain   What do we know about it?
Jenson   Not very much. The dominant life-form in this galaxy is peaceful and intelligent.
Captain   Computer! What's happening?
Computer The spaceship is under attack.

4

Man   So, you're our new waitress.
Waitress Yes, I am.
Man   Have you got experience?
Waitress Yes, I have. But not of being a waitress.
Chef   Coffee for table five!
Waitress I'll do it!
Man   I don't believe it. Look at my trousers.
Waitress I'll sort it out. Here, let me …
Man   Don't touch me! Don't you touch me!

5

Courtier Her majesty, Queen Elizabeth I.
Queen   Ah, my loyal duke. Are you well?
Duke   Yes, your majesty. I am always well when I am in your company. It is a great honour.
Queen   But you are standing strangely.
Duke   Yes, your majesty. Last month, I was injured in the Dolomites.
Queen   How very painful.

Exercise 6 page 34

• Allow a minute for students to work individually.

KEY

2	boring	4	funny	6	violent
3	scary	5	moving	7	entertaining

Exercise 7 page 34 🎧 1.34

• Play the recording. Students listen and check their answers. Have individual students read the completed sentences. Correct and model the pronunciation of adjectives for the class to repeat.

For further practice on types of films and adjectives to describe films, go to:

Vocabulary Builder (part 1): Student's Book page 127

KEY

1 Open answers

2		**3**	
1	comedy	1	funny
2	horror film	2	scary
3	historical drama	3	boring
4	romantic comedy	4	moving
5	war film	5	violent
6	science fiction film	6	gripping
7	musical	7	entertaining

Exercise 8 page 34

• Allow a minute for individual preparation.

Exercise 9 page 34

• Elicit expressions used to agree/disagree (*I agree, I don't think so,* etc.). Students share opinions in pairs. Allow 3–4 minutes.

For practice on –ed and –ing adjectives, go to:

Vocabulary Builder (part 2): Student's Book page 127

KEY

4		**7**	
1	embarrassing	1	boring
2	excited	2	interesting
3	interesting	3	exciting
4	surprised	4	embarrassing
5	confusing	5	annoyed
6	disappointed	6	surprised
7	frightening	7	exhausting
8	exhausted	8	disappointing

5–6 Open answers

➡ Lesson outcome

Ask students: *What have you learned today? What can you do now?* and elicit answers: *I can talk about different types of film. I can describe films and types of film. I can talk about films I like and say why I like them.*

4B GRAMMAR
Comparatives and superlatives

LESSON SUMMARY ●●●○○

Grammar: comparatives and superlatives
Speaking: comparing films; asking and answering questions with superlatives

SHORTCUT *To do the lesson in 30 minutes, set the Grammar Builder for homework and do exercises 2, 4 and 5 as a class.*

➡ Lead-in 4–5 minutes

• Inform the class of the lesson objectives.
• Brainstorm the names of famous Hollywood actors with the class. Ask which of them students like or dislike and why. Finally elicit what students know and think about Tom Hanks.

CULTURE NOTE – TOM HANKS

Some of most famous films that Tom Hanks has starred in include *The Da Vinci Code, The Green Mile, Saving Private Ryan, Philadelphia, Apollo 13* and *Forrest Gump.*

Exercise 1 page 35

• Ask students to try to correct the sentences on their own, then check with the text. Allow 2–3 minutes.
• Focus **fast finishers** on the photo of Tom Hanks. How many sentences can they say about it?
• Check answers, then elicit what students learned about the actor from the text and the photo.

KEY

1 Tom Hanks is one of the richest actors in Hollywood.
2 *You've Got Mail* was one of the biggest comedies of 1998.
3 Tom Hanks isn't the most attractive actor in Hollywood.

Exercise 2 page 35

- Focus students on the table.
- In a **stronger class**, elicit how the forms are made. Ask students to complete the table on their own, then check with the text. In a **weaker class**, reverse the procedure. Students copy the forms from the text into the table. Elicit the rules.

KEY

1 the richest	4 more entertaining
2 the biggest	5 the most attractive
3 funnier	6 the best

LANGUAGE NOTE – SUPERLATIVES

In addition to learning the rules of the adjectives students should also be aware of the way the sentence usually continues after it, especially with the superlative form. Typical follow-on phrases after the superlative are *in the...* (not *of* the), e.g. *the longest river in the world*; *I've ever* plus past participle e.g. *It's the funniest film I've ever seen* and *yet*, e.g. *This is his best film yet*. There are examples of each of these in this lesson.

Point out to students that the use of the possessive, for example, *Spielberg's best film yet.* or Her *most successful film so far.* means that *the* is no longer necessary to form the superlative.

For revision of spelling rules for comparatives and superlatives students can use the Grammar Reference on page 111 of the Student's Book.

OPTIONAL ACTIVITY

Ask students to write three sentences using the following pattern: (person) is one of the most (adjective) (plural noun) I know.

Sample answer: *Tom Hanks is one of the most famous actors I know.*

Exercise 3 page 35

- Read the categories in the table out to the class and elicit which expression from the box matches each category.
- Students can work in pairs for 4 minutes. In a **weaker class**, ask them to write one sentence for each of the six categories. In a **stronger class**, students use all seven expressions from the box.
- Focus **fast finishers** on the stills from both films. Which moments of the films are presented? What is going on? You can check by saying false sentences about the films and eliciting corrections.

KEY

Gladiator was shorter than *The Aviator*.
Gladiator was more popular than *The Aviator*.
Gladiator was more violent than *The Aviator*.
Gladiator was more entertaining than *The Aviator*.
The Aviator was more boring than *Gladiator*.
The Aviator was funnier than *Gladiator*.

For more practice on comparative and superlative forms of adjectives, go to:

Grammar Builder 4B: Student's Book page 110

- Students can find spelling rules in Grammar Reference 4.1

KEY

1

1	larger	3	thinner	5	better	7	hotter
2	taller	4	earlier	6	easier	8	worse

2

1	taller	3	hotter	5	better	7	thinner
2	larger	4	easier	6	earlier	8	worse

3

1 more difficult than	4 more confident than
2 more boring than	5 more entertaining than
3 more successful ... than	6 more exciting than

4

2 Mark is the funniest boy in the class.
3 Russia is the largest country in the world.
4 Hollywood films are the most popular films in the world.
5 Germany has got the biggest population in Europe.
6 Who is the most hard-working student in the class?
7 *Schindler's List* is the most moving film I've ever seen.

Exercise 4 page 35

- Pre-teach *film addicts, thought-provoking, overrated, director.*
- Students work individually for 3 minutes.
- Ask **fast finishers** to list all the titles of Spielberg's films they can remember.
- Check as a class.

KEY

1	best	7	more interesting
2	more gripping	8	most successful
3	earlier	9	the most entertaining
4	better	10	more moving
5	More violent	11	scarier
6	slower		

OPTIONAL ACTIVITY

Elicit what other films directed by Steven Spielberg students can remember. Do students like his films? Is he the best director in the world? Why is he one of the most popular ones?

LANGUAGE NOTE – BEAUTY

Make sure that students are clear that *beautiful* is used to describe women, *good-looking* is usually for men and *attractive* can be used for either.

Exercise 5 page 35

- Work as a class. Ask different students to read out the questions. The rest of the class note them down in their notebooks.

KEY

1 Who's the best looking actor in the world?
2 What's the funniest comedy on TV?
3 Who's the most beautiful actress in the world?
4 What's the most boring programme on TV?
5 Who's the best film director in your country?
6 What's the scariest film you've ever seen?
7 What's the best film you've ever seen?

Exercise 6 page 35

- Students take it in turns to ask and answer the questions. Allow 3 minutes but extend the time if most students are still speaking.

> **OPTIONAL ACTIVITY**
> If there is time left at the end of the lesson, discuss one or more questions with the class.

➡ Lesson outcome

Ask students: *What have you learned today? What can you do now?* and elicit answers: *I can make comparisons. I have learned to use comparative and superlative forms of adjectives to compare films. I can use comparatives and superlatives to express an opinion.*

4C CULTURE Licensed to kill

LESSON SUMMARY ●●●○○

Reading: an article about James Bond; matching
Speaking: asking and answering questions about the Bond films
Listening: a song
Topic: entertainment

SHORTCUT *To do the lesson in 30 minutes, keep a very fast pace in the Lead-in. Do exercise 1 as a class. Do not extend the time limit in exercise 3.*

➡ Lead-in 3–5 minutes

- Inform the class of the lesson objectives.
- Put the following words on the board: *secret service, secret agent, intelligence, secret information, intelligence service, spy.* Elicit three pairs of synonyms (secret agent = spy, intelligence = secret information, secret service = intelligence service).
- Check understanding by asking: *What does the secret service do?* (It collects secret information.) *Who works for the secret service?* (Secret agents.) Then briefly discuss the following questions with the class: *What are spies like? What skills do they have?*

Exercise 1 page 36

- Students can work in pairs for 2 minutes. Elicit what they know about James Bond and his films.

Exercise 2 page 36

- Read the instructions with the class. Remind students that reading the first sentence in each paragraph is a good way of getting a general idea of what it is about. Instruct students to read the rest of the paragraph to confirm their choice. Allow 1–2 minutes.
- Check as a class. Now answer any vocabulary questions students may have about the text.

KEY

A 2   B 1   C 5   D 3

> **OPTIONAL ACTIVITY**
> Ask students to prepare for a 'Memory quiz'. They should read the text carefully again and try to memorise as many details as possible. Allow 2 minutes. Then put students in small groups with books closed. Explain that groups will take turns to answer the questions you ask.
>
> Sample questions: *What is the title of the most famous British romantic comedy? What was the title of the first Bond film? How many Bond films have been made so far? Who wrote the James Bond books? What is Eton?* etc.
>
> In your questions avoid the vocabulary students are not familiar with. Keep a fast pace. Do 2–3 rounds starting with general questions and then moving to the more detailed ones.

Exercise 3 page 36

- Allow 5 minutes for pairwork but extend the time if necessary.
- Ask **fast finishers** to write a short (2–4 sentences) description of a film star without mentioning their name. When most pairs have finished talking, stop pairwork and ask **fast finishers** to read out their descriptions. The class listen and guess the actor.

Exercise 4 page 36 🎧 1.35

- Students work individually for a minute, then compare their answers in pairs. Play the recording for students to check. Answer vocabulary questions.
- Elicit answers to a few comprehension questions, e.g. *How does the spy feel about the singer? How does she feel about him? How does she feel about other men?*

KEY

1 better	4 safe	7 better
2 as good as	5 better	8 as good as
3 the best	6 so good	9 the best

➡ Lesson outcome

Ask students: *What have you learned today? What can you do now?* and elicit answers: *I can talk about a famous film character. I have learned facts about the James Bond films.*

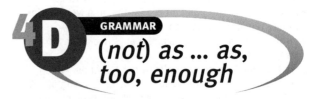

4D GRAMMAR (not) as ... as, too, enough

LESSON SUMMARY ●●●○○

Grammar: *(not) as ... as, too, enough*
Reading: a dialogue about the cinema
Speaking: making excuses

SHORTCUT *To do the lesson in 30 minutes, in a **stronger class,** set the Grammar Builder as homework and skip the preparation for exercises 1 and 8. In a **weaker class,** skip the Lead-in and either exercise 4 or exercises 5 and 6. Do the Grammar Builder as a class. Keep a fast pace.*

→ Lead-in 2–3 minutes

- Inform the class of the lesson objectives.
- Focus students on the picture. Ask: *Who is it?* (Batman) *What sort of films is this character from?* (science fiction and animated films). Elicit answers from the class.
- Have a short discussion about the types of film students enjoy, focusing on the *Batman* films, and asking students to express an opinion using comparatives and revising vocabulary from the previous lessons.

Exercise 1 page 37 🎧 1.36

- Check if students understand *the film is on, book online* and *sold out* by asking: *What films are on at the cinema now? Do you sometimes book cinema tickets online? What do you do when tickets for your film are sold out: do you decide to see another film or do you come again another time?* Play the recording once. Elicit answers.

KEY

1 Jane   2 *Kill Bill*   3 It's too late./There isn't enough time to get there.

Exercise 2 page 37

- In a **weaker class**, first refresh *after, before* and *between* by referring to the students' timetable, then go through the dialogue and underline the adjectives together. Students work individually for a minute. Check as a class.

KEY

1 between   2 before   3 after   4 before

LANGUAGE NOTE – *AS … AS*

The structure *as … as* is more common in the negative form, but it can be used in the affirmative.

Exercise 3 page 37 🎧 1.37

- Play the recording twice to repeat chorally and individually. If students do not know the answer, paraphrase the question: *Which words are stressed/said more clearly and loudly: the words that are underlined or the other ones?*

PRONUNCIATION – WEAK FORMS

Make sure that students understand that the *important* words (i.e. the words that carry the meaning) are strong and the others are weak. They should try to say the weak words as quickly as they can.

N.B. the verb *to be* and auxiliary verbs are usually weak but in their negative form (sentences 1 and 3) they carry an important meaning and are therefore stressed.

For further practice in saying weak (and strong) forms dictate or write these sentences:

History's easier than science.
He's as tall as his brother.
It isn't as long as the last one.

Students mark the stressed syllables. Take the first sentence and read it with them, only saying the stressed syllables. Get them to say it a few times and gradually speed up. Finally ask them to say the full sentence at the same speed. To do this they will need to say the weak words very fast.

Exercise 4 page 37

- Point out that students should use *not as … as* each time. Set a time limit of 2 minutes. If students have a problem with pace, set a limit of 20 seconds per sentence and elicit answers when the time is up.

For more practice on (not) as … as, too *and* enough, *go to:*

> **Grammar Builder 4D:** Student's Book page 110

KEY

5
2 Diana is as old as Mike.
3 Cathy is as intelligent as Joe.
4 The BMW is as fast as the Mercedes.
5 I'm as tired as you (are).
6 I go swimming as often as you (do).

6
2 Science fiction films aren't as gripping as disaster films.
3 *Malcolm in the Middle* isn't as funny as *Friends*.
4 The acting in *Troy* wasn't as good as the acting in *Gladiator*.
5 The cinema in the village isn't as big as the cinema in the town.
6 You aren't as interested in war films as I am.

7

1	too cold	5	too tired
2	too expensive	6	too untidy
3	too sweet	7	too scary
4	too boring		

8

1	enough time	4	enough people
2	funny enough	5	old enough
3	enough exercise	6	enough television

Exercise 5 page 37

- Students work individually for 2–3 minutes. If your class likes competition, you can set it as a contest between small groups. Check as a class.

KEY

1	too busy	4	not old enough
2	not funny enough	5	too expensive
3	too long	6	too violent

Exercise 6 page 37

- Ask students to read the gapped dialogue and find out what *casting directors* do. Elicit an explanation, for example: *They choose actors to play in films.*
- Students can work in pairs. Each student in a pair completes the lines of one director. Then they read the dialogue together and complete the rest of the gaps.

KEY

1	tall enough	4	too old
2	enough experience	5	enough hair
3	as famous as	6	enough time

Exercise 7 page 37 🎧 1.38

- Play the recording for students to check. In a **stronger class**, ask students to underline the stressed syllables in the sentences with *as…as, too* and *enough*. Play the recording again, pause and elicit answers from the class.

Exercise 8 page 37

- Prepare a **weaker class** for the activity. Elicit ways of making suggestions by asking: *What do you say when you invite a friend to the cinema?* Point to sentences in exercise 8 and explain that all of them are suggestions. Read them with the class.
- Focus students on the example. Elicit the difference between *boring* and *bored*. Elicit more excuses – encourage students to use *(not) … enough*
- Students in pairs take it in turns to refuse suggestions. Allow 3 minutes.
- If there is time, check by eliciting different responses to each suggestion. In a **stronger class**, use peer correction to sort out any mistakes.

→ Lesson outcome

Ask students: *What have you learned today? What can you do now?* and elicit answers: *I can use different structures to make comparisons. I have learned how to pronounce the weak forms.*

Notes for Photocopiable activity 4.1

Talk about it

Groupwork or pairwork
Language area: comparatives and superlatives
Materials: one worksheet cut up per pair or group of 3–4 students (Teacher's Book page 130)

- Divide students into pairs or small groups. Give out a set of cut up cards. Ask students to shuffle them and place them face down. Demonstrate the activity by asking a student to turn over the first card and ask you a question. Give an expansive answer.
- Stop the activity when a few pairs have finished and get brief feedback from two or three groups.

4E READING
Crossing cultures

LESSON SUMMARY ●●●○○

Reading: an article about a director; multiple-choice
Vocabulary: film industry vocabulary
Speaking: talking about contemporary films, actors and directors
Topic: entertainment

SHORTCUT *To do the lesson in 30 minutes, do exercises 3 and 5 as a class, and set a time limit of 5 minutes for exercise 6.*

→ Lead-in 2–4 minutes

- Inform the class of the lesson objectives.
- Brainstorm the names of well-known people from your country who are working in the film industry. Elicit what students know about them. Put their jobs on the board (e.g. *director, actor, actress, cameraman, composer*).

Exercise 1 page 38

- Focus students on the photo. If students don't know the man in the centre (Milos Forman), encourage them to look at the photo and make suggestions. Elicit other sentences about the picture. If anybody recognises Forman, elicit what they know about him.

Exercise 2 page 38

- Students work individually. Allow a minute to check information. Elicit answers from different students.

KEY

1 Milos Forman.
2 The Czech Republic (then Czechoslovakia).
3 The USA.
4 Films include *The Fireman's Ball, Black Peter, Taking Off, One Flew Over the Cuckoo's Nest, Ragtime, Amadeus, The People vs. Larry Flint, Goya's Ghosts.*

Exercise 3 page 38

- Students can work in pairs. When most pairs have finished matching, check as a class. Do not answer any other vocabulary questions at this stage. If students insist, explain that they do not need to understand every word to answer multiple-choice questions; on the contrary – the task checks if they understand the text despite unknown vocabulary.

KEY

1 screenplay
2 scene
3 award
4 directors
5 drama
6 film industry
7 documentaries

Exercise 4 page 39

- Read the reading tip on page 38 with the class.
- Allow 10 minutes for students to read the sentences and find the best place for them in the text. Ask them to identify the clues in the surrounding text that confirm their answers.
- In a **weaker class**, do the first one as an example. Ask: *What is* One Flew Over the Cuckoo's Nest*? (A film.) What do you think 'his big breakthrough' means?* (His sudden achievement of major success.) *When did this happen?* (In 1975.) Tell students to look through the text and find the correct gap. Ask: *How do you know the sentence fits here?* Elicit the sequence in dates (1971–1975), the reference to 'The film' in the next sentence and the unusual success of winning five Oscars for it.
- Check answers with the class.

KEY

1 c 2 e 3 g 4 a 5 d 6 b

OPTIONAL ACTIVITY

Focus students on the titles of the lesson and the article. Elicit how they understand *crossing cultures* and *against the odds*. Have they had any experiences which can be described by these expressions?

Exercise 5 page 39

- Model the pronunciation of nationalities and countries for students to repeat. Complete the sentences as a class. Can students add any more names to the list?

KEY

1 Welsh, the USA
2 American, the UK
3 Australian, the USA
4 English, the USA
5 Austrian, the USA

CULTURE NOTE – CELEBRITIES

Catherine Zeta-Jones, actress. (1969–). Films include *The Mask of Zorro, Entrapment, Chicago, Traffic* and *Ocean's Twelve*. She is married to actor Michael Douglas.

Gwyneth Paltrow, actress. (1972–). Films include *Shakespeare in Love, Emma, Seven, Hook* and *The Royal Tenenbaums*. She was engaged to Brad Pitt, and is now married to Chris Martin, the lead singer of British pop group Coldplay.

Nicole Kidman, actress (1967–). Films include *To Die For, Moulin Rouge!, The Others, The Hours* and *Cold Mountain*. In 2006 she became the highest-paid actress in Hollywood. She was married to Tom Cruise but they divorced in 2001.

Alfred Hitchcock, director (1899–1980). Films include *Rebecca, Psycho, Rear Window, North by Northwest, Strangers on a Train* and *The 39 Steps*.

Arnold Schwarzenegger, body-builder, actor and politician (1947–). Films include *The Terminator* films, *Total Recall, Collateral Damage, Last Action Hero* and *True Lies*.

Exercise 6 page 39

- Remind students to speak English but allow them to use their own language for film titles.
- In a **stronger class**, encourage students to add more details and express their opinions of the people and their films.
- When most pairs finish speaking, share answers as a class.

ADDITIONAL SPEAKING ACTIVITY

Brainstorm the films that the people in exercise 5 directed or acted in. Briefly elicit the types of films for some of them and ask students whether they liked them or not.

Choose two films from the list (preferably quite different types of films). Elicit adjectives to describe them. Then brainstorm as many more adjectives for describing films as the students can think of.

Write the following structures on the board: *comparative, superlative, (not) as … as, too, enough*. Work as a class to compare the two films, making two sentences for each of the structures.

Put students in pairs to choose two films in which one of the people from exercise 5 was involved. Their task is to discuss the films and compare them. To stimulate students, put some categories on the board, e.g. *popularity, violence, entertainment, laughs, actors, music, special effects, atmosphere*.

Instruct students to use adjectives from lesson 4A and the structures from lessons 4B and 4D that you have just practised.

Students make notes individually for 2 minutes. Then work in pairs for 3–5 minutes.

If there is time left, ask them to present their comparisons to the class.

➡ Lesson outcome

Ask students: *What have you learned today? What can you do now?* and elicit answers: *I can understand a profile of a famous film director. I have learned new words to talk about the film industry.*

Notes for Photocopiable activity 4.2

What's on?

Class race
Language: film vocabulary
Materials: one copy of the worksheet per student (Teacher's Book page 131)

- As a lead-in, ask students how they read a TV guide. Do they read every word carefully or do they pass their eyes over the text until they find the information they are looking for? What else do they read in this way? (phone books, dictionaries, food labels)
- Tell them that they are going to do an activity to practise fast reading and that they are going to answer 12 questions based on a film guide. The aim is to answer the questions as quickly as they can. In order to do this they will need to scan read.
- Set the activity as a class race. Distribute the worksheets and make sure the students start reading at the same time. Emphasise that although they do not need to write full sentences, their answers must be correctly spelled. The first student to answer all the questions correctly is the winner. (Stop the activity after a few students have finished.)
- Ask students to swap worksheets when you go through the answers.

KEY

1	Two hours and ten minutes	7	*Shrek 2*
2	*Almost Famous*	8	Film Five
3	A comedy	9	No
4	Two	10	No
5	*The Towering Inferno*	11	*King Kong*
6	11 o'clock	12	Three

4F EVERYDAY ENGLISH
Buying tickets

LESSON SUMMARY ●●●●○

Functional English: buying/booking tickets for an event
Reading: a dialogue at the box office
Listening: a dialogue; listening for detail
Speaking: dialogues: buying tickets, booking tickets
Topic: entertainment

SHORTCUT *To do the lesson in 30 minutes, skip exercises 2 and 7.*

➡ Lead-in 3–5 minutes

- Inform the class of the lesson objectives.
- Introduce the topic by asking: *How often do you go to the cinema? Who do you go with? Do you book tickets in advance, or just buy them at the cinema?*
- Put students in pairs. Tell them to imagine they are going to go to the cinema. Ask them to think of all the things that they have to talk about when buying tickets. Allow 2 minutes for students to brainstorm ideas.
- Share ideas as a class.

Exercise 1   page 40   🎧 1.39

- Focus students on the film guide. Explain *OAPs* (old age pensioners).
- In a **stronger class**, ask students to cover the dialogue.
- In a **weaker class**, briefly check understanding of the film guide and revise saying time and prices by asking: *How much is a ticket for a student? At what times are they showing* War of the Worlds? *How many showings of* Batman Begins *are there today?*
- Read the instructions with the class.
- Play the recording once. Students listen, read and mark information. Check as a class.
- Play the recording again, pausing for students to repeat chorally and individually.

KEY

War of the Worlds, 19.30

Exercise 2   page 40

- Allow 3 minutes for students to work in pairs. Remind them to swap roles halfway through. Encourage them to change more details.

Exercise 3   page 40   🎧 1.40

- Read the instructions as a class. Play the recording once and elicit answers.

KEY

1 Will Young's concert   2 £50

Transcript 1.40

Clerk	Good evening, New Theatre box office.
Chris	Oh, hello. Can I book tickets to see Will Young on July 24th?
Clerk	July 24th ... I'm afraid that concert is sold out.
Chris	Oh. What about the 25th? Is that sold out too?
Clerk	Let me see ... We've got tickets at £40 and a few at £25.
Chris	Where are the £25 seats? Are they a long way from the stage?
Clerk	They're at the back of the stalls. In the middle of row M.
Chris	OK. I'd like two tickets at £25, please.
Clerk	That's £50. Can I have your card number, please?
Chris	3675 3795 2649 3321.
Clerk	And the expiry date?
Chris	03, 09.
Clerk	Thank you. And your name and address?
Chris	Chris Brown. 22 Marston Rd, Birmingham B31 4TK.
Clerk	Thank you. I'll put your tickets in the post today.
Chris	Thank you. Goodbye.
Clerk	Goodbye.

Exercise 4   page 40   🎧 1.40

- Play the recording again. Students complete the task. Check as a class.
- If necessary, play the recording once more.
- Ask **fast finishers** to list verbs that collocate with the noun *ticket* (*to buy, to book, to pay for, to pick up, to collect, to sell,* etc.). In a **stronger class**, you can ask students to list nouns that collocate with *ticket* (e.g. *cinema/museum/bus/ train/return/parking ticket*).

KEY

Seats: At the back of the stalls, in the middle of row M
Credit card number: [3675] 3795 [2649] 3321
Expiry date: 03/09
Surname: Brown

Exercise 5   page 40

- Ask students how they react if they do not understand what somebody says to them in English. Elicit possible ways of asking for repetition. Then read the speaking tip as a class. Elicit the phrase from exercise 1 from the class. Conduct a short drill to practise using the phrases: T (quietly): *Maria, what time is it?* Ss: *Pardon?*

KEY

Sorry, did you say ...

Exercise 6   page 40

- In a **weaker class**, go over the instructions as a class. Elicit the meaning of *seats, available* and *expiry date*. Ask students to write down the full dialogues.
- In a **stronger class**, it may be enough for students to make notes.
- When students are writing, go round helping and correcting mistakes.
- Remind students to follow the chart and use the expressions from the lesson.

Exercise 7   page 40

- When students are ready, ask pairs to sit back to back. Remind students that phone conversations are more difficult than face to face conversations as the speakers don't have the benefit of facial expression or gesture. Lack of eye contact will help them imitate the situation of talking on the phone. They should listen carefully and ask for repetition if necessary.

OPTIONAL ACTIVITY

Ask students in pairs to describe the photo. Remind them to talk about the place, time, objects and their positions, people and their actions. Allow 2 minutes.

In a **stronger class**, you can extend the time to 4 minutes and add two questions for students to answer:

- Why is going to the cinema more popular than the theatre or museums?
- Do you like going to the cinema? Why/Why not?

➡ Lesson outcome

Ask students: *What have you learned today? What can you do now?* and elicit answers: *I can book and buy tickets for a concert or a film. I have learned to talk on the phone and ask for repetition.*

4G WRITING A film review

LESSON SUMMARY ●●●○○
Reading: a film review
Writing: a film review
Topic: entertainment

SHORTCUT *To do the lesson in 30 minutes, skip the Lead-in and do exercises 3 and 4 as a class.*

➜ Lead-in 5 minutes

- Inform the class of the lesson objectives.
- Put students in pairs. Ask them to think about films they have seen recently (at the cinema, on TV or on DVD). Ask: *What was the best film and what was the worst? Why?* Give pairs 2–3 minutes to discuss.
- Ask students to share their ideas with the class.

Exercise 1 page 41

- Focus on the photo and elicit answers. If students don't recognise the film, don't mention the title yet.

KEY

Actor: Tom Cruise. Film: *War of the Worlds*

Exercise 2 page 41

- Introduce the word *review* and ask: *What is the purpose of a film review?* (To give some information about the film and to express opinions about it.)
- Students read the text quickly to find the answers to the questions.

KEY

1 *War of the Worlds.*   2 Yes, she did.

Exercise 3 page 41

- **Weaker students** work on the questions in pairs. **Stronger students** work individually, then compare answers in pairs.
- Point out that the first two answers give factual information. Ask students to pick out other facts in the review (*starring Tom Cruise, set in modern times, about alien machines ... etc., plays a father who ... etc.*).
- Now ask students to find adjectives/phrases that express the writer's opinions (*gripping, very good, excellent, not very convincing*, etc.). Check students' understanding of this vocabulary.
- In a **stronger class**, elicit alternative adjectives that the reviewer could have used (e.g. *The story is <u>fascinating/ dramatic</u>*). Then elicit adjectives that could be used to give the opposite opinion (e.g. *The acting is <u>terrible</u>. Tom Cruise is <u>unconvincing</u>. The special effects were <u>not very original</u>.*)

KEY

1 A science fiction film.
2 Over 100 years ago.
3 The story, the acting, the special effects.
4 Dakota Fanning's acting, some scary moments.

Exercise 4 page 41

- Students do the exercise individually.
- Elicit other example sentences using these words/phrases.

KEY

1 starring Tom Cruise	3 plays	5 overall
2 is based on	4 classic	

Exercise 5 page 41

- Read the writing tip as a class.
- When students have found the words, explain that *Nevertheless* means the same as *However*, but it is more formal and more emphatic. Point out that both words usually come at the beginning of a sentence.
- Note that *in spite of* can be followed simply by a noun as well as by *the fact that* + clause (e.g. *In spite of the scary moments, I enjoyed the film.*).

Exercise 6 page 41

- Students do the exercise in pairs.

KEY

1 although
2 However
3 although/in spite of the fact that
4 However
5 although/in spite of the fact that
6 However/Nevertheless
7 However/Nevertheless
8 Although/In spite of the fact that

Exercise 7 page 41

- Go through the plan. Make it clear that students do not have to write about everything suggested in paragraph 3.
- Students plan and write four paragraphs.
- Give students time to check their work, using the checklist.

> **ALTERNATIVE WRITING TASK**
> Write a review of a film or TV drama that you did not enjoy. Follow the writing plan in exercise 7.

➜ Lesson outcome

- Ask students: *What have you learned today? What can you do now?* and elicit answers: *I can write a film review. I have learned words to express contrast.*

1

1	boring	6	expensive
2	enormous	7	modern
3	safe	8	quiet
4	relaxing	9	rich
5	ugly	10	early

2

1	musical	6	rural
2	comedy	7	Traffic lights
3	wood	8	rubbish bin
4	traffic jam	9	historical drama
5	pedestrian crossing	10	cottage

3

2 There are a few street lamps in the village.
3 He isn't old enough to see that film.
4 My sister is the tallest person in her class.
5 Villages are more relaxing than cities.
6 My house is between a hill and a stream.
7 It's not as good as his other films.

4

1	too	6	are
2	much	7	more relaxing
3	than	8	The
4	few	9	a
5	a	10	as

5

1 d 2 a 3 f 4 b 5 e 6 c

6

1 Go to the end of the road.
2 Take the first left.
3 Go past the hospital and turn right.
4 It's on the corner of Park Avenue and South Street.
5 Could you repeat that, please?
6 One adult and two children.
7 Can I have your card number, please?
8 Sorry, did you say £15?

SKILLS ROUND-UP 1–4

Transcript 1.41

Daniel Oh, hi, Joanna!
Joanna Hello, Daniel.
Daniel Are you going into town?
Joanna No, I'm just going to the shop at the end of the road. What about you?
Daniel I'm going to the sports centre to play tennis.
Joanna Oh, you play tennis!
Daniel Yes. Do you?
Joanna Hmm. Not, really.
Daniel Shame. What do you like doing in your free time?
Joanna I like going to the cinema.
Daniel Really? I enjoy going to the cinema, too. What kinds of films do you like?
Joanna Oh, all kinds. Action films, comedies … and horror films are my favourite!
Daniel Do you fancy going to the cinema this evening? They're showing the new Tarantino film.
Joanna Great idea!
Daniel OK. Well, it starts at 6.30. I'll meet you there at 6.15 – by the box office.
Joanna All right. See you later!

Narrator At six o'clock that evening …
Joanna Excuse me. Where's the Palace Cinema?
Woman It's on Green Road.
Joanna Can you tell me how to get there?
Woman Sure. Go past the school and turn left. The cinema is opposite the supermarket.
Joanna Thanks!
Joanna Green Road, Green Road … Ah! Here it is. But where's the cinema? Excuse me. Where's the cinema?
Man It's opposite the supermarket.
Joanna I know, but where's the supermarket?
Man Go straight on, past the traffic lights.
Joanna Thanks! Oh, and do you know what the time is?
Man Yes, it's 6:30.
Joanna Oh no! I'm late.

Joanna Hello.
Daniel Hi, it's Daniel. Where are you?
Joanna I'm sorry. I got lost.
Daniel The film starts in 1 minute!
Joanna Look, buy your ticket and go inside. I'll be there in ten minutes.
Daniel OK. See you soon!

Clerk Can I help you?
Joanna Yes, one ticket for the Tarantino film, please.
Clerk Which showing?
Joanna I'd like the 6:30 showing.
Clerk The film started ten minutes ago.
Joanna I know!
Clerk How old are you?
Joanna Seventeen.
Clerk You can't see that film then. It's an 18 certificate.
Joanna But I'm meeting somebody inside!
Clerk Sorry. There's a new Disney film – screen 3.
Joanna No, thanks.

Narrator A few days later …
Joanna Hi, Maria.
Maria Hi, Joanna. How are you?
Joanna I'm fine. What did you do last weekend?
Maria We had friends to stay. What about you? Did you have a good weekend?
Joanna Not really.
Maria Oh dear. What happened?
Joanna It's a long story …

1 b She's too young.

2

1	Joanna		6	Daniel
2	Daniel		7	Daniel
3	Joanna		8	Joanna
4	Daniel		9	Joanna
5	Joanna			

3

1	today	3	Jim and Sarah's children
2	next weekend	4	last weekend

4

1 Because she's looking after Jim and Sarah's children next Sunday.
2 She doesn't mind.
3 Ellie is quieter than Oliver.
4 In Joanna's opinion, Oliver is shyer.
5 He phoned her after she had a pizza.
6 He thought it was really funny.

5–6 Open answers

EXAM For further exam tasks and practice, go to Workbook page 38. Procedural notes, transcripts and keys for the Workbook can be found on the *Solutions* Teacher's Website at www.oup.com/elt/teacher/solutions.

5 Gifts

A VOCABULARY AND LISTENING
At the shops

THIS UNIT INCLUDES ●●●●
Vocabulary • shops • verbs: shopping and money • special occasions •
buildings • in a shop
Grammar • present perfect • *been* and *gone* • present perfect and past simple
• *How long…?* • *for* and *since*
Speaking • giving and receiving gifts • buying clothes
Writing • an informal letter
WORKBOOK pages 40–46 • Self check 5 page 47

LESSON SUMMARY ●●●○○

Vocabulary: shops; verbs for shopping and money
Listening: short dialogues; listening for specific information
Speaking: talking about shopping and buying gifts
Topic: shops and services

SHORTCUT *To do the lesson in 30 minutes, do exercises 3 and 5 as a class. Skip the Vocabulary Builders or set them for homework.*

➡ Lead-in 2 minutes

- Inform the class of the lesson objectives.
- Ask students to keep their Student's Books closed. Put students in pairs to brainstorm all the shops they can remember in two minutes. Students write down the list in their notebooks.
- Ask students to open their books. The pair with the longest list reads it out to the class. Students listen and underline the words in the box. Ask the class for examples of what they can buy in the shops that have not been read out.

Exercise 1 page 44

- Focus students on the photos. Students match the photos with the words.
- Elicit the names of the items that the people are buying in the photos. In a **stronger class**, encourage students to expand their answers by describing the photos in more detail.

KEY

1 music shop (She is looking at CDs.)
2 butcher's (She is buying meat; they are looking at the sausages.)
3 jeweller's (They are looking at necklaces.)
4 bakery (She is looking at the bread.)

LANGUAGE NOTE – SHOPS

Point out that words like *butcher's* and *jeweller's* have an apostrophe because in the past we used to say *butcher's/ jeweller's shop.*

Exercise 2 page 44 🎧 1.42

- Play the recording for students to listen and check.
- Play the recording again pausing after each item for students to repeat chorally.
- Play the recording a third time. Pause every two or three phrases. Ask individual students to repeat the sets.
- Students check the meanings individually.

Transcript 1.42

1 music shop   2 butcher's   3 jeweller's   4 bakery
Not illustrated: bank, card shop, chemist's, clothes shop, computer shop, electrical store, newsagent's, post office, shoe shop, sports shop, stationery shop, supermarket

Exercise 3 page 44

- Read the list of words with the class. Explain any new vocabulary and work on pronunciation if necessary.
- Model the activity by asking: *Where can you buy a birthday cake?* Elicit answers: *In/At a bakery or a supermarket.*
- Point out that with shops and buildings both *in* and *at* are correct.
- Students work in pairs to ask and answer about where they can buy the other things. Allow 2–3 minutes.
- In a **stronger class**, ask students to cover the vocabulary box in exercise 1 and work from memory.
- Go through the answers as a class.

KEY

(Possible answers)
a birthday cake – bakery, supermarket
meat – butcher's, supermarket
a Christmas card – card shop, newsagent's, post office, supermarket, stationery shop
a magazine – computer shop, music shop, newsagent's, supermarket
a pair of trainers – shoe shop, sports shop, supermarket
a pair of jeans – clothes shop, supermarket
an MP3 player – electrical store, music shop, supermarket, stationery shop
a CD – music shop, supermarket
a watch – electrical store, jeweller's, supermarket
a newspaper – newsagent's, supermarket
a ring – jeweller's
stamps – post office, newsagent's, supermarket
a tennis racquet – sports shop, supermarket
paper – computer shop, post office, supermarket, stationery shop
perfume – chemist's, supermarket
pasta – supermarket
a printer – electrical store, computer shop, supermarket
a jacket – clothes shop, supermarket
aspirins – chemist's, supermarket

OPTIONAL ACTIVITY

Ask students to draw mind maps in their notebooks, with the name of the shop in the centre and the items you can buy there written around it. Encourage students to use their own ideas.

Exercise 4 page 44 🎧 1.43

- Allow a minute for students to read the instructions and the questions.
- Explain that you are going to play the recording straight through once, and then play it again, stopping after each dialogue to check the answers.

Transcript 1.43

1
Girl   Excuse me. Do you sell birthday cakes?
Baker Yes, we do. Who is it for?
Girl   My little brother. He's eight years old on Saturday.
Baker Does he like football?

Girl	Yes, he loves football.
Baker	Well, how about this cake? It's got a picture of a footballer on it.
Girl	How much is it?
Baker	£16
Girl	Hmm. I can't afford £16.
Baker	How much do you want to spend?
Girl	About £10.
Baker	Well, this chocolate cake is £9.50.
Girl	OK! I'll take it.

2

Assistant	This one's nice.
Woman	Yes, it's nice and ... strong. But I don't think it's really me. Have you got anything more ... feminine?
Assistant	How about this? It's called *Empathy*.
Woman	Mmm. Yes, I like that. How much does it cost?
Assistant	£65.
Woman	Ouch!
Assistant	Buy two for £100 and save £30.
Woman	Really?
Assistant	Yes. It's a special offer.
Woman	No, I'm sorry. It's just too expensive. I'll leave it for today.

3

Boy	I need some paper for my printer.
Assistant	White paper?
Boy	Yes.
Assistant	£4.99 a packet.
Boy	Oh. I've only got £3.
Assistant	You need another £1.99 then.
Boy	Just a moment. Maybe I can borrow some money. Mary! Can you lend me £2 to pay for this paper?
Girl	Sorry, I haven't got any money.
Boy	Oh. She hasn't got any money. Can I buy half a packet?
Assistant	No, I'm sorry.
Boy	Oh. Never mind. I'll come back later.

4

Girl	Look at that ring. It's beautiful!
Dad	How much is it?
Girl	Er ... I'm not sure. Just a minute, I'll ask. Excuse me. How much is that ring?
Assistant	It's £55.
Girl	I really like it.
Dad	Have you got enough money with you?
Girl	No, I haven't. But I've got more money at home.
Dad	Do you want to buy it? Are you sure?
Girl	Yes, I'm sure. We'll take it, please.
Assistant	Do you want the box too?
Girl	Yes, please.
Assistant	OK. That's £60 altogether.
Girl	You said £55!
Assistant	We charge £5 for the box.
Girl	Oh. Well, forget the box, then.
Assistant	OK. No box. That's £55.
Dad	I'll use my credit card.
Girl	Thanks, Dad!
Dad	Don't forget, you owe me £55!

KEY

	Person 1	Person 2	Person 3	Person 4
1	bakery	chemist's	stationery shop	jeweller's
2	a birthday cake	perfume	paper	a ring
3	yes	no	no	yes

For more practice on vocabulary related to shopping, go to:

Vocabulary Builder (part 1): Student's Book page 128

KEY

1
a	sports shop			
b	supermarket			
c	chemist's			
d	clothes shop			
e	shoe shop			
f	card shop			
g	newsagent's			
h	electrical store			

2
1 bakery
2 butcher's
3 clothes shop
4 computer shop
5 jeweller's
6 music shop
7 post office

3 Open answers

Exercise 5 page 44

- Write the following verbs on the board: *hate, can't stand, don't mind, like, enjoy, love*. Elicit what verb form follows them (the *-ing* form). Ask: *What do you enjoy/hate buying?* and elicit answers from the class.
- Read the instructions and examples as a class. Students take it in turns to share their opinions in pairs. Get individual students to report on their partner.

Exercise 6 page 44

- Read the instructions as a class. Model the answer saying what three presents you would buy.
- In a **stronger class**, encourage students to add details: describe the gifts, give reasons for choosing this particular present, etc.

Exercise 7 page 44

- Allow 2 minutes for students to plan their answers and another 3 minutes to rehearse in pairs. Get as many students as possible to share their answers with the class.

For practice on collocations related to shops and money, go to:

Vocabulary Builder (part 2): Student's Book page 128

KEY

4
1 sell
2 lend, borrow
3 charged
4 owe
5 bought, cost
6 spends, saves
7 pay for

5
2 but I can't afford it
3 lent me £10
4 cost £10
5 should save that money
6 paid for those CDs
7 did they charge you
8 owe my brother

6 1 from 2 – 3 on 4 for 5 – 6 for 7 from 8 to

➡ Lesson outcome

Ask students: *What have you learned today? What can you do now?* and elicit answers: *I can identify different shops. I can talk about shops and where to buy things. I can talk about buying gifts.*

5B GRAMMAR
Present perfect

LESSON SUMMARY ●●●●●

Grammar: present perfect, *been* and *gone*, *for* and *since*
Reading: a postcard
Speaking: asking and answering questions with *How long?*

SHORTCUT *To do the lesson in 30 minutes, set the Grammar Builder for homework.*

➡ **Lead-in** 2–3 minutes
- Inform the class of the lesson objectives.
- Dictate to students the following list of verbs: *take, spend, go to, see, go* and nouns: *the sights, shopping, a fortune, photos, a museum.* Ask them to match the verbs and nouns to make collocations. Check as a class.
- Ask: *When do you do these activities?* and elicit the answer (on holidays).

Exercise 1 page 45
- Focus students on the photo and ask: *What is it? Which city does it show? What can you do on a holiday there?* Elicit answers from individual students.
- Focus students on the postcard. Students answer the true/false questions individually. Allow 2 minutes.
- **Fast finishers** correct the false statements.

KEY
1 T
2 F Amanda hasn't bought very much.
3 F Suzie's gone to Century 21. / Suzie's in Century 21.

Exercise 2 page 45
- In a **weaker class**, complete the box together. If students need more support, go to Grammar Reference 5.1 and 5.2 and study it with the class.
- In a **stronger class**, students work individually. Check as a class. Elicit how the present perfect is formed.

KEY

affirmative: We've been in New York since Sunday. Suzie has spent a fortune on presents.
negative: I haven't bought very much.
interrogative: Have you fed my fish?

OPTIONAL ACTIVITY

Try the following substitution drill to practise the form of the present perfect.

T *I've taken lots of photos*   Ss *I've taken lots of photos*

Repeat two or three times as a class and then invite individuals to repeat:

T gesture towards a female student   Ss *She's taken lots of photos*

T gesture towards a male student   Ss *He's taken lots of photos*

Exercise 3 page 45
- Read the *Learn this!* box as a class. If students need more support, go to Grammar Reference 5.3.
- Students can work in pairs. Allow 2 minutes.

KEY
1 We've seen all the sights. I've taken lots of photos. We've been shopping. I haven't bought very much. Suzie has spent a fortune on presents. She's gone to Century 21. She's just sent me a text message. She's tried on four pairs of trainers.
2 We've been in New York since Sunday. She's been there for hours.

Exercise 4 page 45
- Read the *Look out!* box as a class. Ask students to look at the postcard again and find examples of *been* and *gone*. Check comprehension by asking: *Has Amanda been to the shops this week? Is she in a shop now? Has Suzie gone to Century 21? Is she still there? What is she buying?*

KEY
We've been shopping.
She's gone to Century 21, a huge clothes shop.

For more practice on the present perfect, go to:

Grammar Builder 5B: Student's Book page 112

KEY
1 1 've found   7 've just looked
      2 've bought   8 haven't decided
      3 hasn't changed   9 Have you started
      4 haven't spoken   10 have
      5 Have you found   11 've given
      6 haven't   12 hasn't paid

2 Open answers

3 1 gone   2 been   3 been   4 gone   5 gone

4 1 for   2 since   3 since   4 for   5 since   6 for

5 2 How long have you lived near the coast? For three years.
      3 How long have you been married? For two years.
      4 How long have you known Mary? Since last Christmas.
      5 How long have you worked in a factory? Since 1994.
      6 How long have you played the piano? Since 2001.
      7 How long have you had a passport? For three years.

Exercise 5 page 45
- Students complete the text messages individually, then check their answers in pairs.
- Check the answers as a class by asking pairs of students to read the messages out.

KEY
1 've tried on   5 's gone
2 Have you bought   6 Has Dad phoned
3 haven't   7 haven't spoken
4 've spent   8 've written

Exercise 6 page 45
- Study the *Learn this!* box as a class. Drill *for* and *since* orally. Use the prompts from exercise 6 or others, for example: *my birthday, two weeks, last summer, ages, a year, July, half a year, five minutes,* etc.
  T: *three weeks* Ss: *for three weeks*

T: *yesterday*   Ss: *since yesterday*

- Students complete the sentences individually then write a few sentences of their own. Check as a class.

KEY

1 since **2** for **3** since **4** since **5** for **6** for **7** since

---

Exercise 7 page 45

- Read the instructions and the example with the class.
- In a **weaker class**, put extra prompts on the board: *be in this classroom?, know your best friend?, live in our town?, study maths?*
- In a **stronger class**, encourage students to use their own ideas.
- Allow 4 minutes. Then share answers as a class. Students can ask and answer in a chain or in random order around the class.

> **OPTIONAL ACTIVITY**
>
> You can use this activity in the class or set it as homework. Ask students to write holiday postcards including the following information:
> - the place they are visiting
> - what they have seen
> - what they have done
> - what they have not done for two days and why
>
> Let pairs exchange and check their postcards before they are read out to the class. Give feedback.

➡ Lesson outcome

Ask students: *What have you learned today? What can you do now?* and elicit answers: *I can talk about recent events. I have learned about the present perfect. I can use* for *and* since.

5C CULTURE
Giving and receiving

LESSON SUMMARY ●●●○○

Reading: an article about gift-giving; true/false questions
Vocabulary: special occasions
Speaking: talking about giving and receiving gifts
Topic: family life and society

SHORTCUT *To do the lesson in 30 minutes, spend 10 minutes on each of the three parts of the lesson: reading, comparing gift-giving traditions and speaking.*

➡ Lead-in 2–4 minutes

- Inform the class of the lesson objectives.
- Focus students on the title and elicit or explain the meaning.
- Ask students to say when people give and receive gifts. When was the last time they received a gift? What was the last gift that they gave?

Exercise 1 page 46

- Put the following words on the board: *adults, exchanged, asleep, receive, guests.*

- Ask students in pairs to read the sentences carefully, find the words and discuss what they mean. Allow 2 minutes. Check and explain any other unknown vocabulary in the sentences.
- Allow students 10 minutes to read the text and answer the questions. Let them compare their answers before checking as a class. Do not explain any vocabulary at this stage but allow students to work independently.
- While checking, get students to read out the relevant parts of the text to support their answers.

KEY

1 T **2** F **3** F **4** T **5** T **6** F **7** T **8** F

> **OPTIONAL ACTIVITY**
>
> Ask **fast finishers** to find in the text the words that mean:
> 1 according to the law
> 2 to give and receive
> 3 something that happens often
> 4 the years when Victoria was Queen of England
> 5 St Nicholas (informal name)
> 6 adults
> 7 the woman getting married at a wedding
> 8 the man getting married at a wedding
>
> Go over the list of words as a class. If students ask, explain other unknown vocabulary from the text.
>
> **Key**
> 1 legally   4 Victorian times   7 bride
> 2 exchange   5 Santa Claus   8 groom
> 3 common   6 grown-ups

Exercise 2 page 46

- Ask students to read the text again and find out which special occasions are mentioned (Christmas, birthdays, New Year's Eve, Twelfth Night, Easter, Mother's Day and weddings). Ask if people in their country exchange gifts on these occasions and what typical gifts are.
- Focus students on the box. Students underline the occasions which are not mentioned in the text. Read out the list and model the pronunciation. Students listen and repeat. Explain any new phrases; for example, by writing dates on the board. Elicit what presents (if any) are given on these days in Britain and in the students' country.
- Remind students of the two different ways to say the date in English (*December the 25th* or *the 25th of December*).

> **CULTURE NOTES – SPECIAL OCCASIONS**
>
> **Halloween** (October 31st) was originally a pagan festival. Children put on costumes and go round houses playing *trick or treat*. They knock on doors and adults give them sweets and fruit (treat) so that they won't cause any mischief (trick).
>
> **Twelfth Night** (January 5th) is the day the three kings arrived at the manger in Bethlehem. In some countries in Europe children get their Christmas presents on this day, and in other countries a special cake is eaten to remember the three kings. In Britain it is not commonly celebrated.
>
> **Mother's Day** is an old celebration. Traditionally it was called 'Mothering Sunday' and female workers were given the day off to go and visit their mothers. They prepared special cakes as gifts. **Father's Day** is much more modern, and originated in America. These days both occasions are celebrated with cards and small gifts like flowers or chocolates.

Valentine's Day is a day for couples. People send cards to their partners or to people they like. Traditionally Valentine's cards were sent anonymously. These days couples often give each other flowers or romantic gifts.

Name days are not celebrated in Britain.

Exercise 3   page 46

• Read the questions with the whole class. Model the intonation. Students listen and repeat.
• Allow 3 minutes for students to look at the questions and prepare what they are going to say. Divide the class into A's and B's and allow 10 minutes for pairs to interview each other. Remind them to swap roles halfway through.

Exercise 4   page 46

• Students report on their partner's answers.
• Put the lists of the best and worst presents students have given and received on the board. Ask individual students what they think about the items on the board. Would they like to receive them? Would they give them to anybody? Have a short class discussion.

→ Lesson outcome

Ask students: *What have you learned today? What can you do now?* and elicit answers: *I have learned words for special occasions. I have learned about gift-giving in Britain. I can talk about giving and receiving gifts on special occasions.*

5D GRAMMAR
Present perfect and past simple

LESSON SUMMARY ●●●○○
Grammar: present perfect and past simple
Reading and Listening: dialogues
Speaking: talking about past experiences

SHORTCUT *To do the lesson in 30 minutes, skip the Lead-in, set the Grammar Builder for homework, do exercises 4 and 5 as a class and skip exercise 6.*

→ Lead-in   2–5 minutes

• Inform the class of the lesson objectives.
• Set a contest to revise vocabulary related to music. Divide the class into two groups and the board into two halves. The groups take it in turns to say words connected with the theme of music. Each time another student comes over to the board and writes the word. Keep a fast pace. The group who writes down the last word is the winner.

Exercise 1   page 47   🎧 1.44

• Ask students to read the sentences. Play the recording once. Students mark their answers. Check as a class.

KEY
1 T   2 T   3 F

Exercise 2   page 47

• In a **weaker class**, look at the verbs in blue together. Elicit the base form of the verbs. Ask the students to tell you the past tense of the base form. Students look at the verbs in blue again and tell you which tense they are in.

KEY
present perfect

Exercise 3   page 47

• Read and explain the information in the *Learn this!* box to the class. In a **weaker class**, go to Grammar reference 5.6 and 5.7 and ask students to study it.
• Go over the dialogue together. Ask individual students to answer the question.

KEY
Have you ever listened – general question, the time is not important
I got – the sentence refers to a specific time in the past
I've seen them – general statement, the time is not important
Were they – now they are talking about a specific time (a specific concert)
They played – now they are talking about a specific time (a specific concert)
I've never been – general negative statement about the past

LANGUAGE NOTE – PRESENT PERFECT AND PAST SIMPLE
The following time lines might help students visualise and understand the difference between finished time and time up to now.

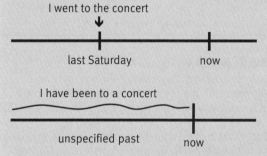

At this point it would be useful to bring together the other three uses of the present perfect from lesson 3B. Elicit these and write them on the board (recent past, experience any time in past, past event with present result). Add to this list the 'new' use (past event at any time until now). Demonstrate that all four uses of the present perfect are in some way connected to now, the present.

The following diagram illustrates very simply and clearly the relationship between the present, the present perfect and the past simple tenses. It is especially useful for visual learners who find it hard to make sense of the grammatical rules. You might want to copy it onto an A4 sheet of paper and keep it permanently on the classroom wall.

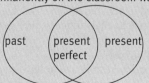

For more practice on the present perfect and past simple, go to:

Grammar Builder 5D: Student's Book page 112

KEY

6 1 Have (you) been
2 visited
3 Did (you) stay
4 Have (you) ever received
5 gave
6 Did (you) say
7 wasn't, opened
8 wrote

7 1 Have you ever been to France or Switzerland?
2 Have you ever swum in the sea?
3 Have you ever broken a bone?
4 Have you ever played a computer game?
5 Have you ever borrowed money from a friend?
6 Have you ever visited a museum?

8 1 She wrote three e-mails last night.
2 correct
3 correct
4 Last Christmas my parents gave me an MP3 player.
5 I have lived in London since last year.
6 'Have you bought any presents yet?'
7 correct, Yes, I went snorkelling last summer.

Exercise 4 page 47

- Students work individually. Remind **weaker students** to look for phrases that refer to time to help them decide which tense is appropriate. Check as a class.

KEY

1 I've received	3 We had	5 She's seen
2 gave	4 I've never eaten	6 We saw

Exercise 5 page 47

- Read the *Look out!* box as a class. Point out that *ever* is typically used with the present perfect whereas the past simple is used with *last summer/weekend,* etc. or *a month/a week ago.*
- Ask students to highlight the time expressions on the page which can't be used with the present perfect: *last month, last weekend, last night, last summer, last year, a few weeks ago.*
- Elicit the past forms of the verbs in the box. Ask which ones have a different past participle and write these on the board. Students complete the gaps individually.

KEY

2 A Have you (ever) seen ...? B ... I saw ...
3 A Have you (ever) met ...? B ... I met ...
4 A Have you (ever) eaten ...? B ... I ate ...
5 A Have you (ever) found ...? B ... I once found ...

Exercise 6 page 47 🎧 1.45

- Play the recording for students to check the forms. If necessary, pause so that students can make corrections.

Exercise 7 page 47

- Pre-teach *department store* and *to have an argument.* Students work individually. Check as a class. Elicit the past participles and write them on the board for students to check the spelling.

KEY

1 bought	4 heard	7 forgotten
2 had	5 received	
3 borrowed	6 seen	

Exercise 8 page 47

- Read the instructions and example with the class. Model the activity with a student. Allow 3 minutes for students to ask and answer in pairs.
- In a **stronger class**, ask students to use their own ideas and continue interviewing each other.

➡ Lesson outcome

Ask students: *What have you learned today? What can you do now?* and elicit answers: *I have learned about present perfect and past simple. I can talk about past experiences and when they happened.*

Notes for Photocopiable activity 5.1

Prove it!

Class survey
Language: present perfect and past simple
Materials: one copy of the worksheet per eight students
(Teacher's Book page 132)

- Dictate or write on the board: *nobody, some of us, everybody, only a few of us* and *most of us.* Elicit or explain their meaning by asking students to order them from the fewest to the most.
- Establish that *only a few of us, some of us* and *most of us* are followed by a plural verb whereas *nobody* and *everybody* are followed by a singular verb.
- Tell the class that they are going to do a class survey but first they have to complete the sentences with either the present perfect or the past simple. Check the answers and explain that they need to find out if the statements are true or false. In order to do this they ask questions to everybody in the class.
- Divide the class into groups of eight and allocate a question to each student in each group. Students can work together to formulate the questions that they need to ask. Elicit the first few questions, e.g. *Did you travel abroad last year?*
- Demonstrate the activity by asking two or three students the first question.
- Ask students to circulate and ask their question to each of their classmates. Suggest that they keep a record of the answers by writing ticks or crosses next to the question.
- When they have spoken to everybody ask them to sit down and work out whether the statements are true or false. Students report their answers.
- If you are short of time, ask half the class to find the answers to the first four and half to find the answers to the other four.

KEY

1 Did you travel abroad last year? (travelled)
2 Have you eaten frog's legs? (has eaten)
3 Did you buy some clothes last weekend? (bought)
4 Did you go to bed after midnight last night? (went)
5 Do you have a job? (has)
6 Have you had the same girlfriend/boyfriend for more than a year? (has had)
7 Have you seen the *Lord of the Rings* films? (have seen)
8 Did you wash your hair yesterday? (washed)

5E READING
Monumental gifts

LESSON SUMMARY ●●●○○

Reading: extracts from a tourist guide; scanning, multiple choice
Vocabulary: types of buildings
Speaking: talking about buildings
Topic: travel and tourism

SHORTCUT *To do the lesson in 30 minutes, keep the Lead-in very brief. Emphasise that exercise 1 requires just a quick read through of the text, and set a time limit for students to find the information. Keep exercise 4 focused and short.*

➡ Lead-in 2–4 minutes
- Inform the class of the lesson objectives.
- Introduce the topic by asking: *What buildings do you like in your town/city? What is special about them? What is the biggest/tallest/smallest building you have seen?*

Exercise 1 page 48
- Read the reading tip with the class and elicit what *scanning* is (to read quickly for particular information) and why it is useful (it helps to deal with reading comprehension tasks and saves time).
- Give students 2 minutes to read the instructions and follow them. Check as a class.

KEY
1 Balmoral Castle
2 The Palace of Culture and Science
3 The Palace of Culture and Science

Exercise 2 page 48
- Read the reading tip with the class. Ask students to find *skyline* in the text and suggest their own explanation or translation, then find the correct meaning in the list a–j.
- Students match the rest of the words with the definitions, then compare answers in pairs. Check answers as a class.

KEY
a	structure	f	construction
b	skyline	g	tower
c	residence	h	ballroom
d	grounds	I	congress hall
e	terrace	j	parade

Exercise 3 page 49
- Ask students to read the questions carefully. Are there any answers which seem obviously right? Ask students to scan the text to confirm their guesses, then read it more carefully to find answers to the rest of the questions. Allow 8 minutes.
- Check by getting individual students to read answers and the relevant fragments of the text.

KEY
1 c   2 c   3 d   4 b   5 a

PRONUNCIATION – SILENT LETTERS
This page contains examples of words with silent letters. For extra practice in this area, write up or dictate the following sentences and ask students to cross out the letters that are silent. Then get them to practise reading the sentences.

She lives in a castle.
I'll see you in half an hour.
They've got a new government.
It's an amazing building.
What are you doing for Christmas?
She never listens to me.
Can you answer my question?
We're going to a Scottish island.

Exercise 4 page 49
- Go over the list of buildings with the class. Explain any new words. Model the pronunciation. Students listen and repeat.
- Ask and answer about the buildings in the pictures as a class (Sydney Opera House, St Peter's Cathedral in Rome, the Leaning Tower of Pisa, the Kremlin). Then ask students to choose three buildings and write answers in their notebooks. Allow 5 minutes. Discuss the answers as a class.

ADDITIONAL SPEAKING ACTIVITY
Tell students that local authorities have decided to add another building to your school. As students, they are asked to share their opinions about the idea. Put students in pairs to discuss the following points:
- where exactly it should be built
- what kind of building is needed (size and type of rooms, architecture, etc.)
- how it will be used (as a gym, canteen, information centre, etc.)
- what benefit it will bring the school (who will use it, what will happen there)

Conduct a 'pyramid' discussion to work out a common design. Put students in pairs to discuss their ideas for 3–4 minutes. Then join pairs in groups of four for another 2–3 minutes to compare their designs. They should try to agree on one idea. Then – depending on the number of students in class – put students in groups of six or eight. Finally bring the class together and decide what building to have. Put the most important features on the board.

If there is time left, ask individual students to make a short oral presentation about the building.

➡ Lesson outcome
Ask students: *What have you learned today? What can you do now?* and elicit answers: *I can understand information in a tourist guide. I have learned words for buildings.*

5F EVERYDAY ENGLISH
Buying clothes

LESSON SUMMARY ●●●○○
Functional English: asking about sizes, prices
Vocabulary: in a shop, prices
Listening: dialogues in a shop; listening for specific information
Speaking: role-play about buying clothes
Topic: shops and services

SHORTCUT *To do the lesson in 30 minutes, replace the Lead-in with questions about the photo (Where is she? What is she doing?) and skip exercises 5 and 10.*

➡ Lead-in 5 minutes
• Inform the class of the lesson objectives.
• Write *clothes* on the board and elicit the correct pronunciation.
• Revise vocabulary for clothes by getting students to describe what they are wearing. Put the words on the board.
• Introduce the topic by asking: *Do you like shopping for clothes? Why/ Why not? Where do you buy clothes? What's your favourite clothes shop?*

Exercise 1 page 50
• Students complete the dialogue in pairs.

KEY

1 jumper	3 black	5 medium
2 jumpers	4 brother	6 £24.99

Exercise 2 page 50 🎧 1.46
• Play the recording. Students listen and repeat.
• In a **weaker class**, play the recording once more. Students listen and read.
• Ask a pair of students to read the dialogue out. Correct any pronunciation or intonation mistakes.

Exercise 3 page 50
• Students match the words to the definitions individually.
• While they are working, write the following on the board:
  I'm looking ... a jumper.
  This jumper is ... the sale.
  Could you come ... to the till?
  Can I bring it ...?
• Check answers as a class, then ask students to cover the dialogue. Elicit the prepositions which complete the sentences on the board (*for, in, over, back*).

KEY

a sale	c till	e receipt
b size	d changing room	f to fit

Exercise 4 page 50
• Ask students to study the information in the box. Encourage individual students to read out the prices.
• If necessary, dictate a few more prices in English. When students have noted them down, put them on the board for students to check. Ask other students to dictate prices. Follow the same procedure. When there are some prices on the board, ask students to read them out.

Exercise 5 page 50
• Go over the vocabulary in the box as a class. Explain any new words. Model the pronunciation for students to repeat.
• Allow 3 minutes to practise reading the dialogue.

Exercise 6 page 50   🎧 1.47
• Read the exam tip with the class. Elicit the meaning of *article of clothing*. Explain that students are going to listen to two people who are looking for clothes. Students listen once and complete the table.

LANGUAGE NOTE – CLOTHES
Explain that *clothes* is a plural word that can't be used in the singular. Instead we tend to refer to the item by its name, e.g. a T-shirt.

KEY

	Article of clothing	Size	Colour
Dialogue 1	shirt	small	white
Dialogue 2	top	14	blue

Transcript 1.47
Dialogue 1

Martin	Excuse me. I'm looking for a white shirt.
Shop assistant	OK. What size are you?
Martin	Um, small, I think.
Shop assistant	How about this one?
Martin	Yes, that looks nice. Can I try it on?
Shop assistant	Of course. The changing rooms are over there.
Martin	Where?
Shop assistant	Next to the till.
Martin	Oh yes.
Martin	I'll take it please.
Shop assistant	That's £25, please ... thank you. And £5 change.
Martin	Thanks.

Dialogue 2

Shop assistant	Can I help you?
Cathy	Yes, I'm looking for a top to go with this skirt.
Shop assistant	How about these blue tops?
Cathy	Hmm. They're quite nice. How much are they?
Shop assistant	The price is on the label.
Cathy	Oh yes. £18. Have you got it in a 14?
Shop assistant	I'll just have a look. Yes, here you are.
Cathy	Thanks. Can I try it on?
Shop assistant	Certainly.
Shop assistant	Is it OK?
Cathy	It's a nice colour, but it doesn't fit very well. I'll leave it. Thanks anyway.
Shop assistant	Thank you. Goodbye.

Exercise 7 page 50
• Students complete the gaps in pairs.

KEY

1 What size	4 price
2 try it on?	5 Have you got
3 to go with	

Exercise 8 page 50 🎧 1.48

- Play the recording again. Students listen and check. Pause the recording so that students can make corrections. Put the words on the board if necessary.
- Ask pairs of students to read the lines out. Help with the pronunciation and intonation.

Exercise 9 page 50

- Students work in pairs to plan a dialogue. Remind them to make notes. Allow a minute.

Exercise 10 page 50

- Allow 5 minutes for students to write dialogues in their notebooks. Go round helping and correcting. Encourage students to use new vocabulary and phrases.
- When the time is up, students read and memorise their dialogues in pairs. Instruct them to keep eye contact as it makes the conversation more natural and prevents them from reading the dialogue.

Exercise 11 page 50

- Arrange a desk in front of the class to represent the till. Ask each pair to face each other and speak without using their notebooks.

➡ Lesson outcome

Ask students: *What have you learned today? What can you do now?* and elicit answers: *I can go shopping for clothes. I have learned vocabulary connected with clothes.*

5G WRITING
An informal letter

LESSON SUMMARY ●●●○○

Writing: a thank-you letter
Vocabulary: colloquial English
Reading: an informal letter
Topic: family life and relationships

SHORTCUT *To do the lesson in 30 minutes, make sure you do not spend more than 15 minutes on preparation, leaving the other half of the lesson for writing. Alternatively, get the students to plan their letters in class, but set the writing for homework.*

➡ Lead-in 2–3 minutes

- Inform the class of the lesson objectives.
- Introduce the topic by asking: *When was the last time you wrote a letter? Who did you write it to? Have you ever received a letter? Who was it from? Why do people write letters?*

Exercise 1 page 51

- Ask students to look at the beginning and ending of the letter and decide (without reading the main body) whether the letter is formal or not.
- Ask students why the letter is informal but do not suggest any answers at this stage. (Possible answers: The person Amy is writing to is her aunt. The letter contains informal phrases: *I hope you're well. Thanks again for the lovely scarf. Lots of love, Amy.* There is no address of the person Amy is writing to.)
- Students read the letter individually and find three things Amy got for her birthday.

KEY

a scarf, some money and a DVD of *The Two Towers*.

Exercise 2 page 51

- Ask: *Has Amy used any informal words or expressions in her letter?* and elicit examples.
- Students work individually to match the words. Check as a class, then give students 2 minutes to test each other on the new vocabulary.

KEY

1 gorgeous	4 the States	7 mates
2 go with	5 I reckon	8 brilliant
3 give back	6 plane	

Exercise 3 page 51

- Read the instructions as a class. Students work individually. Allow 3 minutes.

KEY

Paragraph 1: 1 c, 2 f, 3 g
Paragraph 2: 4 a, 5 d, 6 b
Paragraph 3: 7 e

Exercise 4   page 51

- Read the writing tip as a class. Ask students to draw arrows between the bulleted sentences in the tip and the relevant fragments of the letter or to mark them in some other way.

Exercise 5   page 51

- Read the instructions and the words in the box with the class. Students choose a present.

Exercise 6   page 51

- Read the instructions as a class. Students work individually. Ask them to cover Amy's letter. They can use the information in the writing tip. Allow 10 minutes. While they are working, go round helping.
- If there is time left, ask students to swap letters, read and correct.
- Ask a few students to read their letters out to the class. Give feedback on the content, organisation of ideas and style. Show a few letters to the class and ask what they think of the layout and handwriting. Are the letters easy to read?

ALTERNATIVE WRITING TASK

You had a birthday while you were staying at your cousin's in the UK. Your cousin organised a party and gave you an unusual present. Write a thank-you letter. In the letter:

- thank your cousin for the party and the present
- say how you use the present
- say how you remember the party
- thank them again, invite your cousin to stay in your country and promise to organise a party for him/her

➡ Lesson outcome

Ask students: *What have you learned today? What can you do now?* and elicit answers: *I have learned colloquial words and phrases. I can write a thank-you letter to a friend or relative.*

Notes for Photocopiable activity 5.2

Review

Board game
Language: vocabulary and structures from Unit 5
Materials: one copy of the worksheet per 2–4 students
(Teacher's Book page 133)

- This activity revises the vocabulary and functional language related to Unit 5. It also gives a further opportunity to develop oral fluency. Make one copy of the worksheet, enlarged to A3 if possible, for each group of 2–4 students. You will need 1 dice per group and one counter per student.
- Divide the class into groups. Give each group a copy of the worksheet, dice and counters.
- Look at the board game with the class. Explain that there are two types of task: answering a language question, and talking about a topic for 30 seconds.
- Explain the rules of the game: students throw a dice and move around the board completing the task for the square they land on. If the task is completed successfully, the student continues from that square in the next round. If not, they go to the previous **!** square. If they land directly on a **!** square, they miss a turn.
- Students play the game in groups. The game finishes when the first student reaches the *Finish* square.

EXAM For further exam tasks and practice, go to Workbook page 48. Procedural notes, transcripts and keys for the Workbook can be found on the *Solutions* Teacher's Website at www.oup.com/elt/teacher/solutions.

Get ready for your EXAM 5 & 6

TOPIC ●●●○○
Entertainment

➤ Lead-in   3 minutes

- Inform the class of the lesson objectives.
- Play a round of word tennis using the topic *the theatre*. See page 8 of the Teacher's Book introduction for instructions.
- Play a second round of the game with *music* as the topic.

Exercise 1   page 52   3–4 minutes

- Point out that this question is asking for the overall topic of each review. Remind students that for this type of task they should read quickly, establishing a general sense of what each text is about. Set a time limit of 2 minutes for the task.
- Tell students that in the exam they should always do this preliminary reading themselves, before tackling a more detailed comprehension task.
- In a **stronger class**, ask students to say whether the reviews were generally positive or negative and elicit any other information they picked up about each one.

KEY

A ice show   B play   C rock concert

Exercise 2   page 52   12–15 minutes

E Reading: multiple-choice statements

- Point out that multiple-choice questions require a close and detailed reading of the texts, to identify specific information. Explain that the order of the questions follows the order of the texts. In a **weaker class**, ask students to look at the stem part of each question (at the beginning, in bold) and to say which text the question refers to.
- Advise students to read every part of each question carefully and underline key words. Warn them not to jump to a quick conclusion because they see a word or phrase that appears in the text – the questions include 'traps' that people can fall into if they do not read attentively.
- Students re-read the texts and choose their answers to the questions. Allow them to compare answers in pairs.
- Share answers as a class. Ask students to quote the text fragments which justify their answers.

KEY

1 A   2 D   3 C   4 D   5 A   6 B

Exercise 3   page 52   3–5 minutes

- Ask students to think about their answers, referring back to the texts. Then discuss the questions as a class.

Exercise 4   page 52   8–10 minutes

- Students complete the exercise individually, then compare answers in pairs.
- Elicit example endings to make the incomplete phrases into sentences.
- With the class, elicit a three-line dialogue between friends discussing plans for next Saturday afternoon. Follow this model:
  A: Make a suggestion.
  B: Say no and express a preference for something else.
  A: Accept B's suggestion.
- Put students in pairs to make up and practise a similar dialogue. Tell them to swap roles and practise again.

KEY

Making suggestions: Why don't we …?   Let's …
Expressing dislikes: I'm not keen on …   I don't really want to …
Expressing preferences: I'd rather …   I'd prefer to …
Accepting suggestions: I'd love to.   That's a good idea.

Exercise 5   page 52   6–8 minutes

E Speaking: situational role-play

- Read the exam task and tell students that they will work in pairs. Explain that the discussion should last for about 3 minutes, so they shouldn't reach agreement immediately.
- Put students in different pairs from exercise 4. Give them 3 minutes to plan the general outline of the dialogue and then to consider individually what they will say. Remind them to think about their reasons for making or rejecting a suggestion.
- Model the activity with a strong student.
- Pairs practise their dialogues. At the end, ask them to take a minute or so to discuss ways of improving the dialogue. Then they swap roles and practise again.

➤ Lesson outcome

- Ask students: *What have you learned today? What can you do now?* and elicit answers: *I have practised a multiple-choice reading task. I have learned expressions for making and responding to suggestions. I have practised a role-play.*

Get ready for your EXAM 6

TOPIC ●●●○○
Shops and services

➤ Lead-in   5 minutes

- Inform the class of the lesson objectives.
- Revise vocabulary on the topic of shopping. Ask students to take it in turns around the class to name things connected with shops and shopping.
- Say the following verbs: *sell, look for, look at, afford, try on, fit, pay for*. Elicit an example sentence for each verb in the context of shopping.

Exercise 1   page 53   3–4 minutes

- Students work individually to complete the sentences.
- Ask them to think of two more questions about shopping habits. These could be questions about particular shops or products. **Fast finishers** can be asked to think of more than two.

KEY

1 shopping   2 shops   3 clothes   4 money   5 ages

Exercise 2   page 53   2–3 minutes

- Elicit phrases to express likes and dislikes. If students lack ideas, refer them to the Functions Bank (*Talking about likes and dislikes* Workbook page 100). Encourage students to use the phrases to answer the questions.
- Share ideas as a class.

Get ready for your EXAM 6

Exercise 3 page 53 🎧 1.49 10 minutes

E Listening: matching statements to speakers

- Read the exam task as a class.
- Remind students that it is important to know beforehand what they are listening for. Advise them to underline key words in the sentences as this will help to highlight the meaning and make it easier to match with the recording. Allow a minute for students to get familiar with the task and identify the key words. It is not important that all students underline the same words. Do not elicit any answers at this stage.
- Explain that if two sentences are similar, it is probable that one of them is the unsuitable one. Elicit which sentences in the task are similar (B and E).
- Play the recording twice, pausing for 15–30 seconds between the first and second listening. Allow another 15–30 seconds afterwards so that students can make final decisions.
- Check as a class.

KEY

1 C   2 D   3 A   4 F   5 E

Transcript 🎧 1.49

Announcer Hello and welcome to *Street Talk*. On today's programme we're talking about shopping. Do you love it or hate it? How often do you go shopping? Do you shop alone or with family and friends? We went out on the streets of London and spoke to some teenagers about their shopping habits. Let's find out what they said.

Speaker 1 My boyfriend Chris and I both like shopping and we often go together. I love going to clothes shops and shoe shops – I can spend all day trying on clothes. Chris likes shopping for CDs and DVDs but he doesn't like to spend a long time in the shops – he gets bored more quickly than me.

Speaker 2 My mum makes me go to the supermarket every weekend with her – she has to buy a lot of food so I help her with the bags. Apart from that I never go shopping if I can avoid it. I buy everything I need on the Internet. Occasionally I go into town if I need some trainers or some new jeans.

Speaker 3 My sister can spend ages going round the shops, looking at stuff in the windows. I can't stand that. I only go shopping when I know exactly what I want to buy. I go straight to the shop and buy whatever it is I want, then go home.

Speaker 4 I like shopping but I don't have much money to spend so I don't go that often. I like going to music shops, electrical stores and bookshops. I can spend ages in them. I don't like clothes shops much because I'm not interested in fashion.

Speaker 5 I go shopping every Saturday morning. My friends and I always meet up in town and then we go round the shops. It's great fun. Sometimes I don't buy anything, but I like trying things on and looking at the latest fashions.

Exercise 4 page 53 3–4 minutes

- Explain the meaning of *goods* (products for sale). Point out that this word is not related to the adjective *good* – it is a plural noun, with no singular form.
- Read the words and ask students to identify the parts of speech. Elicit/explain the meaning of *cash* and *faulty*.
- Students complete the task individually.

KEY

1 touch	4 faulty	7 time
2 leave	5 cash	8 shop assistant
3 choice	6 cheaper	

Exercise 5 page 53 3 minutes

- Explain that this is preparation for a speaking task comparing online shopping with going to real shops.
- Do the exercise as a class. Ask follow-up questions, e.g.:
  1 *How do you choose things on the Internet?*
  4 *What do you do if you get faulty goods from a website?*
  5 *How do you pay online?*
  6 *Why are goods more expensive in a shop?*
  7 *When do ordinary shops close?*

KEY

1 real shop	4 real shop	7 online
2 online	5 real shop	8 real shop
3 online	6 online	

Exercise 6 page 53 4 minutes

- Elicit the sentences as a class.
- Ask students to practise in pairs. Encourage **stronger students** to explain the advantages/disadvantages a bit more fully.

Exercise 7 page 53 3 minutes

- Give students a minute to look at the pictures.
- Ask: *What have the photos got in common?* Then elicit answers to the other two questions. Make notes on the board, highlighting contrasts. In a **weaker class**, leave these notes on the board for the exam task.
- Explain that if students are not sure how to interpret the situation in a photo, they can turn this to their advantage by sharing their doubts with the examiner. For example, they might say: *I'm not sure what the man is holding, but I think it's a camcorder.* Refer students to the Functions Bank (*Describing pictures*, Workbook page 101) for useful phrases.

Exercise 8 page 53 10 minutes

E Speaking: picture-based discussion

- Read the exam task as a class and check vocabulary.
- Explain to students that a good way to tackle this task is to start with any points of similarity between the photos, then talk about the differences they can see (as in exercise 7), then discuss advantages/disadvantages (as in exercise 6). They should end by expressing an overall preference or explaining that it is hard to choose one alternative over the other.
- Allow 3 minutes for students to prepare.
- In pairs, students take it in turns to speak for 1–2 minutes. Their partner should only contribute by expressing interest or encouragement.
- At the end, ask students to consider these questions: *Did I feel confident? Did I have enough to say? Was my talk well balanced, or did I talk about one photo more than the other? Did I repeat myself? Where did I run into difficulties? How could I have done better?* Allow pairs to discuss these questions in their own language.
- Discuss difficulties and strategies with the class.

➡ Lesson outcome

- Ask students: *What have you learned today? What can you do now?* and elicit answers: *I have practised a matching listening task. I have compared and contrasted photos as a speaking task.*

6 Technology

THIS UNIT INCLUDES ●●●○○
Vocabulary • electronic devices • phrasal verbs • mobiles: verb + noun phrases • places
Grammar • *will* and *going to* • zero conditional • *may, might* and *could*
Speaking • making predictions • arranging to meet
Writing • a formal letter
WORKBOOK pages 50–56 • Self check 6 page 57

A VOCABULARY AND LISTENING
Useful gadgets

LESSON SUMMARY ●●●○○
Vocabulary: electronic devices, phrasal verbs
Listening: radio advertisements; matching
Speaking: talking about the most useful devices
Topic: science and technology

SHORTCUT *To do the lesson in 30 minutes, set Vocabulary builder part 1 for homework and skip exercises 4 and 7. Keep a fast pace.*

→ Lead-in 2–3 minutes
- Inform the class of the lesson objectives.
- Elicit the meaning of *gadget* (a small, cleverly-designed machine or tool) by putting some examples on the board and getting students to think about what they have in common.
- Ask students in pairs to list all the gadgets they can think of in one minute. Ask students to read out their lists.

Exercise 1 page 54
- Read the instructions with the class. Explain or elicit the meaning of *device* (here: synonym to *gadget*).
- Ask students to put a tick next to the devices they have recently used. As students may not know how to name all the objects yet, do not get any feedback at this stage.

> #### LANGUAGE NOTE – VOCABULARY
> A *device* /dɪˈvaɪs/ is an object that has been designed to do a particular job.
>
> A *gadget* /ˈgædʒɪt/ is a device that is more unusual or cleverly designed than normal technology.

Exercise 2 page 54
- Students can work in pairs. Allow a minute.

KEY

1 satellite TV	5 portable CD player
2 digital camera	6 games console
3 mobile phone	7 calculator
4 stereo	8 MP3 player

Not illustrated: camcorder, digital radio, DVD player, hard disk recorder, video recorder

Exercise 3 page 54 🎧 2.01
- Play the recording once so that students can check their answers.
- Play the recording again. Stop after each expression for students to repeat chorally and individually.
- In a **weaker class**, if students need further practice, play the recording once more. Stop after every two expressions. Students repeat pairs of expressions.

> #### OPTIONAL ACTIVITY
> Focus the class on exercise 1 again. Students work in pairs for a minute telling each other which devices they have used in the last week. Ask a few students to report back on their partners.

For more practice on vocabulary related to electronic devices, go to:

> **Vocabulary Builder (part 1):** Student's Book page 129

KEY
1 a 3   b 4   c 5   d 1   e 2

2 1 MP3 player   4 satellite TV
    2 calculator   5 games console
    3 stereo   6 mobile phone

> #### TECHNOLOGY NOTES
> A **camcorder** is another word for a video camera.
>
> A **games console** is a machine which is designed to play video games either on a television or PC monitor. The most popular brands are Sony's PlayStation, Microsoft's Xbox and Nintendo's Wii (which replaced the earlier Game Cube).
>
> A **hard disk recorder** is a high capacity hard disk which can be used as a DVD recorder.
>
> An **MP3 player** is a device which stores and plays songs which have been compressed into very small files. It is associated with downloading music from the Internet. A computer (but not necessarily the Internet) is needed to download songs. MP3 is the name of the type of computer file. One of the most famous brands of MP3 player is the Apple iPod.

Exercise 4 page 54
- Students work in groups of three or four for 2 minutes. Each works on one of the categories. In a group of four, one student looks for the items which do not belong anywhere.
- Students compare their answers within the group before checking as a class.

KEY
a digital radio, satellite TV, MP3 player, portable CD player, mobile phone, stereo
b camcorder, digital camera, DVD player, satellite TV, mobile phone, video recorder, hard disk recorder
c games console, mobile phone

others: calculator

Exercise 5 page 54 🎧 2.02

- Read the exam tip with the class. Elicit an explanation of *key words* (words or expressions likely to be used in a particular context).
- Elicit what key words may be used in the context of devices. Prompt students by saying that key words may refer to parts, functions, features or a comparison with other devices.
- Play the recording twice. Ask students to note down the key words and identify the devices. Check as a class.

KEY

1 MP3 player (5,000 songs, pocket)
2 mobile phone (play games, make calls)
3 hard disc recorder (press 'record', without a video cassette or a disk)
4 digital radio (digital, the programme)

Transcript 2.02

1

Voice   New, from SuperSound – the 40 gigabyte TrackMate. It can hold more than 5,000 songs and is smaller than a cassette. When you're travelling, working or just relaxing – have 5,000 songs in your pocket with the new TrackMate.

2

Voice   The new F17G is the only gadget you need. You can take photos with it. You can play games on it. You can listen to your favourite music. You can even record video pictures. Oh yes – and you can make calls.

Woman   Hi! Maggie! I simply must tell you about the F17G. Yes, it's new. Yes, you can take photos.

3

Voice   Imagine – you're watching TV – it's your favourite programme.
Man   Great! My favourite programme is starting!
Voice   And then …
Man   Oh … no! I don't want to miss my favourite programme.
Voice   Why don't you record it?
Man   I can't find a video!
Voice   You don't need a video cassette – or a DVD. You just press 'record'!
Man   Really? That's easy!
Voice   Yes! The HDR-360 can record six hours of TV programmes – without a video cassette or a disk!

4

Radio   *And here are the football results.*
Man   Come on Arsenal. Come on Arsenal!
Radio   *Liverpool 1, Chelsea 1.*
Man   Come on Arsenal.
Radio   *Arsenal 2, Manchester United …*
Man   What? I didn't hear the result!! What was the result?
Voice   Don't worry! Because it's digital you can stop the programme, rewind it, and listen to that part again.
Man   Really? That's amazing!
Man   OK, now be quiet! Shh.
Radio   *… football results. Liverpool 1, Chelsea 1.*
Man   COME ON ARSENAL!
Radio   *Arsenal 2, Manchester United 7.*
Man   Oh …

Exercise 6 page 54

- Allow 3–4 minutes for students to discuss in pairs. Remind them to give reasons for their opinions. While they are working, go round helping with any problems.

Exercise 7 page 54

- In a **weaker class**, ask a few students to tell the class their opinion.

- In a **stronger class**, have a short class discussion about the usefulness of the devices in different situations (work, leisure, travel, war, etc.) and for different people (young, old, poor, rich, in different jobs, etc.)
- Students choose the three most useful devices by voting for a maximum of three items. When you say a device, students raise hands. Ask one of the students to count the votes, note them down and announce the results at the end.

For practice on phrasal verbs connected with devices, go to:

Vocabulary Builder (part 2): Student's Book page 129

KEY

3 1 b   2 d   3 a   4 e   5 c

4 1 off   3 up   5 away
    2 down   4 out   6 on

5 1 Can you switch it off?   5 Turn them on!
    2 He put them down.   6 Take it off!
    3 He picked her up.   7 Please put it away.
    4 I put them on.   8 She put him down.

➡ Lesson outcome

Ask students: *What have you learned today? What can you do now?* and elicit answers: *I can describe electronic devices and say why they are useful. I have learned to listen for key words in listening comprehension tasks.*

6B GRAMMAR
will and *going to*

LESSON SUMMARY ●●●●○

Grammar: *will* and *going to*
Functions: expressing plans, intentions, predictions, offers and promises
Speaking: talking about personal plans and intentions

SHORTCUT *This whole lesson can only be done within 30 minutes with a very strong class. It would require keeping a very fast pace, working as a class almost all the time and skipping at least exercises 3 and 6 in the Grammar Builder. In a weaker class, if you have to do this lesson in 30 minutes, do the Grammar Builder and skip exercises 3–6 in the lesson.*

➡ Lead-in 3–4 minutes

- Inform the class of the lesson objectives.
- Ask students in pairs to challenge each other to a verbal duel while describing the photo. They should take it in turns and say one sentence about the photo each time. They must speak as long as they have ideas. The person who says the last sentence is the winner.
- Stop students after 2 minutes. Elicit descriptions from one or two students.

Exercise 1 page 55 🎧 2.03

- In a **stronger class**, ask students to read the dialogue and choose the correct forms. Then play the recording for students to check.
- In a **weaker class**, elicit the meaning of *bring, hurry up, freeze, hit*. Then play the recording. Students listen, read and underline the correct forms in their books.

KEY

1 I'm going to	3 It's going to	5 I'll
2 I'll	4 that'll	

Exercise 2 page 55

- Read the *Learn this!* box with the class explaining the words *prediction, offer, promise, decision* and *intention*. If students have problems, provide more examples or read Grammar Reference 6.2 and 6.4 as a class.
- In a **weaker class**, go over the dialogue in exercise 1 and match examples 1–5 as a class.
- In a **stronger class**, students can work individually. Check as a class.

KEY

1 Predictions with *will*: 4 Do you think that'll help?
2 Offers and promises: 2 I'll lend you my coat.
3 Decisions: 5 I'll call a taxi.
4 Predictions with *going to*: 3 It's going to rain.
5 Intentions: 1 I'm going to use my new mobile phone.

OPTIONAL ACTIVITY

Ask students what a *satellite navigation system* is and in what situations it is useful. (An electronic device that uses satellites to pinpoint its position. They are commonly used now in cars everywhere and can be programmed with software for a certain town or region. They are particularly useful when travelling in an unknown area, or a region that has few reliable landmarks, e.g. a desert or a forest.)

For more practice on will *and* going to go to:

Grammar Builder 6B: Student's Book page 114

- In a **weaker class**, make sure students know how to form sentences with *will* and *going to*. Read Grammar Reference 6.1 and 6.3 with the class and conduct simple drills to practise affirmative and negative sentences with different singular and plural subjects.

KEY

1 I (don't) think all children will have a mobile phone in ten years' time.
I (don't) think camcorders will be very small in ten years' time.
I (don't) think digital cameras will be very expensive in ten years' time.
I (don't) think cars will need petrol in ten years' time.
I (don't) think houses will use solar energy in ten years' time.
I (don't) think watches will include MP3 players in ten years' time.

2–3 Open answers

4 1 c 2 a 3 e 4 d 5 b

5 1 He's going to fall over.
2 She's going to crash/fall off.
3 He's going to steal a mobile phone. The policeman's going to chase him.
4 He's going to frighten her. She's going to scream.

6 Open answers

Exercise 3 page 55

- Students work individually. Allow a minute.
- In a **stronger class**, ask students to explain why they are using *will* or *going to*. Elicit which of the five uses in the *Learn this!* box the dialogues show.

KEY

1 're going to	3 'll	5 's going to
2 'll	4 'm going to	

Exercise 4 page 55 🎧 2.04

- Play the recording for students to check. Then play it again stopping for students to repeat.

PRONUNCIATION – TALKING ABOUT THE FUTURE

Explain to students that *to* in *going to* is a weak form. Elicit or explain that other weak forms include auxiliary verbs, prepositions and articles. Because the syllable is unstressed, its sound becomes the *schwa* /ə/.

In spoken English it is uncommon to use the full form *will*. Much more natural is the contracted form *'ll*. It is pronounced with a dark *l*. This sound is formed towards the back of the mouth. It sounds like *ull* in *pull* rather than the *l* in *lemon*.

Similarly, *going to*, is often pronounced *gonna* in spoken English. This is not slang, lazy or American. (It should not, of course, be written as *gonna*!)

Exercise 5 page 55

- Students work individually for two minutes.
- In a **weaker class**, ask them to write full sentences. While they are working, go round and correct any mistakes.
- In a **stronger class**, encourage students to note down key words only.

Exercise 6 page 55

- Put students in pairs. Instruct them to show interest in what their partner is saying by maintaining eye contact, using *oh?, really?* etc. and asking follow-up questions (see lesson 2F). Demonstrate this in a dialogue with a student:
  S: *I'm going to do some shopping.*
  T: *Really? What are you going to buy?*

➡ Lesson outcome

Ask students: *What have you learned today? What can you do now?* and elicit answers: *I can use different structures to talk about the future. I can express predictions, offers, promises, decisions and intentions in the future. I have learned how to talk about my plans and intentions.*

CULTURE
6C A text education

LESSON SUMMARY ●●●●●

Reading: an article; scanning
Vocabulary: mobile phone vocabulary; verb + noun phrases
Listening: four short statements; matching
Speaking: talking about mobile phones
Topic: science and technology

SHORTCUT *To do the lesson in 30 minutes, keep the discussion in the Lead-in and exercise 1 brief and shorten the class discussion after exercise 6.*

➡ Lead-in 2 minutes
- Inform the class of the lesson objectives.
- Focus them on the main photo and ask: *Who can you see? What is she holding? What is she doing?*

Exercise 1 page 56
- Answer the questions as a class.
- In a **stronger class**, have a short discussion about the popularity of texting in your country. Why don't some people send text messages? In what situations is texting useful?

KEY
Txt means *text*. It is written this way because it is shorter. The language of text messages has evolved to take up less space (particularly because early mobiles had low character limits per message) and to be quicker to type into a mobile phone and send.

Exercise 2 page 56
- Read the instruction with the class and explain *mention*, if necessary.
- All students should be able to do the task without pre-teaching any other vocabulary.
- Allow 5 minutes for reading and matching. Check as a class.
- In a **stronger class**, elicit the context of 1–8 in the text; e.g. 1 James Trusler set a world record in texting while he was appearing in **a TV show** in Australia.

KEY
1 3   2 1   3 2   4 3   5 2   6 3   7 1   8 3

OPTIONAL ACTIVITY
Ask **fast finishers** to go over the article again and underline all expressions with the word *text* in different forms. They should find: *text messages, write in 'txt', language of text, texting, text messaging, texting competitions, world's fastest texter, be addicted to/ spend money on / send texts, text messages.*

Ask **fast finishers** to read the expressions out to the class. Explain or elicit the meanings.

Exercise 3 page 56
- Students work in pairs for a minute. Ask different pairs to write expressions on the board. Can students write any other examples of 'txt' for the rest to decipher?

KEY
1 See you soon.	4 I love you.
2 Call me before tomorrow.	5 I'm at home.
3 You're great.	

LANGUAGE NOTE – TEXT
Text language has evolved as people find new ways to write words based on the way that numbers and letters within the shortened words are pronounced. Common phrases are often reduced to acronyms (e.g. *by the way* is *BTW*). Further examples of text messaging language are:

CYA	See ya (See you)
RUOK?	Are you OK?
SRy	Sorry
WAN2TLK	Want to talk?
some1	someone
XLNT	excellent
HAND	have a nice day
xoxoxoxo	hugs and kisses

Exercise 4 page 56 🎧 2.05
- Ask students to read the instructions on their own. Allow enough time and play the recording once, or twice if necessary. Check answers.

KEY
1 Cindy   2 Darren   3 Paula   4 Ethan

Transcript 2.05
1 Paula I really like mobile phones and I love having the latest model. I usually upgrade my handset every twelve or eighteen months. At the moment, I've got a 3G phone. It's fantastic. I can do instant messaging, play games, watch videos … Look, I've got an episode of *Friends* on here.

2 Ethan I use my phone a lot. I'm not very keen on texting – I prefer to make a voice call, actually. In fact, some of my calls are really long! I use a wireless headset and I walk down the street, talking to my friends – sometimes I talk for twenty or thirty minutes before I realise how much it's costing me! Anyway, my dad pays the bill so I don't … Sorry, excuse me. Oh, hi, Dad. Oh dear, was it? £278! That's impossible. I never talk for more than a few minutes …

3 Darren I use my phone a lot, and I love all the different ringtones you can get. I see adverts for them on MTV – you just dial a number and download a new ringtone. It's easy! It isn't too expensive, either. At the moment, my favourite ringtone is this. Listen.

4 Cindy My friends and I have all got mobiles, and we spend a lot of time texting each other. I love it! It's much cheaper than making voice calls. It costs about 10p to send a text message. Sometimes I send … Just a minute. It's from Michael. Ha ha ha. Cheeky little …

Exercise 5 page 56 🎧 2.05
- In a **weaker class**, play the recording for students to do the matching.
- In a **stronger class**, ask students to try to match the words first, then listen and check their answers. Go over the phrases explaining or eliciting the meaning.

KEY

1 handset	4 number
2 voice call	5 ringtone
3 wireless headset	6 text message

Exercise 6 page 56

* Allow a minute for students to read the questions and make notes of their answers. Then put them in pairs to ask, answer and note down their partner's answers. Allow 3–4 minutes.
* When the time is up, ask one pair to report back on the similarities and differences in the way they use mobile phones. Ask more students to talk. Explain that they should refer to what others have said before.

> **LANGUAGE NOTE**
>
> *Mobile phone* is often shortened to *mobile*: *Call me on my mobile*. In American English mobiles are called *cell phones*.

➡ Lesson outcome

Ask students: *What have you learned today? What can you do now?* and elicit answers: *I can talk about how people use mobile phones. I have learned to 'txt'.*

Notes for Photocopiable activity 6.1

Technology Crossword

Pairwork

Language: gadgets (6A) and mobile phone vocabulary (6C); functional language for describing uses: *You use it to … You can … with it*

Materials: one copy of the worksheet cut up per pair of students (Teacher's Book page 134)

NB the majority of the language is taken from 6A and 6C but there are a small number of new vocabulary items – see below.

* Divide the class into two groups, A and B. Give each student in A a copy of worksheet A and each in B a copy of worksheet B.
* Students work with others in their group to check they know the meaning of the vocabulary in their half of the crossword. Monitor and help, especially with the new words.
* Put students into pairs so that Student A and Student B are working together. They mustn't look at their partner's crossword.
* Students take it in turns to describe the words from their half of the crossword so that their partner can complete their part of the crossword. Draw their attention to the functional language above and demonstrate the first one or two clues together.

New words

* A *PC* is a personal computer. The word is often used to describe a personal computer which is not an Apple MAC.
* A *laptop* is a portable personal computer, so named because you can use it on your lap. It is sometimes called a notebook.
* A *simcard* is a chip inside a mobile phone which contains a person's address list as well as other personal data. It can be transferred from phone to phone.
* A *charger* is plugged into an electricity socket and used to recharge any battery-operated device such as a mobile phone, digital camera or MP3 player.

6D GRAMMAR
Zero conditional

LESSON SUMMARY ●●●○○

Grammar: zero conditional; *may, might, could*

Reading: short texts about modern gadgets

Function: expressing cause and effect

Speaking: talking about cause and effect and about possibility in the present and future in a personal context

---

SHORTCUT *To do this lesson in 30 minutes, do exercise 3 as a class, turn exercise 5 into instant speaking practice omitting preparation in exercise 4, skip both Grammar Builders or set them for homework.*

➡ Lead-in 3–4 minutes

* Inform the class of the lesson objectives.
* Put on the board: *tell the truth, tell a lie* and ask students in pairs to discuss if and how it is possible to tell if a person is lying. Allow 2 minutes. Ask a few students to report back to the class.

Exercise 1 page 57

* In a **weaker class**, pre-teach *to contain, a sign, to measure, an amount, a voice, to come on*.
* In a **stronger class**, encourage students to work out the meaning from the context.
* You can check understanding of the text by asking additional questions, for example: *What happens to your voice when you tell a lie? Can you control your voice when you lie? What does the Truth Machine measure?*

KEY

red

Exercise 2 page 57

* Read the instructions as a class. Put one of the highlighted sentences on the board and label the two clauses with the terms *if clause* and *main clause*.
* Students complete the rules individually.
* Check by asking: *Which tense do we use in zero conditional sentences? Do we use the zero conditional to talk about general truths or future results? When do we use a comma?*

KEY

We use the present simple to describe the action and the present simple to describe the result.

For more practice on the zero conditional, go to:

> **Grammar Builder 6D:** Student's Book page 114

KEY

7 1 d 2 f 3 a 4 c 5 b 6 e

Exercise 3 page 57

- Allow a minute for students to complete the facts. Check as a class. Do students know more facts like these?

KEY

1 … it boils.
2 … your mobile phone's serial number appears on screen.
3 … you get green paint.
4 … you get yellow light.
5 … it dies.
6 … you get 1.234567

OPTIONAL ACTIVITY

Ask students in the same pairs to use their general knowledge and write similar *if* clauses for others to complete. Allow 2–3 minutes. When the time is up, students take it in turns to read their half-sentences out to the class. You can turn it into a contest – the student who finishes most sentences is the winner.

Exercise 4 page 57

- Read through the sentences with the class and check understanding.
- Students work individually for 2 minutes. While they are working, go round and help with any problems. If there are any common mistakes, put them on the board and correct with the class before they start exercise 5.
- Encourage **fast finishers** to write more than one ending where possible.

Exercise 5 page 57

- As this exercise provides valuable speaking practice, use as much time as possible. You will need at least 15 minutes to cover the rest of the lesson.

Exercise 6 page 57

- Look at the artwork and ask students to guess what it is. Explain to students that the Romance Reader is a real product which tells you how the person you are talking to feels about you. Ask students if they would like to have this gadget and why/why not.
- Pre-teach *to find out, embarrassing, to load, romance*.
- Students underline the examples.
- Check understanding of the examples by asking: *Is it certain or possible that she loves him? Is it certain that she doesn't like him? Is it always embarrassing to ask about feelings? Is it certain she won't give a true answer? Is it always a beginning of a big romance?*

KEY

Negative: She may not even like him. She might not give a true answer.

Exercise 7 page 57

- Students complete the rule individually. Check as a class.

KEY

We use *may not* or *might not* for the negative. We don't use *could not*.

LANGUAGE NOTE – *MAY, MIGHT, COULD*

Historically, grammar books have made a distinction between the degrees of probability expressed by *may*, *might* and *could*. In reality, the words mean the same. We express the difference in meaning not through our choice of *may*, *might* or *could* but through intonation. If we want to express a low probability we add extra stress and higher intonation to the modal verb.

Exercise 8 page 57

- Demonstrate the activity by saying a few sentences yourself and eliciting some from students.
- Correct any mistakes paying particular attention to the use of infinitive without *to* after the modal verbs.

For more practice on may, might *and* could, *go to:*

Grammar Builder 6D: Student's Book page 114

- In a **weaker class**, you may need to pre-teach *sales, to decline, illegal, to share files, download, to charge*. In a **stronger class**, you could ask what students think about illegal downloading afterwards.

KEY

8 1 may/might/could happen
2 may/might/could share
3 may/might/could become
4 may/might/could do
5 may/might not want
6 may/might/ prefer

→ Lesson outcome

Ask students: *What have you learned today? What can you do now?* and elicit answers: *I can use the zero conditional and* may, *might and* could. *I can talk about possibilities.*

Notes for Photocopiable activity 6.2

Find somebody who …

A class survey
Language: *going to, will* and *might*
Materials: one copy of the worksheet per student (Teacher's Book page 135)

- Explain to students that they are going to find out about the class's plans and intentions for the future.
- Hand out a copy of the worksheet to each student and deal with any vocabulary questions.
- Explain that they need to make each sentence into a question and then go round the class asking the questions. The other students should answer using short forms, e.g. *Yes, I do* or *No, I'm not*.
- When they find a student who answers *yes* to a question they should write that student's name in the *name* column. They should then ask a follow-up question and note the response in the last column. For example: *'Do you think you'll go to university in the future?' 'Yes, I do.' 'What do you think you'll study?' 'I might study engineering.'*
- They are allowed to write another student's name twice. After that they must move on and talk to other students.

6E READING
Nanotechnology

LESSON SUMMARY ●●●●○

Reading: an article about nanotechnology; detailed reading
Vocabulary: words connected with nanotechnology
Speaking: discussing the influence of technological progress
Topic: science and technology

SHORTCUT *To do this lesson in 30 minutes, work as a class throughout and keep a fast pace.*

➡ Lead-in 2–3 minutes

- Inform the class of the lesson objectives.
- Ask students to write the word *technology* in their notebooks.
  Ask them to work individually for one minute putting down all the words that come to their minds when they think about modern technology. Have students read their words out to the class.

Exercise 1   page 58

- In a **weaker class**, ask students to work in pairs for two minutes first. Then discuss the statement as a class.
- If students need help, put some prompts on the board, e.g. *work, transport, communication, information, free time, pollution, stress, medicine.*

Exercise 2   page 58

- In a **weaker class**, pre-teach *a market, a disease, to inject, damage, to damage, to escape, worries, to worry.* Allow 5 minutes for students to read the text. Complete the sentences as a class.
- In a **stronger class**, students work individually. Check as a class.

KEY

Possible answers:
1 (Paragraph 2) ... cure almost every disease.
2 (Paragraph 3) ... escape and damage the planet.

OPTIONAL ACTIVITY

Put the following sentences on the board for **fast finishers** to complete in their own words:

In the science fiction film *Fantastic Voyage*, nanobots...
In Eric Drexler's *Engines of Creation*, nanobots...
In Michael Crichton's *Prey*, nanobots...

Exercise 3   page 58

- Students work individually. Check as a class. In a **stronger class**, do not explain any other vocabulary until after exercise 4.

KEY

1 tiny	6 patient
2 nightmare	7 entire
3 fantasy	8 cure
4 submarine	9 terrifying
5 environment	

Exercise 4   page 59

- Read the reading tip with the students and encourage them to try the method suggested.

KEY

1 F 2 T 3 F 4 F 5 T 6 F 7 F

Exercise 5   page 59

- Elicit what inventions are presented in the photos. As an example, discuss one of them with the class. Allow 5 minutes for students to work in pairs. Encourage them to use the phrases in the speaking tip box to present their ideas. Extend the time limit if necessary.

ADDITIONAL SPEAKING ACTIVITY

Look again at the photos of modern technology. Ask: *Does technology make our life easier?* Ask students to think of a piece of technology that they use every day. Could they live without it? Share ideas as a class.

As a class, brainstorm as many technological inventions that make our lives easier as the students can think of. If necessary, suggest categories, e.g. transport, in the home, communication, etc. Continue until the board is covered in suggestions.

Put students in pairs to decide which are the five most important/useful inventions. Briefly share ideas as a class.

Now explain to the students that they are planning an Arctic expedition. They are going to spend six months in an extreme environment, but they have a limited budget. They can only choose ten items from the list to use on their expedition. Which are the most important?

Encourage students to think about what they are going to do in the Arctic. What will they need to survive, travel, be comfortable, etc? Remind them that this is a future trip and elicit some sentences with *will* and *going to*. Tell students they need to explain their reasons for taking things. Elicit which structure can be used to talk about outcomes and possibilities (zero conditional) and model a few sentences, for example: *If you have a satellite navigation system, you always know where you are.*

Conduct a pyramid discussion. Allow students a few minutes to decide individually what they would choose. Then put them in pairs to compare answers and agree on a common list. Now put two pairs together to compare again and justify their choices. The aim is to agree on a list of ten in order of importance.

Depending on the size of the class, you may want to increase the group size again to six or eight, or you may wish to bring the class together earlier. Elicit a few lists from different groups and discuss the similarities and differences as a class.

➡ Lesson outcome

Ask students: *What have you learned today? What can you do now?* and elicit answers: *I can understand an article in detail. I can talk about the advantages and disadvantages of advances in technology. I have learned about nanotechnology.*

6F EVERYDAY ENGLISH
Arranging to meet

LESSON SUMMARY ●●●●○

Functional English: making arrangements
Reading: a dialogue
Listening: a dialogue; listening for specific information
Speaking: making arrangements to meet
Topic: relationships

SHORTCUT *To do this lesson in 30 minutes, play the recording in exercise 1 once only, skip the extra comprehension questions in 4 and keep the class performances focused and brief.*

→ Lead-in 3 minutes
- Inform the class of the lesson objectives.
- Explain *to make an arrangement*. Focus students on the picture. Ask them to look at it for 30 seconds, close their books and describe it in pairs. Allow 2 minutes.

Exercise 1 page 60 🎧 2.06
- In a **stronger class**, students keep their books closed. Play the recording once. Students note their answer to the question. In a **weaker class**, students read and listen at the same time.
- Play the recording again. Students listen, read and check. Elicit answers.

KEY
About four o'clock outside the main doors of the department store.

Exercise 2 page 60
- Go over the expressions in the box with the class, explaining any new words.
- Students read the dialogue, then change pairs and roles and read it again.

Exercise 3 page 60
- Students complete the sentences individually. Check as a class.

KEY
1 Do you fancy …   2 Why don't we …   3 Let's …

Exercise 4 page 60 🎧 2.07
- Read the exam tip with the class. Play the recording once. Get the class to answer the question. Encourage individual students to give as much additional information as possible by asking additional questions: *Where is Justin? Where is Tracey? Where does Justin suggest? Why can't they meet at the library?*

Transcript 2.07

Tracey	Hello?
Justin	Hi, Tracey. It's Justin.
Tracey	Oh hi!
Justin	It's 4 o'clock. Where are you?
Tracey	I'm outside the department store. Are you inside?
Justin	No, I'm outside too. I'm standing next to the doors.
Tracey	That's funny. I can't see you.
Justin	I'm by the main doors. You aren't by the side entrance, are you?
Tracey	No. I'm by the main doors too.
Justin	Right. I've just thought of something. What's the name of the department store?
Tracey	Peacock's.
Justin	Peacock's? I've never heard of that. Where is it?
Tracey	It's near the bottom of North Street. Where are you?
Justin	I'm outside Jackson's.
Tracey	Jackson's? Oh, right. That department store. Oh dear. We're at different ends of town. We'll have to meet somewhere else – in the centre.
Justin	OK. Why don't we meet at the library?
Tracey	We can't. It closes in twenty minutes.
Justin	What about the music shop on the High Street? That will be open.
Tracey	OK. See you there at 4.30?
Justin	Fine. Let's meet on the ground floor.
Tracey	No, it'll be too busy there. Let's meet on the top floor.
Justin	OK, no problem. See you at half past four in the music shop, on the top floor.
Tracey	Great. Bye!

KEY
They are at different department stores.

Exercise 5 page 60 🎧 2.07
- Read the instruction with the class explaining any new words in the table. Play the recording again. Check as a class.

KEY
4.30, the music shop, on the top floor

Exercise 6 page 60
- Go through the chart with the class. In a **weaker class**, demonstrate an example with a student and encourage students to write the dialogue down first.
- Students work in pairs for 2 minutes.

Exercise 7 page 60
- Ask students to try and memorise the dialogue. They should not use their notes.

OPTIONAL ACTIVITY
In a **stronger class**, ask students to act out a dialogue based on the situation in the listening in exercise 4. They misunderstood each other and have to make a new arrangement.

→ Lesson outcome
Ask students: *What have you learned today? What can you do now?* and elicit answers: *I can make arrangements to meet someone. I can talk about different meeting places.*

6G WRITING
A formal letter

LESSON SUMMARY ●●●○○

Writing: a letter of complaint
Reading: formal letters
Vocabulary: set phrases for formal letters
Topic: science and technology

SHORTCUT *To do the lesson in 30 minutes, do the preparation work in exercises 1–4 as a class. Emphasise the importance of planning and allow plenty of time to do the writing. Alternatively, spend more class time on preparation and set the writing for homework.*

➡ Lead-in 4–5 minutes

- Inform the class of the lesson objectives.
- Elicit or explain *to complain* (to say or write that you are unhappy about something you bought) and *complaint* (a written or spoken statement in which you complain).
- Put students in groups of three and ask them to brainstorm products one can complain about and possible reasons for complaints. Allow a minute.
- To share answers, ask a group to sugest a product. Another group responds with a possible reason for complaint. Then they read one of their complaints and the third group says the product which matches the problem. Go on matching products with reasons for complaint and vice-versa until all the groups have taken part or the class have run out of ideas.

Exercise 1 page 61

- Students read the letters carefully and make notes. Pairs exchange information for a minute.
- In a **weaker class**, get feedback by going through the questions and both letters as a class. In a **stronger class**, read a few fragments of the text for students to identify the questions the fragments answer. Check vocabulary comprehension by asking students to find the words which mean:
  a problem (fault)
  a song (track)
  to start a machine (to turn it on)
  to stop the machine (to turn off)
  to send something back (to return)
  to fix something so that it works again (to repair)
  to use the Internet (to access the Internet)
  to put something into the envelope together with a letter (to enclose)
  to take back a faulty product and give a new one instead (to replace)
  a small piece of paper you get from a shop when you buy something (a receipt)

KEY

Madeline's letter:
1 Zenon ZK400 MP3 player.
2 From/In/At The Gadget Shop in Newcastle.
3 On 28th April 2007.
4 It sometimes stops in the middle of a track.
5 She wants them to repair the fault or send her a new MP3 player.

Victoria's letter:
1 UltraFast modem.
2 From Computers Online's website.
3 Recently.
4 It does not work.
5 She wants them to replace the modem.

Exercise 2 page 61

- Ask students to read the questions and try to remember the answers. Remind them that the skimming technique will help them check their answers quickly. Allow a minute.

KEY

1 paragraph 2   2 paragraph 1   3 paragraph 3

Exercise 3 page 61

- Students can work individually. To check, ask different students to read the sentences out to the class.
- In a **stronger class**, make students aware of other details of the layout of formal letters by asking: *Whose address do I put in the top right hand corner of the page?* (My address.) *What do I put under my address?* (The date.) *Where do I put the company's address?* (On the left, below the date.) *How do I separate the paragraphs?* (By leaving a blank line.)

KEY

1 date   4 Yours faithfully
2 Dear Sir or Madam   5 full name

Exercise 4 page 61

- Read the writing tip as a class. Put students in the same pairs as for exercise 1 but ask them to look at the other letter this time. Students work quickly to find the phrases.

KEY

Madeline's letter
I am writing to report a fault …
I would be grateful if you could repair the fault.
… could you please send me a new MP3 player?
I look forward to hearing from you.

Victoria's letter
I am writing to complain about …
I am enclosing the modem together with the receipt.
Could you please replace the modem as soon as possible?
I look forward to hearing from you.

Exercise 5 page 61

- Allow students a minute to choose their item and decide on the fault. They can discuss in pairs if necessary.
- In a **weaker class**, elicit some examples and talk about the sorts of problems you can have with different gadgets.

Exercise 6

- Remind students that they must include all the points in the instructions.
- Encourage them to plan their work, and allocate a paragraph to each bullet point.
- Give students time to check their work, using the checklist.
- If there is time, read some of the letters out and ask the class to comment on whether all the points have been appropriately covered. Comment on good use of language from the lesson as well as on mistakes.

➡ Lesson outcome

Ask students: *What have you learned today? What can you do now?* and elicit answers: *I can write a formal letter of complaint. I can return or replace a faulty product.*

LANGUAGE REVIEW 5–6

1
1 bakery e
2 butcher's a
3 chemist's g
4 jeweller's b
5 newsagent's c
6 post office f
7 electrical store d

2
1 camera
2 player
3 console
4 phone
5 TV
6 recorder

3
1 Have (you) enjoyed
2 've had
3 have (you) done
4 've visited
5 Has (the weather) been
6 hasn't rained
7 Have (you) bought
8 've spent

4
1 had
2 met
3 gave
4 hasn't called
5 Have (you) spoken
6 Have (you) seen
7 saw

5
1 'll
2 'm going to
3 'll
4 's going to
5 'll
6 'm going to

6
1 if
2 have
3 might not
4 comes on
5 don't
6 might

7 2, 4, 1, 5, 3

8
1 up
2 in
3 don't
4 What
5 Let's

SKILLS ROUND-UP 1–6

1 1 D   2 C   3 A

2
1 It was a small village.
2 Because they believed that the sea was good for their health.
3 In West Street and Kings Road Arches.
4 Classical music and opera.
5 The Lanes.
6 The independent shops.

3
1 well-known
2 independent
3 fishermen
4 open-air
5 bargains
6 royal palace
7 ideal

Transcript 2.08

Narrator	Joanna is in town. She's looking for a present for Oliver. It's his 8th birthday next week.
Joanna	Hello Maria.
Maria	Hi, Joanna! Where are you?
Joanna	I'm in town. I'm looking for a birthday present for Oliver. What about you?
Maria	I'm at home.
Joanna	What are you up to?
Maria	Nothing much. Do you fancy meeting up?
Joanna	Sure. Where do you want to meet?
Maria	Why don't we meet in the shopping centre?
Joanna	OK. What time?
Maria	About three o'clock.
Joanna	OK. Where exactly are we going to meet?
Maria	By the escalators.
Joanna	Fine. See you at three.
Narrator	It's five to three. Joanna is in a clothes shop.
Assistant	Can I help you?
Joanna	Yes. How much is this T-shirt?
Assistant	It's £11.
Joanna	Have you got it in blue?
Assistant	Yes. What size are you?
Joanna	It isn't for me. It's a present. But I think he's a small.
Assistant	Hmm. Sorry. We've only got it in large and extra large.
Joanna	Oh. OK. I'll keep looking.
Maria	Hi, Joanna. Where are you? It's three o'clock.
Joanna	Sorry! I'm coming. See you in a minute.
Maria	Hi!
Joanna	Hello, Maria. Sorry I'm late.
Maria	That's OK. Have you bought anything for Oliver?
Joanna	No, I haven't. I'm still looking.
Maria	Does he like gadgets?
Joanna	Yes, he does. He loves them.
Maria	I know a great shop, then. Follow me!
Maria	Here we are.
Joanna	Ahh look! A robot dog. He's cute.
RoboDog	*Hello. I'm RoboDog. Woof.*
Joanna	And he can talk!
RoboDog	*I know 350 different words.*
Maria	How much is it?
Joanna	Ninety-five pounds. Too much!
Maria	Look – this is only nine pounds.
Joanna	A pen?
Maria	It's a pen, yes, but it's also a radio.
Joanna	That's cool. Oliver will like that.
Maria	Are you going to buy it?
Joanna	Yes, I am.

4 c a pen/radio

5 1 8   2 3   3 11   4 350   5 95   6 9

6–8 Open answers

EXAM For further exam tasks and practice, go to Workbook page 58. Procedural notes, transcripts and keys for the Workbook can be found on the *Solutions* Teachers' Website at www.oup.com/elt/teacher/solutions.

7 Cultures and customs

THIS UNIT INCLUDES ●●●○
Vocabulary • gestures • phrasal verbs • social activities
Grammar • *must, mustn't* and *needn't* • first conditional
Speaking • making, accepting and declining invitations
Writing • a note
WORKBOOK pages 60–66 • Self check 7 page 67

A VOCABULARY AND LISTENING
Body language

LESSON SUMMARY ●●●○○

Vocabulary: gestures; phrasal verbs
Listening: short texts; listening for gist
Speaking: talking about greetings
Topic: people and society

SHORTCUT *To do the lesson in 30 minutes, skip the Lead-in and Vocabulary Builder part 1. Set exercises 1 and 2 in the Vocabulary Builder for homework if necessary.*

➜ Lead-in 3–5 minutes

- Inform the class of the lesson objectives.
- Put students in pairs and allocate roles: a pair of classmates, student and teacher, child and parent, shop assistant and customer, boss and employee. It is not a problem if more than one pair has the same roles.
- Ask students to act out how their characters greet each other. Allow 30 seconds preparation time.

Exercise 1 page 64

- Focus students on the pictures and ask if they can name any of the gestures.
- Read the expressions from the box to the class and clarify meaning if necessary. Students match the pictures.

KEY

1 bow
2 shake hands
3 shake hands, pat somebody on the back
4 shake hands, kiss
5 kiss
6 wave
7 hug

LANGUAGE NOTE – RECORDING PREPOSITIONS
Encourage students when recording the gesture vocabulary to note down which prepositions are used with the verbs:

beckon **to** somebody
bow **to** somebody
pat somebody **on** the back
skake hands **with** somebody
wave **at** somebody
wink **at** somebody

Exercise 2 page 64 🎧 2.09

- Play the recording for students to listen and repeat chorally and individually.
- Play the recording again. Students perform the gestures.

Exercise 3 page 64

- Put the following on the board: *always, often, sometimes, rarely, never.*
- Discuss as a class. Elicit the context in which the gestures are used in the students' country.

CULTURE NOTE – GREETINGS IN BRITAIN
British people in the past have been shy of physical contact when greeting each other. The traditional form of greeting is a handshake for formal greetings and just the words *Hi* or *How are you?* for informal greetings. In recent years, however, with globalisation, kissing, on one or two cheeks, has become very common, especially for younger generations. There are no fixed rules and British people themselves don't always know what to do. They often wait to see what the other person does.

For more practice on vocabulary related to gestures, go to:

Vocabulary Builder (part 1): Student's Book page 130

KEY

1 a point (at somebody/something)   e shake your head
   b beckon   f nod
   c hold hands   g cross your legs
   d wink   h fold your arms

2 1 shake your head   5 pat you on the back
   2 nod   6 hold hands
   3 beckon   7 hug
   4 wave   8 bow

3 Open answers

Exercise 4 page 64 🎧 2.10

- Read the halves of the sentences as a class. Explain any new words. Play the recording.
- In a **weaker class**, explain the following expressions:
Lucy: t*o treat everybody the same, rules, behaviour*
Haruko: *to show their feelings in public, to expect, to be rude without meaning to, customs, casual, cheek, by mistake*
Ludmila: *to get lost, strangers*
- Play the recording again. Check as a class.
- In a **stronger class**, students guess and match the halves of the sentences before the listening. Play the recording to check.

KEY
1 c   2 a   3 b

Transcript 2.10

Lucy We aren't formal here, not at all. We generally treat everybody the same, whether they're an important company director or a shop assistant. So, for example, when you get in a taxi in Australia, you should sit in the front, with the driver, not in the back. There aren't many rules about behaviour – but of course, you shouldn't be rude. Actually, one thing that's quite rude in Australia, but not in some other countries – in Australia, you shouldn't wink at a woman. If you do, they might get quite angry with you!

Haruko Many people think that the Japanese don't show their feelings in public. I think this is probably true. At least, it's true that we're quite formal. One of the nice things about Japanese people is that they're very polite – and they expect other people to be polite too. Sometimes people are rude without meaning to be, because they don't know the customs. For example, in Japan, you shouldn't cross your legs when you're in a formal situation – crossing your legs is very casual. When you meet a woman for the first time, you should bow to her – you certainly shouldn't kiss her on the cheek, like they do in many European countries. And if you visit somebody's house in Japan, it's rude to look in the kitchen. Many visitors don't know that, and they do it by mistake!

Ludmila Although many parts of Russia are very cold, I think the people are very warm. They're friendly, too – and helpful. If you get lost in Russia, somebody will always help you to find where you're going. In fact, they'll often actually take you there themselves! When Russians meet, they often greet each other with a hug. Men and women do that. Strangers often shake hands, but close friends kiss each other. Traditionally, they give each other three kisses because three is a lucky number in Russia.

Exercise 5 page 64

* Students can work in pairs. Allow a minute.

KEY

1	should	5	kitchen
2	woman	6	and
3	cross your legs	7	three times
4	shouldn't		

Exercise 6 page 64 🎧 2.10

* Play the recording again. Ask students who are confident about their answers to note down more facts. Elicit what students remember from the listening.

Exercise 7 page 64

* Students take it in turns to answer the questions. Allow 5 minutes. While they are working, go round and help with vocabulary. Get feedback.

LANGUAGE NOTE – HIGH FIVE

Explain that a 'high five' is a gesture that originated in North America as an action to celebrate victory or express happiness. Two people raise one arm each and hit their open hands together. It's often accompanied by words such as *Gimme (Give me) five!*

For further practice on phrasal verbs, go to:

Vocabulary Builder (part 2): Student's Book page 130

KEY

4	a	lie down	f	sit down
	b	turn over	g	stand up
	c	bend down	h	put up your hand
	d	turn round	i	hold out your arms
	e	sit up	j	lift up your foot

5	1	held out her arms	5	turned round
	2	turned over	6	put up your hand
	3	lift up your foot	7	Lie down
	4	bent down	8	sat down

OPTIONAL ACTIVITY

Set a class contest. Divide the class into three groups. Students from different groups take it in turns to mime a gesture or an activity from Vocabulary Builder part 2 to the class. Other students try to guess what they are doing. The first group to say the correct expression scores a point. Play nine rounds. The group with the highest score wins.

➡ Lesson outcome

Ask students: *What have you learned today? What can you do now?* and elicit answers: *I can describe how people greet each other in different countries. I have learned phrasal verbs which describe physical activity.*

B **GRAMMAR**
must, mustn't and needn't

LESSON SUMMARY ●●●○○

Grammar: *must, mustn't* and *needn't*
Speaking: talking about customs
Writing: a short note about customs

SHORTCUT *To do the lesson in 30 minutes, set the Grammar Builder and exercise 7 for homework.*

➡ Lead-in 2–3 minutes

* Inform the class of the lesson objectives.
* Focus them on the picture and pre-teach *host, chopsticks, bowl.* Elicit what students know about Chinese food and table manners.

Exercise 1 page 65 🎧 2.11

* Pre-teach: *to pick up, periods of silence, to be considered, to fill the gaps, a proverb.* Allow 30 seconds for students to read the text. Play the recording once. Students fill in the gaps. Check answers.
* Check understanding by asking: *Can you start your food before your host? Can you say 'no' when your host offers you food? Can you be silent?*

KEY

1 mustn't   2 must   3 needn't

Exercise 2 page 65

- In a **weaker class**, complete the rules in the *Learn this!* box together. In a **stronger class**, students work individually. Check as a class. If students need further explanation, go to Grammar Reference 7.

KEY
1 must   2 needn't   3 mustn't

For further practice on must, mustn't *and* needn't, *go to:*

Grammar Builder 7B: Student's Book page 116

KEY

1 1 c   2 a   3 f   4 e   5 d   6 b

2 2 must
3 mustn't
4 must
5 must
6 mustn't
7 must
8 must

3 2 We needn't arrive on time.
3 They needn't phone me.
4 He needn't wear a suit.
5 She needn't cook dinner for me.
6 You needn't wait for me.

PRONUNCIATION – *MUST* AND *MUSTN'T*

Draw students' attention to the fact that the first *t* in *mustn't* is silent: /'mʌsnt/.

Similarly, in normal speech, when *must* is followed by a verb beginning with a consonant, the final *t* is dropped and the 'u' is pronounced /ə/. For example:
I must go. /aɪ məs 'gəʊ/
You must wait. /juː məs 'weɪt/

Exercise 3 page 65

- Go over the expressions in the box with the class, explaining any new words. Students can work in pairs or small groups for 3–4 minutes.
- If possible, distribute large sheets of paper. Students write the school rules down, then hang their posters on the board or around the classroom. Read and compare the rules as a class. Students correct their posters if necessary.

Exercise 4 page 65

- Students work in the same pairs or groups, writing more sentences in their notebooks or on the posters. Allow 2–3 minutes.
- You can ask **fast finishers** to write rules for an imaginary, ideal school.

Exercise 5 page 65

- Put the following on the board: *arrive on time for social events, pat somebody on the head, eat with your right hand, use your index finger to beckon somebody, send a thank-you note, remove your shoes, use a knife and fork, belch.*
- Read the expressions as a class and explain if necessary.
- Students work individually for 2 minutes. Check as a class.

KEY
1	needn't	5	needn't
2	mustn't	6	must
3	must	7	needn't
4	mustn't	8	mustn't

Exercise 6 page 65

- Read the instructions and the expressions in the box with the class. Explain any new words.
- Allow 3–4 minutes for students to discuss in pairs. Share answers as a class by asking students if they agreed with their partners on all the customs. Carefully correct any grammatical mistakes so that students are well prepared for the next exercise.

Exercise 7 page 65

- Students work individually. Allow 5 minutes.
- In a **stronger class**, you can ask students to write notes explaining how to behave in other situations, for example, at a wedding, in a restaurant or theatre.
- Students swap the notes in pairs, read and correct each other's work. Check answers by asking students to read their own notes out to the class.

➡ Lesson outcome

Ask students: *What have you learned today? What can you do now?* and elicit answers: *I can use modal verbs to talk about prohibition and necessity. I can describe customs in different countries. I can describe school rules.*

Notes for Photocopiable activity 7.1

How well do you know your country?
Pairwork
Language: *must, mustn't* and *needn't*
Materials: one copy of the worksheet per student (Teacher's Book page 136)

- Divide the class into pairs. Give each student a copy of the worksheet.
- Ask students to complete the sentences with *must, mustn't* and *needn't* according to their knowledge of laws and customs in their country.
- Go through the answers together and then ask students individually to put a tick or cross against each sentence according to whether they agree with the law.
- Students compare their opinions with a partner.

7C CULTURE
An American festival

LESSON SUMMARY ●●●●●

Reading: an article about Thanksgiving; detailed reading
Listening: the history of Thanksgiving; ordering events
Speaking: asking and answering questions about a festival
Topic: people and society

SHORTCUT *To do the lesson in 30 minutes, skip exercise 1 and keep a fast pace.*

➤ Lead-in 3–5 minutes

• Inform the class of the lesson objectives.
• Focus them on the picture and elicit a description. Put key words on the board. Ask what students know about Thanksgiving in the USA.

Exercise 1 page 66

• In a **weaker class**, pre-teach *according to, apart from, as well as, however.*
• Allow 3–5 minutes for the reading. Remind students to focus on the task and assure them they can do it even if they do not understand all the words in the text.

KEY

dancing

Exercise 2 page 66

• Students work individually. Allow 3–5 minutes. Check as a class.
• Answer students' vocabulary questions after you check answers. This will help students to get used to working with new vocabulary.
• **Fast finishers** can answer the following questions:
Why do Americans travel long distances for Thanksgiving weekend? What other food, apart from turkey, is popular? What do many Americans watch on TV on that day?

KEY

1 In 1621.
2 Roast turkey and vegetables.
3 The person who gets the 'wishbone'.
4 In New York.
5 Because people start buying presents for Christmas.
6 By working in soup kitchens which distribute free food to the poor and homeless.

Exercise 3 page 66 🎧 2.12

• Read the instructions with the class. Remind students that they don't have to understand everything they hear. Encourage them to listen carefully, and focus on the question, but not to worry if there are words that are unfamiliar.

Transcript 2.12

Nearly 400 years ago, people from England went to live in North America. They were called Pilgrims. They wanted to start a new life in a new country, but it was difficult for them. Why? Because they didn't know anything about their new land. They didn't know how to grow food there or build homes. A lot of the Pilgrims became very ill.

One day in spring, the Pilgrims met two Native Americans. Their names were Squanto and Samoset. The Pilgrims were amazed because Squanto and Samoset could speak English! (They learned it from an English explorer.) Squanto and Samoset became friends with the Pilgrims. They gave them lots of advice to make their lives easier. They taught the Pilgrims how to grow food and build better homes.

By autumn, things were going a lot better for the Pilgrims, thanks to the help of Squanto and Samoset . The harvest was good, so they had food for the winter. They also had warm homes. They wanted to say thank you to their Native American friends. They invited three of them and their families to a special meal. The Pilgrims were amazed when ninety people arrived. (The Native Americans had very big families!) It was the first Thanksgiving dinner. They ate turkey, fish, green beans and soup.

Exercise 4 page 66 🎧 2.12

• Read the listening tip with the class. Check understanding by asking: *What should you do before the listening? Why should you do it?*
• In a **weaker class**, pre-teach *the Pilgrims, harvest, the Native Americans, advice.*
• In a **stronger class**, encourage students to remember the order of the events.
• Allow a minute for students to read the events. Play the recording once.
• Students work individually. Let them compare their answers in pairs before they listen again.

KEY

a 5 b 2 c 7 d 1 e 4 f 3 g 6

Exercise 5 page 66 🎧 2.12

• Play the recording again for students to check. If necessary, pause the recording for students to correct their answers.

Exercise 6 page 66

• Elicit the names of different festivals and put them on the board: *Christmas, Easter, Halloween, New Year's Eve, Saint Valentine's Day,* etc.
• Each pair chooses a festival and discusses the questions. Encourage students to make notes, but not to write out full sentences. Allow 6 minutes. Ask individual pairs to tell the class about the way that they celebrate.

➤ Lesson outcome

Ask students: *What have you learned today? What can you do now?* and elicit answers: *I can understand the origins of an American festival. I can talk about a festival that I like.*

7D GRAMMAR
First conditional

LESSON SUMMARY ●●●●●

Grammar: the first conditional
Reading: short texts about superstitions
Speaking: talking about future consequences

SHORTCUT *To do the lesson in 30 minutes, skip the Lead-in and exercise 6 in the Grammar Builder. In exercise 6 in the lesson divide the class into three groups so that each group works on one paragraph for a minute. Share answers briefly after exercise 7.*

➜ Lead-in 3–4 minutes
- Inform the class of the lesson objectives.
- Have a short class discussion about good and bad luck. Ask: *Are you generally a lucky person? Do you know anybody who often has bad luck? What brings good/bad luck?*

Exercise 1 page 67
- Read the questions as a class and check students understand *superstition, superstitious* and *to affect someone's behaviour.* Allow 3 minutes for students to discuss. Share ideas as a class.

Exercise 2 page 67
- Pre-teach *to take chances.* Allow a minute for students to read. Elicit what superstitions are common in their country.

Exercise 3 page 67
- Read the information in the *Learn this!* box as a class. Check understanding of the grammatical terms by asking: *A conditional sentence has two parts; the* if *clause and the main clause. Which clause describes the action? Which clause describes the result? What tense is used in the* if *clause? What tense is used in the main clause?*
- Students find examples of the clauses individually. Allow a minute. Check as a class.

KEY
if **clauses:** if you break a mirror, if you look at the seats of some aeroplanes, if you believe in bad luck
main clauses: you will have seven years of bad luck, you won't find the number 13, you'll probably have it

For more practice on the first conditional, go to:

Grammar Builder 7D: Student's Book page 116

KEY
4 1 b 2 f 3 d 4 a 5 e 6 c

5 1 eats   5 snows
2 asks   6 doesn't come
3 leave
4 work

6 1 'll call   4 'll have
2 won't buy   5 will (you) do
3 'll be   6 will (we) sleep

Exercise 4 page 67
- Do not pre-teach any words here to help students realise they can complete the sentences even if they do not understand everything. Allow 2–3 minutes.

KEY
1 will rain
2 give
3 will make
4 smiles
5 will have
6 sings

Exercise 5 page 67 🎧 2.13
- Play the recording once for students to check their answers. If necessary, stop so that students can make corrections. Explain any new vocabulary.
- Play the recording again for students to repeat chorally and individually.

PRONUNCIATION – *WON'T*

Students are likely to have difficulty distinguishing between *won't* and *want.* Model the diphthong /əʊ/ very clearly, demonstrating how the diphthong is composed of two single vowels and therefore the mouth moves position when uttering it. Contrast this with the single vowel /ɒ/ where the mouth doesn't move when uttering the vowel.

Give extra practice by running a short competition where students in pairs write down as many words containing the /əʊ/ sound as they can in a minute. Repeat with the /ɒ/ sound. The pair with the most words is the winner.

Exercise 6 page 67
- Focus students on the pictures and ask if they have any knowledge or ideas about these superstitions.
- Students work individually for 3 minutes.
- If you are short of time, divide the class into three groups so that each student works on one text only. Allow a minute.
- Check as a class.

KEY
1 see	6 'll have	11 touch
2 'll get	7 leave	12 'll do
3 wash	8 'll have	13 forget
4 won't remember	9 won't be	14 won't pass
5 look	10 look	

Exercise 7 page 67
- Allow 3–5 minutes. In a **stronger class**, ask students to think of more questions to ask each other.

OPTIONAL ACTIVITY

Write the following on the board as examples:
What will happen if you see a black cat?
What will a British person think if their mirror breaks?

Put students in pairs to ask and answer about superstitions.

➜ Lesson outcome
Ask students: *What have you learned today? What can you do now?* and elicit answers: *I can predict the results of an action. I can describe superstitions from different countries.*

Notes for Photocopiable activity 7.2

International body language

Pairwork
Language: body language, first conditional
Materials: one copy cut in half for each pair of students
(Teacher's Book page 137)

- Pre-teach the following as necessary: *gesture, gladiator, thumb, stick out your tongue, warning.*
- Divide the class into pairs. Give out a copy of the cut up worksheet to each pair. Explain to the class that they are going to read about hand gestures and that they have different information from their partner.
- Students read the text and find half the answers. They then ask their partner questions to find the rest of the information. Encourage the students to answer the questions from memory.

Alternative procedure

- Instead of pre-teaching the vocabulary, ask students to try to work out the meaning of the unknown words, then check in the dictionary.
- When they have finished the information sharing stage of the task, they should teach the new vocabulary to their partners.

KEY

1 Everything's OK.	a Peace.
2 No.	b In photos.
3 Kill him.	c In Britain.
4 I don't believe you.	d OK.
5 No.	e Zero.
6 Be careful.	f I need change.

E READING
Unusual festivals

LESSON SUMMARY ●●●●●

Reading: an article about unusual festivals; matching
Vocabulary: words for talking about events
Speaking: talking about festivals
Topic: people and society

SHORTCUT *To do the lesson in 30 minutes, set exercise 3 for homework.*

➡ Lead-in 3–4 minutes

- Inform the class of the lesson objectives.
- Put the word *tradition* on the board and elicit students' associations. Ask what traditions students dislike and do not/are not going to observe in their adult lives.

Exercise 1   page 68

- Students can work in pairs to prepare their answers before sharing their ideas with the class. Encourage students to describe what is going on in the photos and speculate about the possible significance (using *may, might* and *could*).

Exercise 2   page 69

- Focus students on the photos and headlines. In a **weaker class**, you may have to explain the key words *to ban, to throw* and *to roll*. Instruct students to read the texts quite quickly, then elicit a brief statement about what each text is about.

- Read the exam tip with the class. Check comprehension by asking: *What should you do first when you're doing a matching task? What do you do next?*
- In a **weaker class**, go over the questions as a group, explaining any new vocabulary.
- Allow 5 minutes. Remind students to find the relevant fragment of the text rather than make conclusions.

KEY

1 CR   2 WT   3 CR   4 BR   5 BR   6 WT   7 CR
8 WT   9 BR

Exercise 3   page 69

- Students work individually for a minute. Check as a class.
- Explain or elicit the meaning of any other unknown words individual students ask about.

KEY

1 at risk	4 participants	7 casualties
2 buckets	5 concerned	8 horns
3 reduce	6 sign up	9 spectators

Exercise 4   page 69

- Focus students on one of the photos. Describe it as a class. Read the questions together. Point out that students should use the present simple to answer them.
- Students each choose one of the festivals and make notes of their answers.
- Allow 3 minutes for the speaking. Check answers as a class.

ADDITIONAL SPEAKING ACTIVITY

Look again at the three festivals presented in the lesson. Ask students why they think they are popular with tourists.

Inform students that their task is to invent an unusual festival. They should decide when and where their festival takes place, who participates and what the participants do.

If necessary, brainstorm ideas for an unusual festival as a class. For example, call it *The Great Jam Party of Budapest* and decide what it involves.

Use the language from lesson 7B to describe the rules of the festival, what participants must do, what they must not do, what the role of the spectators is. For example: *Participant must wear hats. The spectators needn't eat the jam, but they must vote for the best hat.*

Inform students that their festival also has three superstitions attached to the day of the event. They should use the first conditional to express their superstitions. For example: *If it rains on the morning of the festival, the jam will not set.*

Put students in small groups. Allow 5 minutes to discuss and make notes. When the time is up, each group presents their festival to the class.

➡ Lesson outcome

Ask students: *What have you learned today? What can you do now?* and elicit answers: *I can understand a description of different cultural traditions. I have learned new words related to festivals. I can describe a festival.*

EVERYDAY ENGLISH
Making invitations

LESSON SUMMARY ●●●○○

Functional English: making, accepting and declining invitations
Reading and Listening: dialogues; true/false questions, matching
Topic: relationships

SHORTCUT *To do the lesson in 30 minutes, do the Lead-in briefly as a class and keep a fast pace. Limit or skip the performances in exercise 6.*

→ Lead-in 4–5 minutes

• Inform the class of the lesson objectives.
• Put students in pairs to describe the picture. Pre-teach *popcorn* if necessary. Allow a minute.
• Bring the class back together, focus them on the title of the lesson and ask: *Where do you meet friends? Do you stay at home or go out? Do you watch DVDs and have food or do something else? Do you sometimes cook for your friends?*

Exercise 1 page 70 🎧 2.14

• Focus students on the dialogue. Play the recording straight through once. Allow a moment for students to decide on the true/false sentences. Ask them to read out the sentences and the relevant lines of the dialogues to check.

KEY

1 T   2 F   3 F

LANGUAGE NOTE – USAGE

Draw attention to the following language points in the dialogue:

In the expression, *have someone over*, *over* means *to my home*. We can also say *ask someone over*, e.g. *Let's ask the Smiths over* and *go over*, e.g. *I'm going over to John's (house)*.

The use of *then* in *Shall I bring some food, then?* is very different from the time marker *then*, e.g. *I had a shower. Then I had breakfast*. In this dialogue it has the same meaning as *so*: *So shall I bring some food?*

Exercise 2 page 70 🎧 2.15

• Explain that *social activities* are activities with friends. Go over the expressions in the box as a class. If there are any pronunciation problems, continue choral and individual repetition until students are confident.
• Play the recording once. Check as a class.

KEY

2	go shopping	5	have a barbecue
3	go to the cinema	6	play basketball
4	have a party		

Transcript 2.15

1
Boy   Hi!
Girl   Hello. How are you?
Boy   Fine thanks. Hey, I'm going to watch a football match tomorrow evening. Would you like to come?
Girl   I'd love to, thanks! What time are you meeting?
Boy   At 7.00, at the bus stop. The match starts at 7.45, and we don't want to be late.
Girl   OK, see you tomorrow at 7 o'clock.
Boy   Great! See you there!

2
Girl 1   Hello.
Girl 2   Hi! Are you all right?
Girl 1   Yes, I'm fine. I'm just going into town. I'm going shopping with my sister. Do you fancy joining us?
Girl 2   I'm sorry, I can't.
Girl 1   Oh. That's a shame.
Girl 2   I've got lots of homework for tomorrow. I really need to start!

3
Boy   Are you going into town?
Girl   Yes, I am. I'm going to the cinema with a couple of friends.
Boy   What are you going to see?
Girl   We haven't decided yet. Hey, why don't you come along?
Boy   I'd love to, but I can't. I'm going to a party tonight.
Girl   Oh well. Sorry you can't make it.
Boy   See you soon.

4
Girl   Hi! Are you around this weekend?
Boy   Yes, I am. Why?
Girl   I'm having a party on Saturday night. Would you like to come?
Boy   Yes. That sounds great!
Girl   Good. Oh, it's fancy dress, by the way.
Boy   Right.
Girl   Glad you can make it!
Boy   See you on Saturday.

5
Boy   What are your plans for the weekend.
Girl   My family is having a barbecue on Sunday.
Boy   Really? That sounds fun.
Girl   Why don't you come along?
Boy   Sorry, but I won't be able to make it.
Girl   That's a shame. Why not?
Boy   I'm going to visit my grandparents on Sunday.
Girl   Oh. Sorry you can't make it.

6
Boy 1   What are you doing tomorrow?
Boy 2   I'm meeting some friends at the park. We're going to play basketball.
Boy 1   I love basketball.
Boy 2   Yes, so do I. Do you fancy joining us?
Boy 1   Thanks. I'll definitely be there.
Boy 2   Great! See you there.

Exercise 3 page 70 🎧 2.15

• Play the recording again. Students make notes of the answers. Check as a class.

KEY

2 no   3 no   4 yes   5 no   6 yes

Exercise 4 page 70 🎧 2.16

- In a **weaker class** ask students to close their books and play the recording twice. Pause after each item. The first time, students repeat chorally. The second time, ask for individual repetitions. When students are confident, ask students to open their books and read the phrases out.
- In a **stronger class**, play the tape once for students to repeat chorally and individually. Then ask them to close their books and check that they remember the phrases. Read parts of phrases and elicit the endings from the class:
  T: *Would you ...*
  Ss: *Would you like to come?*

Exercise 5 page 70

- In a **weaker class**, ask students to write their dialogues down first. While they are working, go round the class and correct any mistakes. Allow 5 minutes. Then ask students to say their dialogues in pairs, using their notes as little as possible. Allow 3 minutes.
- In a **stronger class**, students can agree on the details orally. Remind them to use the phrases from exercise 4. Allow 3 minutes.

Exercise 6 page 70

- Ask students to close their books and notebooks. Remind them to keep eye contact and speak at natural speed.

➡ Lesson outcome

Ask students: *What have you learned today? What can you do now?* and elicit answers: *I can make and accept or decline an invitation. I can invite friends to do various social activities together.*

WRITING
G A note

LESSON SUMMARY ●●●●○

Reading: notes; reading for gist, detailed reading
Vocabulary: abbreviations
Writing: a reply to an invitation
Topic: relationships

SHORTCUT *To do the lesson in 30 minutes, shorten the Lead-in to identifying what celebration is in the picture, skip exercise 5 and ask students to choose and write one note instead of two in exercises 6–7.*

➡ Lead-in 3–5 minutes

- Inform the class of the objectives.
- Focus students on the picture. Elicit what sort of party it shows. Ask what people wear, eat and do at a Halloween party. Ask the class: *Have you ever been invited to a Halloween party? Did you accept or decline the invitation? Do you like Halloween parties?*

Exercise 1 page 71

- Read the instructions as a class. Ask students to focus on the task while reading the texts. Allow 3 minutes. Check as a class.

KEY

1 c   2 a   3 b

Exercise 2 page 71

- Students read the texts again.
- In a **weaker class** or if you are short of time, answer the questions as a class.
- In a **stronger class**, you can set a memory quiz. Ask students to cover the texts. Read the questions out. Pause after each one so that students can note down their answers. When you have finished, ask students to swap their answers and check them quickly with the texts. How many students got everything right?

KEY

1 A Halloween party.
2 She's going to have dinner with her family at a restaurant to celebrate her grandmother's birthday.
3 She loves them.
4 He's going to invite some mates and have a barbecue.
5 A few CDs.
6 It's on New Year's Eve.
7 It's 'Hollywood'.

Exercise 3 page 71

- Briefly ask why we use abbreviations. Are there any that are also used in the students' language?
- Focus students on the box and the chart. Students can work in pairs for a minute. Check as a class.

KEY

1 compact disc	5 Please reply
2 Road	6 and so on
3 telephone number	7 I also want to say
4 for example	8 as soon as possible

Exercise 4 page 71

- Ask: *Are the notes formal or informal? Why? What words or expressions in the notes are informal?* Elicit examples.
- Students work individually. Allow a minute. Check as a class.

KEY

1 mates	4 rubbish
2 make it	5 too bad
3 hear from you	

Exercise 5 page 71

- Work as a class. The student who finds the phrase first reads it out to the class.

KEY

1 I'm afraid I won't be able to make it.
2 Would you like to come?
3 I'll definitely be there!

Exercise 6 page 71

- Read the instructions as a class. Elicit example phrases from the class to make sure students understand.

Exercise 7 page 71

- Allow 10 minutes for students to write their notes. While they are working, go round and help with any problems.
- Give students time to check their work, using the checklist.
- **Fast finishers** can form pairs and check each other's work. They then exchange comments, offering any suggestions that could improve their partner's work.
- Ask individual students to read their notes out to the class.

OPTIONAL ACTIVITY

Put students in pairs to do a role-play. One student takes the role of an answerphone machine. The other one phones to accept or decline an invitation. Allow a minute for students to prepare what they are going to say. They can use their notes from exercise 6.

ALTERNATIVE WRITING TASK

Ask students to read Louise's and Gloria's notes again and write one of the notes they received. In the note they should:

- invite Gloria/Louise to the party
- describe briefly what kind of party it is
- encourage her to wear a costume
- say what preparations you have made
- say that you want her to come very much

➡ Lesson outcome

Ask students: *What have you learned today? What can you do now?* and elicit answers: *I can write a note replying to an invitation. I have learned to understand abbreviations.*

EXAM For further exam tasks and practice, go to Workbook page 68. Procedural notes, transcripts and keys for the Workbook can be found on the *Solutions* Teacher's Website at www.oup.com/elt/teacher/solutions.

TOPIC ●●●●○

Science and technology

➡ Lead-in 3–5 minutes
- Inform the class of the lesson objectives.
- Brainstorm the biggest inventions in human history. Put the words on the board.
- Elicit how some of the things where invented, by whom and what problem the invention solved.

Exercise 1 page 72 1–2 minutes
- Explain that it is important to have a general idea of the contents of the text before starting to do a more in-depth task.

KEY

1 A 2 C 3 B

Exercise 2 page 72 12 minutes
E Reading: multiple matching

- Read the exam task as a class. Check comprehension by asking: *What are 'the toys'?* (LEGO, Razor Scooter and Monopoly.) *If you think a sentence is describing Monopoly, what answer will you write?* (C.) *Where will you write it?* (In the box next to the sentence.)
- Give students 2 minutes to read the sentences and underline key words. Encourage them to pencil in any answers they think they know from the first reading.
- Advise them to narrow down the choices where possible. For example, for question 2 a quick scan of the texts will show that the time in B is much later than the 1930s, so the choice is between texts A and C. At this point students will have to look carefully at each of these texts to locate the right information. Advise them to underline the relevant text fragments.
- Allow 8 minutes for the task. **Fast finishers** can form pairs to compare and discuss answers. Check as a class.

KEY

1 B 2 C 3 B 4 C 5 A 6 C 7 C 8 A 9 B

Exercise 3 page 72 2–4 minutes
- Ask students to read the instructions. Elicit the meaning of *domestic appliances*.
- Explain that the topic of inventions and domestic appliances often appears in the exam questions and students should make sure they know the vocabulary.
- Students work individually. Check as a class.

KEY

For food and drink

1 fridge   3 juicer   5 microwave   7 toaster
2 freezer   4 kettle   6 oven

For cleaning, washing and clothes

1 dishwasher   3 tumble dryer   5 washing machine
2 iron   4 vacuum cleaner

Exercise 4 page 72 🎧 2.17 3 minutes
- Read the questions as a class. Ask students to predict the answer to the second question.
- Play the recording through once.

KEY

They discuss vacuum cleaners, microwaves, washing machines and dishwashers. They decide that a washing machine is the most important appliance.

Transcript 🎧 2.17

Robert	Which domestic appliance do you think is the most useful and important?
Laura	How about vacuum cleaners?
Robert	Mmm. I think that microwaves are more useful. I use a microwave all the time.
Laura	I'm afraid I don't agree. A microwave isn't essential. It's a luxury. Anyway, you should learn to cook properly. Vacuum cleaners are much more useful than microwaves.
Robert	Do you think so?
Laura	Yes, of course. They help you to keep the house clean.
Robert	I suppose you're right. Now that you mention cleaning, I think washing machines are even more useful than vacuum cleaners.
Laura	Yes, that's true. But are they as useful as dishwashers?
Robert	Of course. If you don't have a dishwasher, you can always wash up plates and cups by hand in the sink, but …
Laura	You can wash clothes by hand in the sink, too.
Robert	That may be true, but it takes much longer to wash clothes, and it's much harder work.
Laura	OK. I agree with you. Washing machines are the most useful appliance.

Exercise 5 page 72 🎧 2.17 8 minutes
- Read through the expressions. Then play the recording again. Students tick the expressions as they hear them.
- Explain that *That's right* and *That's true* are used very commonly in conversation. *I couldn't agree with you more* is very emphatic, while *I suppose you're right* is a more uncertain or reluctant form of agreement.

KEY

I'm afraid I don't agree.   I suppose you're right.
Yes, that's true.   That may be true, but …   I agree with you.

Exercise 6 page 72 10–15 minutes
E Speaking: topic-based discussion

- Read the task as a class. Tell students that this conversation should last for 3–5 minutes, so they will need to talk about their choices in some detail. Warn them not to move away too quickly from discussion of each appliance – even if they agree about it, they should discuss it fully.
- Give students 3 minutes to plan. Encourage **stronger students** to do this without making notes.
- Students discuss in pairs.
- Choose a strong pair to do the task in front of the class. Ask the others to jot down any expressions the speakers use to respond to each other and to keep the conversation moving. Ask: *Which appliances did they choose? Did they give reasons? Did one person speak more than the other?*

➡ Lesson outcome
- Ask students: *What have you learned today? What can you do now?* and elicit answers: *I have practised a multiple-matching reading task. I have learned new words for domestic appliances. I have practised discussing a topic.*

TOPIC ●●●●○○○○

Food and drink

➡ Lead-in 3–5 minutes

• Inform the class of the lesson objectives.
• Elicit how many meals students eat throughout the day, what food they usually eat and what their favourite dishes are. Put the words on the board.

Exercise 1 page 73 4 minutes

• Tell students they are preparing for a listening task on restaurants. Let them discuss the questions in pairs.
• Ask different students to ask and answer across the class.

Exercise 2 page 73 3–5 minutes

• Do the matching as a class, providing or eliciting translations. Elicit example sentences using the four expressions.

KEY

1 c 2 a 3 d 4 b

Exercise 3 page 73 3–4 minutes

• Explain that only one word is to go in each gap.
• Explain that on the recording the information will not be expressed in exactly the same way as it is in the sentences. It is important for students to prepare beforehand and predict what kind of answers they will hear.
• As they identify the parts of speech, ask students to think of possible words to fit the gaps. **Weaker students** do the exercise in pairs. **Stronger students** work individually.

KEY

1 noun	5 noun	8 verb
2 verb	6 noun	9 noun
3 noun	7 adjective	10 noun
4 noun		

Exercise 4 page 73 🎧 2.18 6–8 minutes

E Listening: completing statements

• Tell students that they will hear the recording twice. The first time, they should fill in as many answers as they can. During the pause they should look at sentences that remain unanswered so that they can focus on these in the second listening.
• Play the recording through twice, pausing for 15 seconds before and after the second listening. Check as a class.

KEY

1 Tuesday	5 bill	8 booked
2 drove	6 meal	9 poster
3 mechanic	7 hot	10 family
4 card		

Transcript 🎧 2.18

Thomas

It was my friend Christina's birthday last Tuesday so we decided to go out for a meal. We booked a table for six o'clock at a nice restaurant in town and arranged to meet at five to six, outside the restaurant. I live in a small village about six kilometres from the town and my dad kindly offered to drive me to the restaurant.

Unfortunately, his car broke down on the way, and we had to wait for the garage to send out a mechanic to get the car started again. Anyway, that made me very late. Everyone else was there and was already eating. It was then that I realised that I didn't have Christina's present or card with me – they were in Dad's car. I felt awful as everyone else gave Christina something for her birthday. Everything went fine after that – until the end of the meal. We got the bill and were working out how much each person had to pay when I realised that I didn't have my wallet with me either. I had to borrow some money from one of my friends. Everyone thought it was very funny, but I was really embarrassed.

Rachel

Last Friday evening my mum and dad wanted to take us all out for a meal. My brother wanted to go to an Indian restaurant and have a curry and I wanted a Chinese meal. As Dad doesn't like Chinese food very much, we agreed to go for a curry. I don't mind curries as long they aren't too hot. Anyway, Dad rang up and booked a table for eight o'clock at The Spice House, one of the Indian restaurants in town. We left the house at about quarter to eight and arrived at the restaurant ten minutes later. But when we went in, the waiter said there wasn't a table for us. My dad argued with him, and said he phoned the restaurant earlier and booked a table. But the restaurant had no record of the call. Then suddenly I saw a poster on the wall of the restaurant. It was advertising another restaurant, also called The Spice House, on the other side of town. The waiter explained that his family had two restaurants. It turned out that Dad booked a table at the other restaurant by mistake. The waiter was very understanding and he managed to find a table for us after all. Then he rang the other restaurant to let them know what happened.

Exercise 5 page 73 5–8 minutes

E Use of English: open cloze

• Tell students to read the whole text before they focus on the gapped words.
• Ask them to check by re-reading the completed sentences. Do they make sense? Is the grammar correct? Let them compare answers in pairs before you check with the class.

KEY

1 for 2 on 3 who 4 to 5 has 6 him

Exercise 6 page 73 5–7 minutes

• Read the sentences and explain new vocabulary.
• Explain that the sentences present different ways of saying 'Maybe/Probably this is true'. Ask students to pick out the sentence in which the speaker is most sure (5).
• Students discuss in pairs, then share ideas as a class.
• Elicit other sentences, using the same structures with different adjectives.

Exercise 7 page 73 8 minutes

E Speaking: picture-based discussion

• Students prepare beforehand, then speak in pairs. For more detailed procedures, see the notes for picture-based discussion on pages 43, 44 and 66 of the Teacher's Book.

➡ Lesson outcome

• Ask students: *What have you learned today? What can you do now?* and elicit answers: *I have practised completing statements as a listening task. I have practised an open cloze. I have learned expressions for making speculations. I have compared and contrasted photos as a speaking task.*

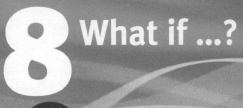

8 What if ...?

THIS UNIT INCLUDES ●●●●
Vocabulary • global issues • word formation: noun suffixes
Grammar • second conditional • *I wish...*
Speaking • discussing global issues • giving advice
Writing • an essay
WORKBOOK pages 70–76 • Self check 8 page 77

A VOCABULARY AND LISTENING
Global issues

LESSON SUMMARY ●●●●●
Vocabulary: global issues
Listening: radio programmes; listening for gist
Speaking: discussing global issues
Topic: people and society

SHORTCUT *To do the lesson in 30 minutes, set the Vocabulary Builder (part 1) for homework and do exercise 3 as a class.*

➡ Lead-in   4 minutes
• Inform the class of the lesson objectives.
• Focus them on the title of the lesson. Explain that *a global issue* is a problem which affects the whole world. Ask: *What problems can we call global issues?* Put the suggestions on the board.

Exercise 1   page 74
• Read the speaking tip as a class. Check comprehension by asking: *What should you do before you start describing the photo? Why should you think of the words in English, not in your own language?*
• Brainstorm vocabulary connected with photo 1 as a class. Put all students' ideas on the board.

Exercise 2   page 74
• Read the questions as a class. Elicit what tense is used to describe a photo.
• Students can work in pairs for 2 minutes. Get class feedback.

OPTIONAL ACTIVITY
Ask students in pairs to note down words related to the other photographs. Allow 3 minutes.

Share ideas as a class. Students listen and add to their notes.

Put students in five groups and allocate a different photo to each group. Allow 2–3 minutes for students to talk about the photo.

Share ideas as a class.

Exercise 3   page 74
• Students can work in pairs. Check as a class.
• In a **weaker class**, ask students to use the Wordlist at the back of the Workbook.

KEY
1	homelessness	4	pollution
2	child labour	5	poverty
3	endangered species	6	war

not illustrated: the arms trade, disease, famine, global warming, racism, terrorism

PRONUNCIATION – THE LETTER 'A'
The words in exercise 3 exemplify four different sounds for the letter 'a'. For further practice, write the following words in a word pool on the board and ask students to find pairs with the same vowel sound.

<u>fa</u>mine   <u>ar</u>ms   <u>la</u>bour   <u>fa</u>ther   end<u>a</u>ngered
w<u>ar</u>   Engl<u>a</u>nd   <u>a</u>ction   w<u>ar</u>ming   glob<u>a</u>l

Key
famine, action /æ/
arms, father /ɑː/
labour, endangered /eɪ/
war, warming /ɔː/
England, global /ə/

Exercise 4   page 74   🎧 2.19
• Play the recording. Students listen and repeat chorally and individually.
• Play the recording again. Students listen and read.
• Students check the meaning of the words individually.
• Ask **fast finishers** to copy the words into their notebooks and group them under four headings: *health, political, social* and *environmental*. Check as a class.

For more practice on vocabulary related to global issues, go to:

Vocabulary Builder (part 1): Student's Book page 131

KEY
1 a the arms trade
    b disease
    c famine
    d global warming

2 a terrorism
    b the arms trade
    c racism
    d homelessness
    e war
    f disease
    g poverty
    h global warming

Exercise 5   page 74   🎧 2.20
• Read the instructions as a class.
• Remind students that thinking about the words they might hear is a great way to prepare for the listening. Students can work in pairs, taking it in turns to say the words they associate with each of the issues. Allow 2 minutes.
• Play the recording twice. Students listen and note down their answers.
• Ask **fast finishers** to note down the words connected with the issues which helped them make their decisions.

- You may wish to teach some of the words; for example: *lynx, deer* (1), *argument, divorced* (2), *to suspect, a motive* (3), *died, to grow crops* (4), *soldiers, destroyed, fighting* (5), *conditions* (6). If so, put them on the board, explain them and model the pronunciation for students to repeat. Then play the recording again. Pause after each issue and elicit the connection between the new word and the issue.

KEY

1	endangered species	4	famine
2	homelessness	5	war
3	racism	6	child labour

Transcript 2.20

1 The European lynx is a type of wild cat. These beautiful animals became extinct in many European countries over 100 years ago, but they were later successfully reintroduced into some European forests. They eat rabbits and small deer and sometimes …

2 Nobody knows exactly how many homeless people there are in Britain. But we know that many of them are teenagers who have left home after a family argument or because their parents have divorced. They sleep in parks and on the streets …

3 Late last night two young black men were attacked in south London. They were leaving a disco when four white men came up to them and asked for money. The police suspect a racist motive …

4 It hasn't rained here for two years. The animals have all died and it's impossible to grow crops. The people are all very hungry. If we don't get some food to this region soon, many people will die …

5 Government soldiers attacked the town again last night. They destroyed a lot of buildings and killed at least fifteen people. The fighting lasted for three hours …

6 These football shirts are made in Bangladesh. The children that make them receive only $1 a day … that is why they are so cheap. But these children work very long hours in difficult conditions …

Exercise 6 page 74

- Pre-teach *serious*.
- Allow 5 minutes. Encourage students to give reasons for their choices.
- Share ideas as a class.
- In a **stronger class**, discuss and choose the most serious issues as a class. Check if everybody agrees by asking individual students about particular issues: *Why do you think X is more serious than Y? Why is X not serious in our country?*

For practice on word formation (noun suffixes), go to:

> **Vocabulary Builder (part 2):** Student's Book page 131

- For exercise 5 make students aware that when we make words longer by adding a suffix it can sometimes change the word stress. With the suffix *-ness* it doesn't change but when a suffix with *-ion* is added the stress is always on the second last syllable:

  in**form**   infor**ma**tion   **ed**ucate   edu**ca**tion

KEY

3	pollution		homelessness
4 1	information	4	suggestion
2	education	5	sadness
3	action	6	goodness
5	Students listen and repeat.		

Transcript 🎧 2.28

inf**orm**	infor**ma**tion
educate	edu**ca**tion
act	**ac**tion
sug**gest**	sug**ges**tion
sad	**sad**ness
good	**good**ness

6 1 information   5 education
2 goodness   6 darkness
3 suggestion   7 organisation
4 discussion

➜ Lesson outcome

Ask students: *What have you learned today? What can you do now?* and elicit answers: *I can identify global problems. I can talk about a photograph from a newspaper.*

8B GRAMMAR
Second conditional

LESSON SUMMARY ●●●●●

Grammar: second conditional
Speaking: predicting the results of imaginary situations

SHORTCUT *To do the lesson in 30 minutes, skip the Grammar Builder (in a **stronger class**) or exercises 3 and 6 (in a **weaker class**).*

➜ Lead-in 3–4 minutes

- Inform the class of the lesson objectives.
- Put the following on the board: *environment, car, pollution, petrol, CO_2, vegetable oil, renewable energy.* Model the pronunciation. Students listen and repeat.
- Ask students in small groups to discuss the meaning of words and how they are connected. Allow 2 minutes.
- Share ideas. Explain any words which are still unclear.

LANGUAGE NOTE – CHEMICALS

Make sure that students can say the abbreviation CO_2 correctly: /ˌsiː əʊ ˈtuː/. Similarly, H_2O is pronounced /ˌeɪtʃ tuː ˈəʊ/.

Exercise 1 page 75   🎧 2.21

- Students read the instructions and the text individually. In a **stronger class**, ask students to try and complete the text before they listen.
- Play the recording once. Students complete the gaps. In a **weaker class**, ask a student to read the text out. Correct pronunciation and explain any other unknown words.

KEY

1	used	3	had
2	wouldn't produce	4	would earn

Vegetable oil is better than petrol because it produces very little CO_2. It is also an example of a renewable fuel.

Exercise 2   page 75

- Read the *Learn this!* box as a class.
- Check comprehension by asking: *Does the second conditional describe a real situation or an imaginary situation? What tense do we use to describe the imaginary situation? What tense do we use to describe its result?*
- In a **weaker class**, if students find it difficult to answer, let them read Grammar Reference 8.1 and 8.2, then ask again.
- Students can complete the sentences in pairs. Check by asking individual students to read out full sentences starting with, *If the world were a village of 100 people …*
- In a **stronger class**, you can do oral drilling practice using the numbers from the sentences: T: *61* Ss: *If the world were a village of 100 people, 61 would be Asian*. After a while, ask students to cover the exercise and work from memory.

KEY

61 would be Asian and 12 would be European.
22 would speak Chinese and 9 would speak English.
20 would earn less than $1 a day.
24 wouldn't have any electricity in their home.
7 would own a car.
20 would consume 80% of the energy.
67 wouldn't be able to read.

For more practice on the second conditional, go to:

Grammar Builder 8B: Student's Book page 118

KEY

1 1 had
2 owed
3 had
4 knew
5 didn't live
6 copied
7 didn't stay up
8 didn't smoke

2 1 lived, would be
2 would play, was/were
3 had, would watch
4 could, didn't spend
5 would happen, didn't go
6 wouldn't be, didn't invite
7 found, would take
8 would you feel, didn't pass

3 2 If Ben didn't have to get up early on Mondays, he would go out on Sunday evenings.
3 If Kate had a ticket for the Madonna concert, she would be going.
4 If there was/were a football match on TV this evening, they wouldn't be going out.
5 If I didn't have a lot of homework, I wouldn't stay in this evening.
6 If we had to help with the cooking, we couldn't watch a DVD.

Exercise 3   page 75

- In a **weaker class**, ask students to match the halves of the sentences first. Check as a class. Students complete the sentences. Check together.
- In a **stronger class**, students complete the sentences and match the halves. Check as a class.
- **Fast finishers** can complete the halves 1–5 with their own ideas. Briefly discuss as a class.

KEY

1 c didn't produce, would reduce
2 d would give, was/were
3 a would save, were able to
4 e would be, stopped
5 b didn't pollute, would be

Exercise 4   page 75

- As this exercise contains core vocabulary and states important facts, make sure students understand both. Put the following on the board: *plastic bottles, to recycle, to burn oil, greenhouse gases, atmosphere, global warming, climate change*. Elicit or explain the meaning. Point out that *oil* refers to mineral liquid from which petrol is produced and does not mean *vegetable oil* as in exercise 1.
- Ask students in pairs to try and explain in what way plastic bottles influence the earth's climate. Allow a minute.
- Ask students to read the gapped sentences and check their ideas. Were they right?
- Students complete the gaps individually. Check as a class.

KEY

1 recycled
2 wouldn't have to
3 produced
4 would burn
5 burned
6 wouldn't be
7 weren't
8 would be able to
9 reduced
10 wouldn't change

Exercise 5 page 75

- Allow 2 minutes for students to make notes. While they are working, go round and help with any vocabulary problems.
- Students work in pairs for 3–4 minutes. If the class gets involved, extend the time limit.
- You can ask **fast finishers** to work in the same pairs trying to guess what their partner would do in the following situations: if he/she could make one miracle / woke up aged 50 one morning / had to cook dinner for twelve people / learned about a classmate's secret, etc. They can only ask specific questions (*Would you...?*) and answer *yes* or *no*.

Exercise 6 page 75

- Keep a fairly fast pace. Go through the sentences as a class, eliciting answers from different students.
- Choose one of the sentences (preferably a controversial one, e.g. 3, 6 or 7) and elicit answers from all the students. Would they react the same? Why would they behave differently? Have a short class discussion.

➡ Lesson outcome

Ask students: *What have you learned today? What can you do now?* and elicit answers: *I can predict the result of an imaginary situation. I have learned about global warming.*

Notes for Photocopiable activity 8.1

Moral dilemmas

Pairwork
Language: second conditional
Materials: one copy of the cut-up worksheet between 3–4 students (Teacher's Book page 138), *Yes/No* cards

- Pre-teach the following vocabulary as necessary: *act suspiciously   sell-by date   exploit workers   put something out of its misery*
- Divide students into groups of 3–4. Give each group a pile of the cut-up questions which are placed face down on the desk. Give out a *Yes* and a *No* card to each student in the class. (Students can make their own if necessary.)
- The first student takes a card and reads out the question. The other players have to decide whether they think the first student would answer *Yes* or *No* to the question. To do this the other students simultaneously put a *Yes* or *No* card face down on the table. They mustn't see each other's cards.
- The first student then tells the group whether they would or wouldn't do the action on the card. The other students then turn over their *Yes* or *No* cards. They receive a point for a correct guess.
- The next student takes a card and the activity is repeated until all the cards are used up.

8C CULTURE
Going green

Reading: a short text about the Youth Eco Parliament; gap-fill
Vocabulary: the environment
Listening: quiz; listening for specific information
Speaking: discussing ways of improving the environment
Writing: an e-mail
Topic: nature and the environment

SHORTCUT *To do the lesson in 30 minutes, set the e-mail for homework.*

➡ Lead-in 3–5 minutes

- Inform the class of the lesson objectives.
- Focus students on the pictures. Elicit what problem is illustrated (the pollution of the environment). Ask students if they think it is a serious problem.
- Put three nouns on the board: *the environment, rubbish, energy.* Dictate the following verbs: *to use, to improve, to waste, to pick up, to save, to recycle, to pollute, to drop, to protect.* Ask students in pairs to match each of the nouns on the board with three of the verbs. Check as a class. Put the verbs on the board in the three columns.

Exercise 1 page 76 🎧 2.22

- Pre-teach *the ozone layer, ultra-violet light* and *pesticides.* Students read the quiz. Ask: *In what ways do people pollute the environment?* Elicit answers encouraging the class to use their general knowledge as well as the facts from the previous lessons.
- Students do the quiz individually. Play the recording once to check answers.

Transcript and key 2.22

1   The answer is C. Plastic bags can take up to 1,000 years to decompose. When we go shopping we should take a bag with us.
2   The answer is A. The ozone layer stops ultra-violet light from the sun. It's between 15 and 17 kilometres above the surface of the Earth.
3   The answer is C. About 90% of the world's energy comes from oil, coal and gas. One problem is that they are not renewable – they will eventually run out. Another problem is that when we burn them they cause global warming.
4   The answer is B. At the moment the EU only recycles about 45% of its rubbish. It wants to recycle between 50 and 80 per cent of its waste.
5   The answer is all of them. More than 400 pesticides are regularly used in non-organic farming. The pesticides can kill wild animals and birds, and also cause water pollution.

Exercise 2 page 76 🎧 2.22

- Pre-teach *above, surface, to cause, non-organic farming, to run out, waste* (= rubbish).
- Allow a minute for students to read the questions. Play the recording again. Students listen and note down the answers. Check answers as a class.

KEY

1 We should take a bag with us.
2 Between 15 and 17 kilometres.
3 It causes global warming.
4 Between 50 and 80%.
5 More than 400.

Exercise 3 page 76

- Read the instructions as a class. Allow 2 minutes for students to read the text and complete the gaps. Check as a class.
- Check comprehension of the text by asking: *How old were the members of the first Youth Eco Parliament? What plans did they make? What problems did they focus on? Why did they meet in Berlin? Which of their suggestions are easy to follow?*

KEY

1 countries	5 rubbish
2 environment	6 turn off
3 energy	7 Use
4 letters	

Exercise 4 page 76

- In a **stronger class**, put three words on the board: *locally, nationally, globally*. Divide the class into 3 or 6 groups. Each group (or two groups) discusses the suggestions from a different perspective.
- In a **weaker class**, ask students to suggest what teenagers can do to help improve the environment around them.
- Allow 5 minutes. Remind students to use the second conditional where appropriate. Share ideas as a class.

Exercise 5 page 76

- In a **weaker class**, students can work in pairs. In a **stronger class**, students work individually. Allow 5–10 minutes.
- **Fast finishers** can go round and help others finish their e-mails.
- Ask individual students to read their e-mails out to the class. Make notes of mistakes and correct them with the class at the end of the lesson.

➡ Lesson outcome

Ask students: *What have you learned today? What can you do now?* and elicit answers: *I can talk about the environment. I have learned how to improve the environment.*

8D GRAMMAR
I wish ...

LESSON SUMMARY ●●●●●

Grammar: *I wish*
Listening: a song
Speaking: talking about wishes

SHORTCUT *To do the lesson in 30 minutes, skip the Grammar Builder or exercise 3. Do not share ideas as a class after exercise 6 but go round monitoring when students are working on exercise 5.*

➡ Lead-in 3–5 minutes

- Inform the class of the lesson objectives.
- Ask students in pairs to discuss what they dislike about their lives and what they would like to change. They can note their ideas down under the headings *complaints* and *dreams*.
- Allow 2 minutes. Share ideas.

Exercise 1 page 77

- Focus students on the cartoons. Ask: *Are the characters happy about their situations or would they like to change them?*
- Students answer the questions individually. Check as a class.

KEY

1 Yes 2 No 3 No

Exercise 2 page 77

- In a **weaker class**, students can read Grammar Reference 8.3 and 8.4 on page 119, then work together. In a **stronger class**, students complete the rule individually.
- Point out that after *wish* we can use the past simple (for general facts and regular activities) or past continuous (if we want the situation to change at the moment of speaking).

LANGUAGE NOTE – *I WISH*

As with the second conditional, students might find it strange to be using a past tense to talk about the present after *I wish*. Therefore it is important to emphasise that these sentences do not refer to the past but to an imaginary situation.

For more practice on I wish, *go to:*

Grammar Builder 8D: Student's Book page 118

KEY

4 1 I wish I were taller.
  2 I wish we had tickets.
  3 I wish I lived in the country.
  4 I wish you could talk.
  5 I wish the music wasn't so loud.
  6 I wish I could buy that jacket.

5			
1 didn't have		5 didn't hate
2 were		6 were
3 could		7 could
4 wasn't/weren't		8 didn't have to

Exercise 3   page 77

- Students work individually for 3 minutes.
- Ask **fast finishers** to use their notes from the Lead-in to write more sentences.
- Check as a class.

KEY

2 I wish I had a dog.
3 I wish I liked vegetables.
4 I wish I was/were good at maths.
5 I wish I could speak French.
6 I wish I could play the guitar.
7 I wish I didn't have a lot of homework.
8 I wish I were taller.

Exercise 4   page 77   🎧 2.23

- Read the instructions and the phrases from the box to the class. You may wish to pre-teach *break all the chains, remove all the bars, share all the love*. Ask students to read the glossary below the text.
- Play the recording. Students listen and complete the song.
- Play the recording again for students to check.

KEY

1 break all the chains	5 be like a bird
2 say all the things	6 soar to the sun
3 share all the love	7 break all the chains
4 know how it feels	8 say all the things

LANGUAGE NOTE – *GONNA*

Explain to students that it is usual in fast speech to shorten *want to* to *wanna* and *because* to *cos*. These words and others such as *gonna* and *gotta* are commonly seen in song lyrics but shouldn't otherwise be used in written English.

Exercise 5   page 77

- Ask students to think about their own life and complete the sentences. Allow 3 minutes.
- **Fast finishers** can come back to the song and complete the sentences on behalf of the singer.

Exercise 6   page 77

- Allow 5 minutes. If there is time left, share answers as a class.
- In a **stronger class**, encourage students to ask follow-up questions and use second conditional to answer them, for example:
  S1: *I wish I were older.*
  S2: *Why do you wish you were older?*
  S1: *Because if I were older, I would have more freedom.*

➡ Lesson outcome

Ask students: *What have you learned today? What can you do now?* and elicit answers: *I can talk about situations I would like to change. I have learned to use* wish.

8E   READING   Disaster!

LESSON SUMMARY ●●●●●

Vocabulary: words for natural disasters
Reading: an article about a volcano; scanning, reading for detail
Topic: nature and the environment

SHORTCUT *To do the lesson in 30 minutes, do exercises 4, 5 and 6 as a class.*

➡ Lead-in   3–5 minutes

- Inform the class of the lesson objectives.
- Elicit or explain the meaning of *disaster*. Ask students about types of disasters and the greatest disasters in history. What happened? What were the consequences?

Exercise 1   page 78

- Allow 30 seconds, then check as a class.
- Can students name any other volcanoes? For example: Mount St. Helen's (USA); Mount Kilimanjaro (Tanzania).

KEY

1 Japan   2 Italy   3 Indonesia   4 Mexico

Exercise 2   page 78

- In a **weaker class**, pre-teach *to collapse, to fall, to cover, weak, deep, flat*.
- Students work individually for a minute. Check as a class.

KEY

1 F   2 T   3 F

Exercise 3   page 78

- Read the reading tip with the class. Students look at the diagrams. Elicit what they show. Ask some questions about the numbers and locations to check understanding.
- Students can work in pairs. Ask them to find and underline the relevant sentences in the text.
- In a **weaker class**, check by having students read answers out from the book.
- In a **stronger class**, ask the questions with books closed and elicit answers.

KEY

1 The water next to the volcano is about six kilometres deep.
2 If the volcano collapsed, 500 billion tonnes of rock would fall into the sea.
3 The wave would travel away from the Canary Islands in all directions at about 800 km/h.
4 In less than an hour a 90-metre wave would hit north-west Africa.
5 Eight hours after the eruption it would hit the east coast of America.

Exercise 4   page 78

- Students work individually. Allow 2–3 minutes to read the text in detail.
- In a **weaker class**, answer vocabulary questions, but encourage students to try to work out meaning from context first.

KEY

1 Scientists fear that when the volcano erupts, one side of the volcano could collapse and fall into the sea. It would cause the biggest tsunami ever recorded in history.
2 Less than an hour.
3 Because the side of the volcano faces west, across the Atlantic.
4 It would be 12 metres high.
5 Because the coast is very flat.
6 They can put better equipment on Cumbre Vieja.

Exercise 5 page 78

• Work as a class.

KEY

1 huge, enormous   2 devastate, destroy

Exercise 6 page 78

Students can work in pairs. Check as a class.

KEY

1 destroy   4 predict
2 devastate   5 protect
3 erupt

Exercise 7 page 78

• Ask students to make notes on the consequences of a Cumbre Vieja eruption. Allow 2 minutes.
• Put students in pairs. They take it in turns to say sentences using the words from the box.
• Bring the class together. Elicit answers.

ADDITIONAL SPEAKING ACTIVITY

Briefly brainstorm other types of disaster as a class. For example: forest fires, flooding, hurricanes, earthquakes. Talk about the consequences in towns and cities.

Inform the students that they are on the council in their town. They have been warned that a natural disaster is about to happen. They need to plan a response. It is up to them to protect the inhabitants of their town.

Put the following categories on the board: transport, communication, first aid, accommodation.

Students in pairs brainstorm ideas for what they would need in the disaster situation.

Remind students to use the conditional tenses to talk about possibilities, imaginary situations and their consequences.

Ask a few pairs to share some ideas. For example: *If there was a hurricane coming, we would contact people by telephone to warn them.* In a **stronger class**, invent problems to stretch the students, for example: T: *The telephone lines are broken.* Ss: *If the telephone lines were broken, we would use local radio and television.*

Allow pairs to continue working for a few more minutes. Then combine pairs in groups of four to agree on a disaster and finalise their response. Allow 5 minutes.

Get a few groups to present their solution to the class.

➡ Lesson outcome

Ask students: *What have you learned today? What can you do now?* and elicit answers: *I have learned words connected with volcanic eruption. I can talk about a global disaster.*

Notes for Photocopiable activity 8.2

Word formation

Vocabulary practice
Language: noun suffixes
Materials: one copy of the worksheet per student (Teacher's Book page 139)

Students can work through the worksheet individually. Allow them to compare answers in pairs before checking as a class. This worksheet could be set for homework if necessary.

KEY

1 happiness, homelessness, ambition, similarity, weakness, poverty, rudeness, globality, popularity, education, recycling, pollution, government, arrangement, spelling, production, employment, improvement

2   1 Homelessness   5 arrangement   9 ambitious
    2 similarities   6 employs   10 spelling
    3 recycle   7 improvement   11 weak
    4 happiness   8 produces   12 pollution

8F EVERYDAY ENGLISH
Giving advice

LESSON SUMMARY ●●●●●

Functional English: describing a problem and giving advice
Listening: a dialogue; true/false questions
Speaking: giving advice
Topic: relationships

SHORTCUT *To do the lesson in 30 minutes, skip exercises 2, 3 and 10. You can speed up the pace in exercise 7 if you allow 15 seconds to write each piece of advice and get answers immediately from 2–3 students.*

➡ Lead-in 3–5 minutes

• Inform the class of the lesson objectives.
• Write *advice* and *advise* on the board. Model the pronunciation for students to repeat. Elicit which is a noun and which is a verb. Point out that *advice* is uncountable and so we can talk of *some advice* or *a piece of advice*.
• Ask students in pairs to list the advice their parents and teachers often give them. Allow 2 minutes. Get class feedback.

Exercise 1 page 80 🎧 2.24

• Write *lend, borrow* and *pay back* on the board. Elicit what can be lent, borrowed and paid back (money). Elicit the difference between *lend* and *borrow* by asking: *Who gives the money back, the person who lends it or the person who borrows it?* (The person who borrows it.)
• Students complete the gaps individually. Allow a minute.
• Play the recording to check. In a **stronger class**, elicit the meaning of *embarrassing, upset, short of money*. In a **weaker class**, explain the words.
• Read the *Learn this!* with the class. Ask students to underline the uses of *should* in the dialogue. Which one is used for advice? (*I think you should ask him to pay you back.*) Which one is used to give an opinion? (*He shouldn't get upset at that.*)
• Point out that it is more natural in English to say *I don't think you should …* than *I think you shouldn't …*

KEY

1 advice	4 borrowed
2 lent	5 idea
3 upset	

CULTURE AND LANGUAGE NOTE

Draw students' attention to the use of 'softening' language which people in the UK use to sound less direct and more polite. Explain that what might be considered perfectly polite in some countries may sometimes be considered too direct in the UK.

I'm *a bit* short of money. is preferred to I'm short of money.

When *do you think you could* pay me back? rather than When will you pay me back?

He *shouldn't* get upset. Here the modal verb *should* is used to mean *very probably won't*.

Exercise 2 page 80

- In a **weaker class**, play the recording again. Students listen and read. Ask a pair of students to read the dialogue out. Work on pronunciation problems as a class. When students are confident, allow a minute to work in pairs.
- In a **stronger class**, students read the dialogue in pairs. Then change roles and read it again.

Exercise 3 page 80

- Work as a class. Encourage students to start with *I would/wouldn't tell him to …* or *I think/don't think he should/ought to …*
- In a **stronger class**, take the role of Mark and ask different students directly for advice. Ask the class to comment on their friends' ideas.

Exercise 4 page 80 🎧 2.25

- Read the listening tip with the class. Check comprehension by asking: *Should you worry if there are a lot of words you do not understand in the recording? What should you try to do when you listen to the recording for the first time?*
- Play the recording once. Elicit what Will's problem is.

KEY

Will's parents won't let him stay out after nine o'clock.

Transcript 2.25

Susan Hello, Will.
Will Hi, Susan. Can I ask your advice about something?
Susan Sure. What is it?
Will My parents won't let me stay out after nine o'clock in the evening. All my friends can stay out till about ten.
Susan Why won't they let you stay out?
Will Well, one day last week I got home very late because I missed the last bus. It was nearly midnight, and they were very cross because I didn't ring them or answer my mobile.
Susan Did you apologise?
Will They didn't give me a chance. We just got into a big argument.
Susan Hmm. If I were you, I'd say sorry for being late last week, and tell them you'll make sure you're always back before ten.
Will OK. I'll give it a try.

Exercise 5 page 80 🎧 2.25

- Put *to miss, to be cross, to apologise* on the board. Explain or elicit the meaning.

- Ask students to read the sentences carefully on their own. Point out that in most false sentences some information is true, so attention to detail is important.
- Play the recording again. Students mark their answers.
- Check as a class.

KEY

1 T
2 F They were cross because he didn't ring or answer the phone.
3 F He didn't apologise because his parents didn't give him a chance.
4 T

Exercise 6 page 80 🎧 2.26

- Play the recording. Students read, listen and repeat.

PRONUNCIATION – *SHOULD*

Make sure students pronounce the 'ou' in *should/shouldn't*, *would/wouldn't* as an /ə/ sound and that they don't pronounce the 'l'.

Exercise 7 page 80

- Students can work in pairs. Allow 2 minutes.
- Share answers as a class. You read a problem. Students read out their advice. Correct mistakes. Try to keep a fast pace.

Exercise 8 page 80

- Allow a minute to choose a problem and brainstorm possible advice.
- In a **stronger class**, you can put some students in groups of three. Two students prepare contradictory advice. They will try to persuade the third one to follow it. The third student thinks of reasons why he/she can't do it.

Exercise 9 page 80

- Remind students to use various phrases to give advice.
- Allow 3–5 minutes for the writing and one more to read the dialogues through. Help with any problems.

Exercise 10 page 80

- In a **weaker class**, students act their dialogues out for the class. Discuss the advice as a class.
- In a **stronger class**, divide students into 2–3 groups. Students act their dialogues out and discuss the advice in groups.

OPTIONAL ACTIVITY

To revise the functional language for giving advice at a later date, try the following activity, which works well as a warmer at the beginning of a lesson.

Ask a student to sit at the front with his/her back to the board. Write a problem on the board, such as *I can't sleep well at night*. The other students call out advice, e.g. *I don't think you should take pills. Why don't you read a book? If I were you I'd have a glass of milk before you go to bed*. and the student has to guess the problem. Alternatively, you could write problems on post-it notes and stick them to students' backs. They mingle, giving and receiving advice, and try to guess their problems.

➡ Lesson outcome

Ask students: *What have you learned today? What can you do now?* and elicit answers: *I can use different structures to give advice. I have learned what to say if someone asks me for advice. I can describe a problem.*

8G WRITING — An essay

LESSON SUMMARY ●●●●●

Reading: an essay
Vocabulary: phrases for expressing opinions, expressions with *make*
Writing: an essay on an ideal world
Topic: people and society

SHORTCUT *To do the lesson in 30 minutes, skip the Lead-in and keep exercise 2 brief. Skip exercise 4 and introduce the structures yourself at the start of exercise 5.*

➜ Lead-in 4–5 minutes
- Inform the class of the lesson objectives.
- Ask the class: *What's been in the news lately?* Elicit a range of answers and note them on the board. Introduce the phrase *global issues* and ask students to say which of the news events listed are global issues and which are local ones.
- Ask students to say which news story they think is the most important and to give reasons.

Exercise 1 page 81
- Focus on the essay title and explain the meaning. Point out that this is an imaginary situation, so the second conditional is used.
- Students read the essay and choose the issues.
- While they are working, write the following on the board: *prevent, the developing world, vaccinate, drugs companies, invest in, solar power, illegal, ban, reduce.* Ask **fast finishers** to find some or all of the words and work out their meaning.
- Check as a class. Elicit/Explain the meaning of the words.

KEY

disease, famine, global warming

Exercise 2 page 81
- Students answer the questions. Allow them to work in pairs.
- As you check the answers, ask some follow-up comprehension questions, e.g. 1 *What's the situation now? 2 What result would this have? 3 What else would she do to help stop global warming?* etc.

KEY

1 She would make sure they could sell their food to the rest of the world.
2 Vaccinate children.
3 Because we need to stop global warming.
4 Rap music.
5 Sports.
6 Change his socks every day.

Exercise 3 page 81
- Read the tip as a class. Tell students that all the expressions are useful for the fairly formal style of essay writing.
- When students have found the phrases in the text, discuss translations. Explain that *I believe* and *I'm convinced that* are stronger than *I think*.
- Focus on the use of *I don't think/believe*. Explain that it is normal to say, for example, *I don't think sports programmes are interesting* rather than *I think sports programmes aren't interesting.*

KEY

In my opinion, I believe, In my view, I think

Exercise 4 page 81
- Students find the structures with *make*. Elicit translations and ask students to suggest other examples, e.g. *I'd make people pay more for petrol. I'd make solar power cheaper. I'd make sure that every town and village had recycling bins.*

Exercise 5 page 81
- In a **weaker class**, go through the sentences and elicit the parts of speech needed. Students complete the exercise in pairs.
- In a **stronger class**, students work individually. **Fast finishers** can form pairs to check their answers.
- Ask students for their opinions. Do they agree or disagree strongly with any of these ideas? How possible are the actions and what would the results be?

KEY

1	illegal	3	reduce	5	pick up	7	optional
2	found	4	smaller	6	was	8	stop

Exercise 6 page 81
- Ask students to look back at the organisation of the model essay. Ask: *What is the theme of each paragraph?* (1 famine and disease in the developing world, 2 global warming, 3 less serious ideas.) Point out that in each paragraph the writer identifies problems and says what she would do about them.
- Students plan and write a first draft of their essay in three paragraphs. Go round helping as needed.
- Ask students to exchange essays and check their partner's work, using the checklist. Encourage them to make constructive comments and suggestions.
- Students write their final version of the essay, either in class or for homework.

ALTERNATIVE WRITING TASK
Write an essay about what you would do if you were the head teacher of your school with plenty of money to spend on improvements. Write 130–150 words.

➜ Lesson outcome
- Ask students: *What have you learned today? What can you do now?* and elicit answers: *I can write an essay about an imaginary situation. I have learned some new phrases for expressing opinions. I have learned expressions with* make.

LANGUAGE REVIEW 7-8

1 1 legs 2 arms 3 hands 4 head 5 back

2 1 homelessness   5 global warming
    2 racism   6 endangered species
    3 child labour   7 disease
    4 pollution   8 famine

3 1 needn't   4 must
    2 mustn't   5 must
    3 needn't   6 mustn't

4 1 c You won't pass your exam if you don't study.
    2 f We won't have a barbecue if it rains.
    3 a If he invites me to the party, I'll accept.
    4 b If they leave now, they'll get home before 8 o'clock.
    5 e I won't be angry if you forget my birthday.
    6 d If I buy a new MP3 player, I'll give you my old one.

5 1 had, would buy   4 wouldn't do, were
    2 would have, wasn't   5 spoke, would be able to
    3 would be, did   6 weren't, wouldn't get

6 2 I wish the supermarket wasn't shut.
    3 I wish I had my mobile phone.
    4 I wish my homework wasn't (so) difficult.
    5 I wish I could find my bag.
    6 I wish it wasn't Monday.
    7 I wish we didn't have an exam tomorrow.

7 1 d   2 e   3 c   4 b   5 a

8 1 advice   5 were
    2 course   6 borrow
    3 problem   7 should
    4 afford   8 understand

SKILLS ROUND-UP 1-8

Transcript 2.27

Joanna Hi, Maria.
Maria Hi, Joanna. How are you?
Joanna I'm fine, thanks.
Maria What did you do at the weekend?
Joanna Nothing much. I went to the cinema on Saturday evening.
Maria With Daniel, your neighbour?
Joanna Huh! No. I went by myself. I haven't spoken to Daniel for ages. I never see him!
Maria That's a shame.
Joanna I know. I really like him – and I'm sure he likes me.
Maria Well, I think you ought to arrange something.
Joanna What do you mean?
Maria Well, you should plan to do something – and then invite him.
Joanna Actually, it's the Notting Hill carnival next weekend. I'm going there on Sunday with Jim, Sarah and the children.
Maria If I were you, I'd invite Daniel to that. I'm sure he'd love to go.
Joanna Good idea!

Daniel Hello!
Joanna Hi! How are you?
Daniel Fine thanks. And you?
Joanna Yes, I'm fine. Great weather, isn't it?
Daniel Yes, it is. Are you working today?
Joanna No, I'm not. I don't usually work at weekends.
Daniel Really? Well, we're having a barbecue next Sunday. Would you like to come?
Joanna I'd love to, thanks. What time?
Daniel About one o'clock.
Joanna That's great! Shall I bring some food?
Daniel You needn't bring anything. We've got lots of food.
Joanna OK. Thanks!

Narrator It's Wednesday evening. Joanna is at her English class.
Maria So, Joanna … did you invite Daniel to the carnival?
Joanna Not exactly. He invited me to a barbecue.
Maria Fantastic!
Joanna Hmm.
Maria What's the problem?
Joanna Well, I accepted his invitation. But I've already told Jim and Sarah that I'll go with them to the carnival in London next Sunday.
Maria Ah.
Joanna I don't know what to do! I really want to go to Daniel's barbecue, but I don't want Jim and Sarah to be angry with me.
Maria Hmm. That's difficult.

1 2 She wants to go to Daniel's barbecue but she's already arranged to go to the carnival with the family.

2 1 F   2 T   3 F   4 F   5 T   6 F

3–5 Open answers

6 1 d   2 c   3 a

7 1 In August.
    2 There is a competition between groups of musicians who play steel drums.
    3 Members of the Caribbean community.
    4 The carnival moved outdoors.
    5 About 1.5 million.
    6 Because the crowds are large.

8–9 Open answers

EXAM For further exam tasks and practice, go to Workbook page 78. Procedural notes, transcripts and keys for the Workbook can be found on the *Solutions* Teacher's Website at www.oup.com/elt/teacher/solutions.

9 Crime scene

A VOCABULARY AND LISTENING
Crimes and criminals

THIS UNIT INCLUDES ●●●○
Vocabulary • crimes and criminals • crime verbs • extreme adjectives
• word formation: noun suffixes *-er*, *-ist* and *-ian* • colloquial expressions
Grammar • past perfect • reported speech
Speaking • asking and replying to personal questions • reporting a theft
• giving opinions
Writing • a story
WORKBOOK pages 80–86 • Self check 9 page 87

LESSON SUMMARY ●●●○○
Vocabulary: crimes and criminals, crime verbs
Listening: dialogues; multiple-choice
Speaking: assessing crimes
Topic: people and society

SHORTCUT *To do the lesson in 30 minutes, do exercises 1–3 quickly as a class, set Vocabulary Builder (part 1) for homework, doing Vocabulary Builder (part 2) in class instead.*

➡ Lead-in 2–4 minutes
• Inform the class of the lesson objectives.
• Write on the board for students to copy: *crime scene, crime* and *criminal*. Elicit the meaning. If students have a problem, help by asking: *Which is the word for illegal activity? / a person who acts against the law? / a place where illegal activity happened?*
• Briefly brainstorm types of crimes and criminals students are familiar with. Put the words on the board.

Exercise 1 page 84
• Focus students on the photos. Elicit any other words students know for the crimes, criminals and their activities in the photos. Do not teach any new words at this stage.

KEY

1 burglary	4 drug dealing
2 vandalism	5 shoplifting
3 joyriding	6 bank robbery

Exercise 2 page 84
• Students can work in pairs. Check as a class.
• In a **weaker class**, check understanding of the core vocabulary by asking: *Who breaks shop windows, a vandal or a shoplifter? Who steals cars, a joyrider or a drug dealer?* etc.

KEY

a 3 b 2 c 5 d 4 e 1 f 6

Exercise 3 page 84
• In a **weaker class**, work together. Ask individual students to share their opinions.
• In a **stronger class,** put students in small groups to discuss the crimes. Allow 3 minutes. Share ideas.
• Encourage students to justify their answers.

Exercise 4 page 84
• Students work individually. Allow a minute.

KEY

1 burglary	5 robbery
2 sell	6 steal
3 joyriding	7 theft
4 murder	8 vandalise

Not in the photos: murder, theft

Exercise 5 page 84 🎧 2.29
• Play the recording to check. Then play it again for students to repeat.
• Use a drilling technique to help students remember the words.
• Read the *Look out!* box as a class. Elicit what else one can steal (money, a watch, a bag, etc.) and rob (a shop, a post office, an old lady, etc.).

For more practice on vocabulary connected with crime go to:

Vocabulary Builder (part 1): Student's Book page 132

KEY

1 1 -ing 2 -ing 3 -ism 4 -ing 5 -ery 6 -ary
   7 -er 8 -ft

2

1 murderer	4 burglar	7 thief
2 shoplifter	5 vandal	8 robber
3 drug dealer	6 joyrider	

3

1 murder	4 burglary	7 theft
2 shoplifting	5 vandalism	8 robbery
3 drug dealing	6 joyriding	

4

1 robbed	4 burgled
2 stole	5 murdered
3 vandalised, sprayed	6 went joyriding

Exercise 6 page 84 🎧 2.30
• In a **weaker class**, allow 30 seconds to read the task and check vocabulary.
• Play the recording twice. Students listen and mark their answers. Remind them not to worry about the unknown words but to try to get the general meaning. Check as a class.

KEY

1 b vandalism	4 b shoplifting
2 a robbery	5 a joyriding
3 a drug dealing	

Transcript 2.30

1
A Somebody broke into the school in the middle of the night.
B Broke into the school? Really? Do you know how they got in?
A They climbed through a window.
B Did they steal anything?
A No, but they smashed lots of desks and chairs.
B That's terrible. Do they know who did it?
A Well the police arrested two boys this morning.

2
A Did you hear about Mark?
B No. What?
A Two teenagers stopped him in the street last night when he was walking home. They stole his wallet and his mobile.
B Is he OK?
A Yes, they didn't hurt him.

3
A I saw two men selling drugs at the end of our road.
B Really? How do you know they were selling drugs?
A A car stopped near the men, and a man in the car gave them some money. And they gave him something. I couldn't see, because it was dark, but I'm sure they were drugs.

4
A Kate's son stole a CD from the department store in town last weekend.
B Yes, I heard. A shop assistant called the police.
B I don't think that was necessary. It was only a CD.
A But he shouldn't steal from shops, should he?
B I know, but he's only 16.

5
A Some boys took our neighbour's car last night.
B Really?
A Yes. They didn't steal it, but they drove it round the streets for an hour, and then left it near the park.
A Did the police catch them?
A Yes, they're questioning two local boys at the police station.

Exercise 7   page 84
- Allow 3 minutes. Remind students to give reasons for their choice.

Exercise 8   page 84
- Ask individual students to present their opinion.
- In a **stronger class**, encourage students to comment on other students' opinions.

For practice on vocabulary formation (noun suffixes) go to:

> **Vocabulary Builder (part 2):** Student's Book page 132

KEY
5 drug dealer, joyrider, murderer, robber, shoplifter

6 1 -ian 2 -er 3 -er 4 -ist 5 -ian 6 -ist
　　 7 -ist 8 -er

7 a 5 b 1 c 8 d 6 e 3 f 2 g 7 h 4

→ Lesson outcome
Ask students: *What have you learned today? What can you do now?* and elicit answers: *I can describe different crimes. I have learned nouns and verbs to talk about crime, criminals and their actions.*

GRAMMAR
Past perfect

LESSON SUMMARY ●●●●●
Grammar: past perfect
Reading: accounts of crimes
Speaking: describing past events

SHORTCUT *To do the lesson in 30 minutes, skip exercises 4, 7 and 8.*

→ Lead-in 2–3 minutes
- Inform the class of the lesson objectives.
- Ask students if they listen to the radio, what radio stations and programmes are their favourite and if they have taken part in a phone-in programme. Elicit details.

Exercise 1   page 85
- Pre-teach *to confess, to describe, to be proud of, to discover.*
- Students read the text individually. Elicit the answer.

KEY
Because he confessed to a serious crime on the radio, which led to his arrest.

Exercise 2   page 85
- In a **weaker class**, ask more comprehension questions first, for example: *What happened at the bank? When was the radio programme? Why did the man phone? What did the police do?* Put these on the board for students to order chronologically: *the radio programme, the police arrest, the bank robbery.*
- Focus students on the verbs in blue. Elicit the answer.

KEY
had asked	before
had committed	before
had gone	before
had stolen	before
had helped	before

Exercise 3   page 85
- Students complete the rule individually.
- Read the rules as a class and check.
- Point out that in the past perfect we use *had* for all grammatical persons. Explain that the past participle of regular verbs is formed with the ending *-d* / *-ed* whereas that of irregular verbs has to be looked up in a dictionary. The past participle is the same in the present perfect and past perfect.
- Use the comparison with the present perfect to show that the concept of 'before' is crucial in both tenses. 'I have bought a CD' and 'I had bought a CD' both mean that the action of buying happened before a certain moment in time – before now or before some moment in the past. 'Now' does not need to be defined and so the sentence 'I have bought a CD' is complete and clear. But in the other sentence the moment in the past needs to be described and that is why 'I had bought a CD' is usually completed by another clause, for example, '... before my dad gave me an MP3 player.' That is why the past perfect is often used in complex sentences together with the past simple.

LANGUAGE NOTE – PAST PERFECT

The form and concept of the past perfect tense shouldn't cause much difficulty in isolation but students need to understand the relationship between the past perfect and the past simple. The following timeline might help illustrate this.

We ran to the station but the train had already left.

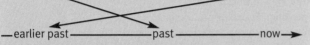

—earlier past————————past————————now—→

Highlight the fact that *'d* is the contracted form of both *had* and *would*. Give students practice in identifying which is which by calling out sentences with both contractions and asking students to say either *had* or *would*.

For more practice on the past perfect go to:

Grammar Builder 9B: Student's Book page 120

KEY

1 1 had seen
2 had eaten
3 had broken down
4 hadn't finished
5 hadn't had

6 had bought
7 had promised
8 hadn't visited
9 had written
10 had done

2 2 When Paul phoned, I had gone to bed.
3 When the police arrived, the shoplifter had run away.
4 When Mum got home, Dad had cooked dinner.
5 When the police caught the vandals, they had sprayed graffiti on the wall.
6 When we arrived at the cinema, the film had started.
7 When we left the beach, it had started to rain.
8 When we got to the station, the train had left.

Exercise 4 page 85

• Read the instructions and example with the class.
• In a **weaker class**, do the activity as a class first.
• In a **stronger class**, get feedback by asking individual students what they had done by the time they arrived at school this morning.

OPTIONAL ACTIVITY

Read the following questions out to the class:

How many teachers had you had by the time you came to this school?
How many cities had you visited by the time you came to this school?
How many books had you read by the time you came to this school?
How many gadgets had you bought by the time you came to this school?

Students listen and note down their answers. Put students in pairs and ask them to compare their answers and recreate the questions together. Allow 3 minutes. Share answers.

Exercise 5 page 85

• In a **weaker class**, pre-teach *to chase, to catch up with, to run out of, to keep up, to order, an owner, a petrol station, fuel*. In a **stronger class**, ask students in pairs to read the text and work out the meaning from the context. Check as a class.
• Ask students to read the story. Check understanding by asking: *Who stole the car? Where did they stop for petrol? Why did the owner of the petrol station call the police? How far did they chase the joyriders? How did they catch them?*
• Students can work individually. Let them use the list of irregular verbs at the back of the Workbook. Check as a class.

KEY

1 had stolen
2 had (then) stopped
3 had not paid

4 had run out of
5 had realised
6 had ordered

Exercise 6 page 85

• Put the following on the board:
I was upset because I had failed the exam.
I was upset because I didn't know the answer to the exam question.
• Make sure students understand how to use the past perfect by asking: *In which sentence was the speaker upset during the exam? In which sentence was the speaker upset after the exam? Which tense do we use to talk about earlier events? Can we use the past perfect to talk about events which happen at the same time?*
• Students work individually. Allow 3 minutes. Get class feedback.
• **Fast finishers** can be offered more sentences to finish, e.g. *I didn't know that …, I wanted to cry because …*, etc.

Exercise 7 page 85

• Read the instructions and examples as a class.
• Allow 30 seconds for students to write down their own idea. Tell them not to copy the examples.

Exercise 8 page 85

• Students read the instructions individually.
• In a **weaker class**, you can ask students to play the game in groups of 4–6 first.
• Play as a class. If the sentence gets too long for students to repeat, start all over again with another student. Make sure everybody has taken part.

➡ Lesson outcome

Ask students: *What have you learned today? What can you do now?* and elicit answers: *I can describe an event using different past tenses. I have learned how to use the past perfect.*

9C CULTURE
Sherlock Holmes

LESSON SUMMARY ●●●●○

Reading: an article about Sherlock Holmes; true/false questions
Listening: a story – putting events in order
Speaking: asking and answering about crime stories
Topic: literature

SHORTCUT

To do the lesson in 30 minutes, skip the Lead-in and exercise 6. Focus on the reading and listening tasks and do not spend much time teaching vocabulary. Keep a fast pace.

➡ Lead-in 3–5 minutes
- Inform the class of the lesson objectives.
- Ask students in pairs to write down the names of famous detectives – real ones and characters from books and films. Allow 2 minutes. Get feedback.
- Ask: *What are detectives like?* Brainstorm typical features and put them on the board. If students lack ideas, prompt them with suitable and unsuitable adjectives to choose from. Use lesson 1A for ideas.

Exercise 1 page 86
- Put the following on the board: *deerstalker, pipe*. Explain the meaning. Ask a student to describe the photo.
- Elicit anything the students know about the character, Sherlock Holmes.

KEY
fictional

Exercise 2 page 86
- Ask students to scan the text to find a description of Holmes. Explain any new vocabulary in the exercise. What else can they say about the character in the photo now?
- Focus students on the task. Explain that one of the sentences 1–4 is not completely true. Allow 2–3 minutes for individual work. Check as a class.

KEY
4

Exercise 3 page 86
- Do not pre-teach any vocabulary from paragraphs 1, 2 and 4.
- Students work individually for 5 minutes. Let them compare their answers in pairs before checking as a class.
- **Fast finishers** can work on collocations. Put the following on the board and ask students to find nouns which complete the phrases: *detective* (story), *spare* (time), *private* (detective), *deerstalker* (hat), *magnifying* (glass), *dark* (side), *everyday* (life), *short* (story).

KEY
1 T 2 F 3 F 4 T 5 T 6 F

Exercise 4 page 86 🎧 2.31
- Explain *speckled* (lightly spotted) and *band* (a thin flat strip of colour or pattern). Ask students to guess what they think the title refers to. Do not give any answers at the moment.

- Ask students to read the task carefully and underline the characters in the story. Put the list on the board: *Helen Stoner, her mother, her father, her sister Julia, Doctor Roylott, a servant*. Elicit what is the relationship between Helen and Doctor Roylott (he married her mother who was a widow; he's Helen's step-father).
- Read the listening tip with the class. Ask them to read the events again and think logically about the order of the events.
- Play the recording twice. Students listen and mark their answers. Check in class.

KEY
1 Her father dies.
2 Her mother marries Doctor Roylott.
3 Somebody burgles their house in India.
4 Doctor Roylott murders a servant.
5 Doctor Roylott goes to prison.
6 The family returns to England.
7 Helen's mother dies.
8 Helen's twin sister, Julia, dies in her bedroom.

Transcript 2.31

At 7.15 in the morning, Sherlock Holmes wakes Doctor Watson and tells him that there is a visitor downstairs: a young woman called Helen Stoner. She is very frightened, and she has come to see Sherlock Holmes to ask for help. He asks her to explain why she is frightened.

Helen Stoner tells Holmes that she lives in the south of England with her step-father, Doctor Roylott. Doctor Roylott met Helen's mother, a widow, when they were both in India. Her father had died a few months earlier. Helen and her twin sister Julia were only two years old when their mother married Doctor Roylott.

Helen Stoner explains to Holmes that her step-father is a violent man. While they were living in India, somebody burgled their house and Doctor Roylott was so angry that he murdered one of his own servants. He spent a long time in prison for his crime. Then he came back to England with his wife and daughters. Soon after they got back to England, Helen's mother died in an accident. This was eight years ago.

Six years later, the sisters were no longer children. Julia was planning to get married. One evening, two weeks before the wedding, Helen was in Julia's room, talking to her. Julia mentioned a strange sound – a whistle – that she sometimes heard at night. Helen said she hadn't heard it. She left the room and went to bed. Later that night, Helen woke up when she heard her sister scream. She ran to Julia's room. Julia opened the door. She was in terrible pain. She said something about a 'speckled band'. Their step-father came, but he couldn't do anything to help Julia. She died in a few minutes. What had she meant when she talked about the speckled band? It was a mystery.

Exercise 5 page 86 🎧 2.32
- Ask students what they think has happened to Julia and what happens next in the story. Encourage them to share ideas but do not comment on them.
- Pre-teach *a whistle, a rope, a stick, a scream*. Play the recording once. Check answers.
- If students are not sure, play the recording again. Ask more questions, for example: *Why is the story called* The Speckled Band? *How did Holmes discover the mystery?*
- Return to the students' predictions about the title. What do they think it refers to now? (The snake, the pattern on its skin.)

KEY
1 Dr Roylott trained a poisonous snake which went down the rope from his room to her bedroom and killed her.
2 When Holmes hits the rope with his stick, it scares the snake which goes back to Dr Roylott's room and bites him. He dies within 10 seconds.

Transcript 2.32

Now, two years later, Helen is planning to get married. She is frightened because she has started to hear a strange sound at night – a whistle – just like her sister mentioned before she died! Helen thinks that her own life is now in danger too.
Sherlock Holmes visits the house. He examines the room where Julia was sleeping when she died. He notices that there is a rope by the bed. This room is now Helen's bedroom. Gradually, Holmes works out what has happened. He agrees that Helen's life is in danger and tells her that she cannot sleep in the room tonight. Holmes and Watson wait in the room overnight, while Helen sleeps in another room. For hours, nothing happens. Then suddenly they hear a whistle. Holmes jumps up and hits the rope by the bed with his stick. A few seconds later, they hear a terrible scream. They go next door and find Dr Roylott sitting in a chair, dead. Around his head is something that looks like a band of speckled or spotty material. Then it moves. It's a snake! Holmes recognises it as the most poisonous kind of snake in India.
Holmes reveals that it was Doctor Roylott who murdered Julia and was planning to murder Helen. He had brought the snake back from India and trained it to go from his room, down the rope, to the other bedroom. He gave it instructions by whistling! When Holmes frightened the snake by hitting the rope with his stick, it went back and attacked Doctor Roylott. One bite was enough to kill him in ten seconds.

Exercise 6 page 86

- Students can work in groups of 3–4. Allow 5 minutes. Share ideas as a class.

➡ Lesson outcome

Ask students: *What have you learned today? What can you do now?* and elicit answers: *I can understand a story about a fictional character. I have learned about Arthur Conan Doyle and his work. I have listened to a Sherlock Holmes story.*

9D GRAMMAR
Reported speech

LESSON SUMMARY ●●●○○
Grammar: reported speech
Reading: funny crime stories
Speaking: reporting what other people said

SHORTCUT *To do the lesson in 30 minutes, skip exercises 4, 7 and 8.*

➡ Lead-in 5 minutes

- Inform the class of the lesson objectives.
- Dictate the following: a *bank form, a queue, a robbery, a bank assistant, spelling mistakes.* If necessary, spell the words and explain the meaning.
- Ask students in pairs to talk and invent a story using all the words. Allow 3 minutes. Share ideas as a class.

Exercise 1 page 87

- Students read the story individually. Elicit the answer.

KEY

No, he wasn't.

Exercise 2 page 87

- Read the instructions as a class. Explain *quotation* (a sentence which somebody else said).
- Allow a minute for individual work. Check as a class.
- Elicit which sentences (the quotations or the underlined sentences) are examples of reported speech.

KEY

1 He ... said that he was robbing a bank. (the robber)
2 She said that he was in the Wells Fargo Bank. (the bank assistant)
3 She said that he needed to take the form to the Bank of America. (the bank assistant)
4 She told the police that a man had tried to rob the bank. (the bank assistant)

Exercise 3 page 87

- Focus students on the underlined sentences and the quotations again. Elicit what tenses are used. Students note them down.
- Go through the questions in the *Learn this!* box as a class. Elicit the answers. Ask students to read out the pair of sentences which illustrate each rule.

KEY

1 b 2 b 3 a 4 b

LANGUAGE NOTE – REPORTED SPEECH

The guidelines presented in the Student's Book mention that the verbs *usually* go back one tense. If somebody said something that is still true when it is reported, the tenses don't always change:

He said that he liked / likes techno music.

Draw attention to the fact that we can use *say* and *tell* in reported speech. *Tell* must have a personal object but *say* doesn't need one.

Point out that *that* after *say* or *tell* is optional.

Exercise 4 page 87

- Read the instructions and analyse the example as a class.
- In a **weaker class**, let students read Grammar Reference 9.3 on page 121. Then identify the tenses in sentences 1–8 as a class.
- Students can work in pairs for 2 minutes. Check as a class.

KEY

2 He said that she had stolen a CD from the music shop.
3 She said that the police had arrested a drug dealer.
4 He said that he went joyriding at weekends.
5 The policeman said that they were questioning two teenagers about the burglary.
6 My sister said that a boy in her class had vandalised a phone box.
7 Mark said that Jake was a drug dealer.
8 She said that the police were looking for the bank robbers.

For more practice on reported speech go to:

Grammar Builder 9D: Student's Book page 120

KEY

3
2	had stolen	6	was
3	were selling	7	had robbed
4	was getting	8	stole
5	had smashed		

4 1 she 2 they 3 he, his 4 me, I 5 he, her

5
2 Fiona said that she hadn't had any breakfast.
3 Fiona said that she wanted a banana.
4 Fiona said that she was going out.
5 Fiona said that her friend was meeting her at the cinema.
6 Fiona said that her friend's name was Tom.
7 Fiona said that she had first met him last year.
8 Fiona said that they were going to see a Johnny Depp film.

6
2 'Last month joyriders stole my car,' she said.
3 'I need a holiday,' he said.
4 'I am going to Tom's party this evening,' you said.
5 'I saw the robbers leaving the bank,' he said.
6 'You are greedy,' she said.
7 'I've had lunch,' you said.
8 'I'm feeling ill,' he said.

Exercise 5   page 87
- Ask students to take it in turns around the class to say different English verbs.
- Students write sentences individually.

Exercise 6   page 87
- Students practise reporting in pairs for 2 minutes.
- Check answers as a class. Instruct students in pairs to speak loud and clear. Other students listen and correct any mistakes.

Exercise 7   page 87
- Pre-teach *to get in/out of the car, to run away, to fit, to point out, terrified, frightened, nearby, accidentally.*
- Students can work in pairs. In a **stronger class**, they can work individually.

KEY
The old lady said to the men, 'You're sitting in my car.'
She said, 'I want you to get out!'
The old lady said to her friend, 'It's the wrong key. It doesn't fit!'
Than she said, 'This is not my car!'
The old lady and her friend said to the police officer, 'We accidentally stole a car.'
The police officer said, 'The four men arrived at the police station a few minutes ago and reported the theft of the car by two dangerous old ladies.'

LANGUAGE NOTE – QUOTATION MARKS
Explain that speech marks are called 'quotation marks' or 'inverted commas'.

The rules for writing direct speech are as follows:

Speech marks can be single or double: ' ' or " ".

What people actually say starts and finishes with speech marks.

If the reporting sentence continues, there is a comma before the closing speech marks.

The reporting verb, e.g. *said,* can go before or after the subject if it is a noun.

'The thief was arrested,' said John.
'The thief was arrested,' John said.

Exercise 8   page 87
- Students can work in groups of 4–5: two ladies, two men and a police officer. Ask them to prepare lines for all actors in a group. Allow 5 minutes for writing and rehearsing.

OPTIONAL ACTIVITY – CONTRADICTIONS
Reported speech is often used to contradict another person. Practise using reported speech in this context by saying statements to the class and asking students to contradict you.

Examples

T: *I can't come to the party.* SS: *But you said you could come to the party.*

T: *The exam's in June.* SS: *But you said the exam was in July.*

Ask students to write five sentences. They read them out to their partner who contradicts them.

➡ Lesson outcome
Ask students: *What have you learned today? What can you do now?* and elicit answers: *I can report what other people have said. I have learned about reported speech.*

9E READING
Computer crime

LESSON SUMMARY ●●●○○
Reading: an article about computer crime; multiple choice
Vocabulary: extreme adjectives
Speaking: discussing computer crime
Topic: people and society

SHORTCUT *To do the lesson in 30 minutes, skip one stage from the Lead-in and keep the planning and discussion in exercises 6 and 7 brief.*

➡ Lead-in 5 minutes
- Inform the class of the lesson objectives.
- Ask students in small groups to note down vocabulary related to computers. Allow 2 minutes. When the time is up, ask a strong student from each group to write their lists on the board.
- While they are writing, ask the class what crimes can be committed using computers. If necessary, prompt with questions: *Can you rob a bank using a computer? Can you steal from a person? Can you vandalise a place? Can you deal drugs?* etc.
- Read the words from the board as a class. Correct any mistakes.

Exercise 1 page 88
- Remind students that scanning the text for information without focusing on unknown vocabulary is an important examination skill.
- Allow 30 seconds. Check as a class. Ask a student to read the relevant sentence from the text: *He was found guilty of putting the terrible 'Sasser' computer virus on the Internet and received a 21-month suspended sentence.*
- Elicit the meaning of *guilty* and *suspended sentence*.

KEY
2

CULTURE NOTE – LEGAL TERMS
Criminal damage is a legal term for the crime of damaging somebody's property deliberately.

A *suspended sentence* is a punishment given to a criminal in court which means that they will only go to prison if they commit another crime within a particular time.

Exercise 2 page 88
- In a **weaker class**, pre-teach any unknown vocabulary used in the questions, e.g. *to spread, to admit, guilt, to release, to cause damage, to be caught, a reward.* In a **stronger class**, instruct students to read the question, locate the relevant fragment of the text, compare vocabulary in the text and in the questions and work out the meaning.
- Allow up to 10 minutes. Focus **fast finishers** on the photos below the text and ask: *What information do you get from the photos? Are computer viruses dangerous?* Students write sentences in their notebooks.
- Check the multiple-choice questions as a class.

KEY
1 b 2 a 3 c 4 a 5 b

Exercise 3 page 88
- Students work individually for a minute. The first student to match all adjectives reads them out to the class.

KEY
1	vital	6	delighted
2	enormous	7	terrible
3	tiny	8	terrific
4	astonished	9	terrified
5	brilliant		

Exercise 4 page 89 🎧 2.33
- Explain that in communication using correct intonation is as important as using correct words. You may demonstrate it by reading the questions in the bubbles with flat intonation.
- Play the recording for students to repeat.

PRONUNCIATION – INTONATION
When using extreme adjectives the stress is strong and intonation high to show strong feeling. People often use a flat voice with strong adjectives to mean the opposite, e.g. *great* or *brilliant* as a response to something bad: *He's lost his keys. Great.* If students don't add extra stress and high intonation to the adjective they will sound as if they don't mean it.

Exercise 5 page 89 🎧 2.34
- Students work in pairs for a minute. Then instruct them to change roles and go over the questions again.
- Play the recording for students to check and repeat. If they need more practice, play it again. Stop after each question, ask a student to respond, than play the response.

Transcript 2.34
1 Is Jane's computer very small?
  Small? It's tiny!
2 Were you happy with your exam results?
  Happy? I was delighted!
3 Is this information important?
  Important? It's vital!
4 Is she clever?
  Clever? She's brilliant!
5 Are you scared of spiders?
  Scared? I'm terrified!
6 Was the film bad?
  Bad? It was terrible!
7 Is their house big?
  Big? It's enormous!

Exercise 6 page 89
- Focus students on the photos.
- Write two example sentences on the board to refresh the second conditional: *If a virus caused every computer system in the country to crash, we wouldn't do any shopping / driving would become dangerous.*
- In a **weaker class**, work together. Feed in any necessary vocabulary.
- In a **stronger class**, students can work in pairs. Get feedback.

Exercise 7 page 89

- Ask students to read the instructions on their own.
- Allow 5 minutes for pairwork.
- Share ideas as a class. If there is time left, have a short class discussion.

→ Lesson outcome

Ask students: *What have you learned today? What can you do now?* and elicit answers: *I can understand and react to an article about a crime. I have learned extreme adjectives and how to use them. I have learned about computer viruses.*

EVERYDAY ENGLISH
Reporting a theft

LESSON SUMMARY ●●●●○

Vocabulary: words to describe lost property
Functional English: reporting and describing lost property
Listening: dialogues – multiple choice
Speaking: reporting a theft
Topic: people and society

SHORTCUT *To do the lesson in 30 minutes, skip the Lead-in and exercise 6. Keep a fast pace.*

→ Lead-in 3–5 minutes

- Inform the class of the lesson objectives.
- Play a game with the class. Tell students that you have ten things in your bag and you want them to guess what they are. The things are all typical (e.g. a pen, a pencil, a wallet, identification, keys, a book, a notebook, a pocket calendar, a packet of tissues). Each student can ask one *yes/no* question, for example: *Do you have a pen in your bag?* When everyone has had a turn, tell students the things they didn't guess.
- Students can do the same in pairs now. Each asks ten questions to find out what their partner keeps in their schoolbag. At the end students tell each other what else is there.
- Share answers as a class. Who guessed the most items? Are there any unusual things students admit to carrying with them?

Exercise 1 page 90 🎧 2.35

- Ask students what bags are made of. Elicit or teach *canvas, leather, plastic,* etc.
- Play the recording for students to listen and read.
- In a **weaker class**, work on pronunciation of the more difficult words, e.g. *details, café, straight, identification.*
- Elicit answers.
- In a **stronger class**, focus students on the picture and the lesson title. What else can they say about Sarah? What is she doing at the police station?

KEY

Sarah's bag.
In a café about an hour ago.

Exercise 2 page 90

- Read the instructions and the information box as a class. Explain any new vocabulary.
- Students in pairs read the dialogue twice, changing roles. Allow 2 minutes.

Exercise 3 page 90 🎧 2.36

- Go over the items with the class. Explain any new words.
- Play the recording once. Check as a class.

KEY

Lenka: wallet, £9, credit cards, traveller's cheques
Malcolm: mobile phone, bus pass

Transcript 2.36

1
Officer	Good morning. Can I help you?
Lenka	Good morning. Yes, someone has stolen my wallet from my bag.
Officer	OK. Can you give me your name, please?
Lenka	Lenka Paulerova. That's P-A-U-L-E-R-O-V-A.
Officer	Thank you. Now, when did this happen?
Lenka	I noticed it was missing about half an hour ago. I was going to pay for some postcards and it wasn't there.
Officer	What was in the wallet?
Lenka	About £9, my credit cards ... oh yes and some traveller's cheques.
Officer	OK. You should ring your credit card company and tell them what's happened. They'll stop the card so that nobody can use it.
Lenka	OK.
Officer	And you need to get in touch with your bank and tell them about the travellers' cheques.
Lenka	OK.
Officer	Can you describe the wallet?
Lenka	Yes, it's black, made of leather.
Officer	OK. I'll just take some more details. Where are you staying?

2
Officer	Good afternoon.
Malcolm	Hello. I'd like to report a theft.
Officer	Oh yes?
Malcolm	Someone has stolen my mobile. Actually they took my schoolbag, but I found the schoolbag later. They'd thrown it into someone's garden. But the mobile was missing.
Officer	The mobile was in the bag?
Malcolm	Yes.
Officer	What was the make and model?
Malcolm	It was a Nokia 6060.
Officer	Colour?
Malcolm	Black.
Officer	Have you phoned your network?
Malcolm	No, not yet.
Officer	Well, you must do that as soon as possible. Now, did they take anything else from the bag?
Malcolm	Yes, my bus pass ... Do you think I'll get the mobile back?
Officer	I'm afraid it's unlikely. Now, could you fill in this form, please?

Exercise 4 page 90 🎧 2.36

- Ask students to read the questions carefully. Allow a minute.
- Play the recording again. Check as a class. If students have problems answering, play the recording a third time, pausing to check each question.

KEY

1 b 2 b 3 c 4 a 5 b 6 c

Exercise 5 page 90

- Allow 3–5 minutes to prepare and rehearse a dialogue. Ask students to make notes on the chart rather than write full dialogues in their notebooks.
- **Fast finishers** can prepare another dialogue describing unusual or funny lost property, e.g. a pet, a younger brother, a take-away pizza, etc.

Exercise 6 page 90

- Ask as many pairs as possible to present their dialogue to the class.
- If there is time left, ask students if they have ever reported stolen property, if they have ever got anything back, etc. What advice would they give to people who have had something stolen?

➡ Lesson outcome

Ask students: *What have you learned today? What can you do now?* and elicit answers: *I can describe a stolen item and report a theft. I have learned words for the items which get stolen.*

Notes for Photocopiable activity 9.1

The O.A.P. shoplifter

Pairwork
Language: past perfect, reported speech and crime vocabulary
Materials: one copy of the cut-up worksheet per pair of students (Teacher's Book page 140)

- An information gap activity in the form of a mutual dictation where students dictate alternate sentences to each other and then rearrange the sentences to make a news story.
- If necessary, pre-teach the following vocabulary:
  O.A.P. bite pensioner harm
- Divide the class into pairs of Student A and Student B. Give a copy of worksheet A to all Students A and worksheet B to all Students B. Explain that they each have half of the sentences from a news story. They must not look at each other's worksheets.
- Student A dictates the first line for B to write down. Student B dictates the second line and so on. They shouldn't spell out any words except for names.
- When they have finished dictating the sentences, students compare what they have written with the original.
- Finally, they arrange the lines in order to form a news story.

Alternative procedure – shouting dictation

- As an alternative method to the standard dictation method, organise the desks so that Student As are sitting at a distance from Student Bs. They then have to shout their sentences to their partners. Point out that this is useful practice for them since it creates a situation that they might face in the future where the listening conditions are not ideal, e.g. a noisy bar or a poor telephone line.

KEY

1 a An eighty-year-old shoplifter tried to escape arrest
2 e by biting a policeman before he realised that
3 j he had left his false teeth at home
4 c Gilles Durand attacked the policeman who
5 h caught the man as he ran out of an electrical shop in Marseilles after he
6 b had stolen a box of CDs.
7 i But, instead of biting the police officer's arms
8 k he was only able to leave a wet mark from his mouth.
9 f Police spokesman Jean-Claude Rousseau said the pensioner
10 g had tried to bite the police officer several times but
11 d hadn't caused him any harm.

9G WRITING
A story

LESSON SUMMARY ●●●●●
Reading: a crime story
Vocabulary: time expressions
Writing: a crime story
Topic: people and society

SHORTCUT *To do the lesson in 30 minutes, skip the Lead-in. Do the translation in exercise 3 and the whole of exercise 4 as a class. Skip the pairwork practice in exercise 5.*

➡ Lead-in 3 minutes

- Inform the class of the lesson objectives.
- Divide the class into two teams and quickly revise irregular past verb forms. For each team in turn, say a verb and elicit the past simple and past participle forms. Award a point for each correct answer. Now and then, interrupt the flow by calling for a sentence using the verb in one form or the other, for which the team scores a bonus point. Include verbs which students will use in the lesson: *steal, find, buy, give, get, go, ring, see, send, leave.*

Exercise 1 page 91

- Write the story title (*The careless thief*) on the board. Elicit the meaning of *careless*. Then ask: *What sort of story do you expect this to be? Sad? Funny? Tragic? Frightening?*
- Before students read, establish the meaning of *sat nav, insurance company* and *online auction.*

KEY

Because a thief had stolen his old sat nav system from his car.

Exercise 2 page 91

- Make it clear to students that they need to work out the order in which the events happened. This is different from the order in which they appear in the story.
- Students work in pairs. Ask them to guess any unknown words from the context.
- Check as a class, and elicit the meaning of *second-hand, locked/unlocked, refuse, replace, astonished, collect.*

KEY

1 Jeremy left his car unlocked.
2 A thief stole Jeremy's sat nav system.
3 The insurance company refused to pay for a new sat nav system.
4 Jeremy found an auction site that had sat nav systems for sale.
5 Jeremy saw his own sat nav system for sale and bought it.
6 Jeremy sent an e-mail to the thief.
7 Jeremy rang the police.
8 A police officer went to the thief's house and arrested him.
9 Jeremy got his old sat nav system back.

Exercise 3 page 91

- When students have found the expressions, ask them to discuss translations in pairs before checking as a class. Ask **fast finishers** to find another expression which is not in the list (*the next day*).
- Elicit other words that can replace the words in brackets (e.g. one <u>day/morning</u>, an <u>hour/six months/three years</u> earlier, the following <u>morning/year</u>).

KEY

All expressions except *soon*, *at first* and *while* are in the story.

Exercise 4 page 91

- Students work individually. Check as a class.

KEY

1	immediately	4	At first, in the end
2	a week earlier	5	as soon as
3	as		

Exercise 5 page 91

- Read the tip and emphasise the importance of time expressions when telling a story. They are signals telling the reader when things happened and linking one event with the next.
- Work as a class, with students taking it in turns to tell part of the story. In a **weaker class**, write the verbs from exercise 2 on the board for reference.
- Ask students to retell the story in pairs.

Exercise 6 page 91

- Make sure that students plan before they start to write. When they have made notes in answer to the questions, they should have a basic framework for their story. Ask them to add information about the time and place.
- Allow 15 minutes for the writing. Go round giving help where needed. Encourage **stronger students** to use descriptive techniques to enrich their writing. This could mean adding details about the appearance of the people and the place or using adverbs and strong verbs to describe actions.
- Tell students to check their work, using the checklist.
- If you have time, ask a few students to read out their stories to the class. Give feedback.

> ### ALTERNATIVE WRITING TASK
>
> Write a story of 130–150 words about a dangerous situation that you had to face. It can be a real situation or an imaginary one. Write four paragraphs:
>
> 1 What were you doing at the time? What had you done before that?
> 2 What happened? Why was it dangerous?
> 3 What happened next? How did you feel?
> 4 How did you escape from the situation?

➡ Lesson outcome

- Ask students: *What have you learned today? What can you do now?* and elicit answers: *I can write a crime story. I have learned to use time expressions to tell a story.*

Notes for Photocopiable activity 9.2

Crime questionnaire

Group work

Language: crime vocabulary, functional language for expressing opinions

Materials: one copy of the worksheet per student (Teacher's Book page 141)

- If necessary, pre-teach the following vocabulary: *capital punishment   hit   chewing gum   illegal*
- Give each student a copy of the worksheet and ask them to read the sentences and tick the correct column according to the scale shown.
- Read the first statement and ask if anybody agrees or disagrees strongly. Ask them to explain why. Encourage a discussion across the class. Next elicit language for giving opinions, agreeing and disagreeing and write it on the board for students to refer to during the activity.
  Giving opinions
  I think/don't think … should
  In my opinion …
  Agreeing
  I agree (with you).
  I think so too.
  Absolutely.
  Disagreeing
  I don't agree./I disagree (with you).
  Do you think so? (polite)
  That's rubbish! (strong disagreement and not polite)
- Students work in groups of 2–4. They take it in turn to read the statements and discuss them with the others in the group, giving reasons for their opinions.

EXAM For further exam tasks and practice, go to Workbook page 88. Procedural notes, transcripts and keys for the Workbook can be found on the *Solutions* Teacher's Website at www.oup.com/elt/teacher/solutions.

Get ready for your EXAM 9

TOPIC ●●●○

Nature and the environment

➜ Lead-in 2–4 minutes

- Inform the class of the lesson objectives.
- Elicit words for natural disasters from the class. Which disasters do they remember from the news? Where did they happen?

Exercise 1 page 92 2–4 minutes

- Students can work in pairs. Check as a class.
- Work on the pronunciation with the class.

KEY

1 hurricane   2 flood   3 earthquake   4 forest fire

Exercise 2 page 92 🎧 2.37 10 minutes

E Listening: true/false statements

- Refer students to the listening tip in lesson 8F, exercise 3. Point out that in listening comprehension tasks students should focus on the information they understand as it is often enough to answer the questions. Explain that thinking about the unknown words while listening to the recording is pointless and distracting.
- Ask students to read the sentences individually. Encourage them to try to predict the answers using their general knowledge and logical thinking.
- Play the recording twice, pausing for 15 seconds before and after the second listening.
- Check as a class. Elicit corrections of the false sentences.

KEY

1 T   2 F   3 T   4 T   5 F

Transcript 🎧 2.37

Presenter	Good evening and welcome to *Earthwatch*. In the programme tonight, we're going to talk about hurricanes. In the studio with me is Professor Rachel Keane. Welcome to the programme, Professor.
Prof Keane	Thank you.
Presenter	Professor, what exactly is a hurricane?
Prof Keane	Well, a hurricane is a very powerful storm. You only find hurricanes in the tropics, where there is very warm water, and they always start out at sea.
Presenter	And when do we use the word 'hurricane', as opposed to just 'storm'?
Prof Keane	When the winds in a tropical storm reach speeds of over 115 km/h, we call it a hurricane. Every year about 50 tropical storms become hurricanes.
Presenter	And how dangerous are they?
Prof Keane	Hurricanes cause strong winds, enormous waves, and heavy flooding. In 2005, Hurricane Katrina produced 175 km/h winds, killed over 1,600 people and devastated the southern states of America, in particular New Orleans.
Presenter	We give hurricanes names, like Katrina or Gilbert. Why is that?
Prof Keane	It helps us to identify them and to keep track of them. Each year there's a list of 26 names, one name for each letter of the alphabet. So for example, the first four Atlantic hurricanes in 2007 were Andrea, Barry, Chantal and Dean. They alternate boys' and girls' names.
Presenter	How do hurricanes happen?
Prof Keane	Well, imagine a beautiful, blue, warm tropical ocean ... as the sun heats it, the warm water evaporates and

rises quickly into the air. As the air rises, it turns around and around. This creates low pressure in the centre – this is the eye of the storm. You can clearly see the eye of a hurricane on a satellite photo. It's relatively calm in the eye of a hurricane, but around the eye you have very strong winds, thunder and lightning, and incredibly heavy rain, moving very slowly across the ocean.

Presenter	Hurricanes move slowly, then?
Prof Keane	Oh, yes. At about 30 to 40 km/h. But when they hit land they cause terrible flooding if the coast is very flat. The flooding is caused by the low pressure at the eye of the hurricane. It lifts the surface of the sea by up to four metres ...
Presenter	The sea actually rises?
Prof Keane	Yes, in the centre of the hurricane the water is higher, and the storm pushes the water along. When it reaches shallow water near the coast, huge waves form and flood the land. We call this a storm surge. In addition to the storm surge, the torrential rain can also cause flooding. It can be devastating.
Presenter	And do they travel inland?
Prof Keane	Not very far, no. They need warm water to power themselves, so they quickly lose strength.
Presenter	Thank you very much, Professor Keane. And now the weather forecast for tomorrow ...

Exercise 3 page 92 3–4 minutes

- Elicit answers to the questions. Encourage students to think about their own situations after a big storm, forest fire or flood. What disaster would be the most devastating in their area?

Exercise 4 page 92 2–4 minutes

- Read the words as a class, working on the pronunciation.
- Students can work in pairs. Check as a class. To elicit other words for geographical features, ask students to think of different regions in their own country and elsewhere in the world.

KEY

1 mountains	4 river
2 forest	5 lake
3 sand dunes	6 island

not illustrated: cave

Exercise 5 page 92 4–5 minutes

- Explain the meaning of *crops*, *drown*, *rise*, *river bank*, *starve*, and model the pronunciation for students to repeat.
- Do the matching as a class, accepting a variety of answers. Elicit short sentences using the words to describe one photo or the other.

KEY

Suggested answers

Photo 1: boat, drown, flood, rise

Photo 2: drought, dry

The other words could be used for either photo.

Exercise 6 page 92 4 minutes

- Students can work in pairs on the sentences.
- Check students' understanding of the structures. Ask: *Which sentence describes the present situation?* (1) *Which describes an event in the recent past?* (5) *Which describes a past action?* (3) *Which describes a situation that started in*

the past and still exists now? (4) *Which describes a possibility in the future?* (2) Ask these questions in the students' language if you prefer.

KEY

1	c (both)	4	d (drought)
2	e (flood)	5	b (flood)
3	a (flood)		

Exercise 7 page 92 10–12 minutes
E Speaking: picture-based discussion

- As revision, quickly brainstorm useful expressions for describing a photo and giving opinions (e.g. *In the first photo there is / I can see ..., The people are ...ing, They look ..., They must be ..., I think ..., In my opinion ..., Perhaps ...*).
- Give students 3 minutes to plan what they will say. Ask them to do this without making notes.
- Put students in pairs. Student A speaks for 1–2 minutes while student B listens. Allow 2 minutes for pair discussion afterwards. Then ask them to form new A/B pairs and repeat the task, with B speaking and A listening.
- Ask a strong student to speak in front of the class. Give feedback.

➡ Lesson outcome
- Ask students: *What have you learned today? What can you do now?* and elicit answers: *I have practised a true/false listening task. I have learned some new words connected with natural disasters. I have compared and contrasted photos as a speaking task.*

Get ready for your EXAM 10

TOPIC ●●●○○
People and society

➡ Lead-in 3–4 minutes
- Inform the class of the lesson objectives.
- Write a short list of crimes on the board, e.g. *bank robbery, murder, shoplifting, assault, vandalism*. Ask students to rank them in order from 1 (the most serious) to 5 (the least serious) and to say what penalty they think there should be for each one. Should people go to prison for all/any of these crimes?
- Ask: *What is the purpose of a prison? Do you think there are any disadvantages in locking people in prison? If you were in prison, what would you miss most?* Discuss the questions with the class.

Exercise 1 page 93 4–5 minutes
- Ask students if they have heard of Alcatraz. If possible, elicit some basic information about this prison.
- Students read the sentences and then read the text quickly to find the information. Ask them to read out sentences from the text to show why one answer is true and the other two are false.
- Ask students to cover the text. Elicit any other information they picked up about Alcatraz from their first reading.

KEY
Sentence 3 is true.

Exercise 2 page 93 15 minutes
E Reading: missing sentences

- Read the task as a class. Check comprehension by asking: *Where do the seven sentences come from? What do you have to do with them? Where do you write your answer? What do you write in the box?*
- Explain that to do this type of matching task, it is crucial to understand the text well. Instruct students to read it through again carefully, trying to work out unknown vocabulary.
- Ask students to consider the topic of each paragraph – this will help them to predict what kind of information is missing. Elicit the following topics for this text:
  Paragraph 1: introduction to Alcatraz
  Paragraph 2: location and early history
  Paragraph 3: prisoners' conditions
  Paragraph 4: escapes from Alcatraz
  Paragraph 5: conclusion
- Students read sentences a–h and connect them with the paragraph topics. They match seven of the sentences with the numbered gaps. Tell them to read each completed paragraph to check that each sentence fits. Finally, advise them to check that the remaining sentence does not fit any of the gaps.
- Ask **fast finishers** to compare answers in pairs and then to check the meaning of new words.

KEY
1 d 2 h 3 b 4 c 5 f 6 a 7 g

Exercise 3 page 93 6 minutes
- Refer back to the text as necessary to elicit the meaning of new words in the list. Practise the pronunciation.
- Students work in pairs. Ask them to make sentences using the words to describe one photo or the other, or to describe similarities between them.
- Check with the class and elicit other useful words.

KEY
Suggested answers
Photo 1: cell, clothes, food, guard, lonely, prison, prisoner, punish, uniform, visitor
Photo 2: clothes, food, free, happy

Exercise 4 page 93 10 minutes
E Speaking: picture-based discussion

- Read the task as a class. Point out that here students should focus on one photo in detail first. Tell them not to spend too long on this, however – they must leave room to make a comparison between the photos.
- Remind students to use the present continuous to describe what people are doing in a photo.
- Students plan and then take it turns to speak and listen, working in two different pairs. See the teaching notes above for *Get ready for your exam 9*, exercise 7.
- Choose two students to speak in front of the class, each starting with a different picture. Give feedback

➡ Lesson outcome
- Ask students: *What have you learned today? What can you do now?* and elicit answers: *I have practised fitting missing sentences into a reading text. I have learned some new words connected with prisons. I have compared and contrasted photos as a speaking task.*

10 The written word

THIS UNIT INCLUDES ●●●○
Vocabulary • publications • books and text • styles of fiction • bookshop departments • talking about stories
Grammar • the passive (present simple) • the passive (other tenses)
Speaking • talking about reading habits • in a bookshop
Writing • a book review
WORKBOOK pages 90–96 • Self check 10 page 97

A VOCABULARY AND LISTENING
Publications

LESSON SUMMARY ●●●●○
Vocabulary: publications
Listening: a dialogue; multiple-choice
Speaking: asking and answering about reading habits
Topic: literature and entertainment

SHORTCUT *To do the lesson in 30 minutes, set exercises 1 and 2 and Vocabulary Builder (part 1) for homework.*

➡ Lead-in 3–5 minutes
• Inform the class of the lesson objectives.
• Ask students to think of the advantages of the fact that they can read. Explain that you want to hear at least as many advantages as there are students in the class. Ask all students the same question: *How is reading useful?* Keep asking until students have run out of ideas.

Exercise 1 page 94
• In a **weaker class**, work as a class. Ask: *Who wrote ...?* and elicit answers.
• In a **stronger class**, students work in pairs. Set it as a contest. The first pair to match the authors with the books reads the answers out to the class. Correct any pronunciation errors for students to repeat.
• Introduce the phrase *was written by* and ask students to use it while reading the answers.

KEY
1 William Shakespeare	5 J. K. Rowling
2 Agatha Christie	6 Stephen King
3 J. R. R. Tolkien	7 Jane Austen
4 Charles Dickens	8 Joseph Conrad

CULTURE NOTE – AUTHORS
Jane Austen (1775–1815) wrote novels about the personal relationships and social life of the English upper middle class. Her best-known books are *Sense and Sensibility, Pride and Prejudice, Emma* and *Persuasion.* Many of her novels have been made into films.

Agatha Christie (1890–1976) wrote 67 books (mainly detective stories) and 16 plays, the most famous of which include *Death on the Nile* and *Murder on the Orient Express.* She created the detectives Hercule Poirot and Miss Marple.

Joseph Conrad (1857–1924) was born Teodor Josef Konrad Korzeniowski in Poland. He left home at 17 to go to sea, where he joined a British ship. He became a British citizen in 1886. His most famous novels include *Lord Jim* and *Heart of Darkness.*

Charles Dickens (1812–70) was the author of many books about life in Victorian England which often describe the difficult conditions in which poor people lived. Many of his characters have become famous, such as Scrooge and Fagin. His best-known books include *Oliver Twist, David Copperfield, A Tale of Two Cities* and *Great Expectations.*

Stephen King (1947–) is a very popular writer of horror stories. Several of his books have been made into films, including *Carrie, The Shining, Misery* and *The Shawshank Redemption.*

J. K. Rowling (1965–) is the author of the successful *Harry Potter* series consisting of seven books. The books are *Harry Potter and the Philosopher's Stone, Harry Potter and the Chamber of Secrets, Harry Potter and the Prisoner of Azkaban, Harry Potter and the Goblet of Fire, Harry Potter and the Order of the Phoenix, Harry Potter and the Half Blood Prince* and *Harry Potter and the Deathly Hallows.*

J. R. R. Tolkien (1882–1973) is best known as the author of *The Hobbit* and *The Lord of the Rings.* He was a professor at Oxford University.

William Shakespeare (1564–1616) was a poet and playwright, often considered the best writer in the English language. His plays are performed all over the world. In Britain they are often performed by the Royal Shakespeare Company in Stratford-upon-Avon and at the Globe Theatre in London.

Exercise 2 page 94
• Work as a class. You may wish to ask more questions, for example: *Which of the books have been made into films? Have you seen any of the films? What characters do you remember? What other famous characters did the authors create?* etc.

Exercise 3 page 94 🎧 2.38
• Elicit or explain the meaning of *publications.*
• Focus students on the photos. Elicit what types of books they can name.
• Play the recording once. Students listen and underline the stresses. Play it again for students to repeat.
• Focus students on the photos again. Identify the rest of the books as a class.

KEY
<u>a</u>tlas auto<u>bi</u>ography bi<u>og</u>raphy <u>com</u>ic <u>cook</u>book <u>dic</u>tionary encyclo<u>pae</u>dia <u>guide</u>book maga<u>zine</u> <u>man</u>ual <u>news</u>paper <u>nov</u>el <u>play</u> <u>text</u>book

PRONUNCIATION – THE *SCHWA* /ə/
Explain that the *schwa* is the most common sound in the English language and that it is always in weak or unstressed syllables. Demonstrate how the sound is produced with the mouth muscles in a relaxed position.

Before students repeat the words in exercise 3 ask them to mark the *schwa* sound with a *schwa* symbol.

Key

publicətions atlas(ə) autobiəgraphy(ə) biography(ə) comic
cookbook dictionəry(ə ə) enclyclopaediə(ə) guidebook(ə)
magazine manuəl(ə) newspaper(ə) novel(ə) play textbook

Exercise 4 page 94

• Students can work in pairs. Check as a class.
• To revise the second conditional, ask students to answer with full sentences.

KEY

1 atlas	8 guidebook
2 dictionary	9 cookbook
3 encyclopaedia	10 newspaper
4 manual	11 autobiography
5 magazine	12 biography
6 comic	13 novel
7 textbook	14 play

For more practice on vocabulary related to publications go to:

Vocabulary Builder (part 1): Student's Book page 133

KEY

1
1 guidebook	5 cookbook
2 novel	6 magazine
3 atlas	7 autobiography
4 newspaper	

2
1 manual	5 biography
2 comic	6 play
3 textbook	7 encyclopaedia
4 dictionary	

3 Open answers

Exercise 5 page 94 🎧 2.39

• Read the instructions as a class. Explain that the questionnaire is about reading books. Focus students on the questions.
• In a **stronger class**, ask students in pairs to fill in the gaps before the listening. Play the recording to check.
• In a **weaker class**, students listen and complete the questions. Pause the recording if necessary.

KEY

1 Who are your	4 you like to
2 do you read?	5 would you write
3 do you read?	

Transcript 2.39

India   Hi, Josh. What are you reading?
Josh   It's a magazine article about how to become a famous author.
India   Is it interesting?
Josh   Yes, it is actually. And there's a short questionnaire, too.
India   Great! I love questionnaires. Let's do it. Ask me the first question.
Josh   OK. Who are your favourite authors?
India   Hmm. Stephen King and Agatha Christie.
Josh   How much do you read?
India   Probably about an hour a day.
Josh   When do you read?
India   In the evening, if there's nothing on TV.
Josh   Would you like to write?
India   Yes, I would!
Josh   What would you write about?
India   I'd write books about crime and violence.
Josh   Really?
India   Yes.
Josh   Now you ask me.
India   OK. Who are your favourite authors?

Josh   I like Charles Dickens – and Jane Austen – she's my other favourite.
India   OK. How much do you read?
Josh   About two hours a day.
India   That's a lot!
Josh   Yes, I know!
India   So when do you read?
Josh   I read on the way to school, and on the way home. I get the train to school, so I've got lots of time.
India   Would you like to write?
Josh   Yes, I would.
India   What would you write about?
Josh   I'd write about love and romance and people who …
India   Boring!

Exercise 6 page 94 🎧 2.39

• Allow a minute for students to read the instructions and the task.
• Play the recording once. Students listen and mark their answers. Check as a class.

KEY

India:	1 a	2 a	3 b	4 a	5 a
Josh:	1 b	2 b	3 a	4 a	5 b

Exercise 7 page 94

• Students work in pairs for 3 minutes.
• Share answers. Alternatively, ask students to note their partner's answers on a piece of paper, collect them and read them out to the class in a random order. The pair whose note is being read remains silent. The rest try to guess who the note refers to.

For more practice on vocabulary related to books and text go to

Vocabulary Builder (part 2): Student's Book page 133

KEY

4
1 the back cover	5 a hardback book
2 the spine	6 a paperback book
3 the front cover	7 a chapter
4 the title	8 the contents page

5 (sample answers)
THE FINAL – capital letters	? – question mark
noise – lower case letters	" – quotation marks
. – full stop	– – dash
, – comma	! – exclamation mark

6
1 *A Summer Romance*	4 no
2 the title and author's name	5 five
3 sixteen	

➡ Lesson outcome

Ask students: *What have you learned today? What can you do now?* and elicit answers: *I can identify and talk about different publications. I have learned the titles of famous books written by English and American writers.*

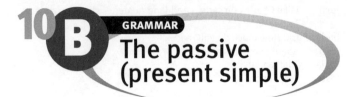

10 B GRAMMAR
The passive (present simple)

LESSON SUMMARY ●●●●●

Grammar: present simple passive
Vocabulary: words for printing and publishing

SHORTCUT *To do the lesson in 30 minutes, do exercise 4 and the Grammar Builder quickly as a class and skip stage 2 in exercise 6. Keep a fast pace.*

➡ Lead-in 3–5 minutes

- Inform the class of the lesson objectives.
- Put the following words on the board: *accuracy, quality, journalism, to appear, to publish, to print.* Ask what kind of publication students associate with the words. Elicit *paper* or *newspaper*. Explain unknown words from the board.
- Ask about newspapers: *What are newspapers for? What kinds of information do we get from them?* Find out how many of your students regularly read newspapers. Ask them why (not).

Exercise 1 page 95

- Focus students on the instructions. Ask different students to read out the numbers. Help and correct if necessary.
- Students read and check the information individually. Check as a class.

KEY

1 *The New York Times* first appeared in 1851.
2 The New York Times Company publishes 40 other newspapers.
3 Over 1.3 million copies of *The New York Times* are printed every day.

Exercise 2 page 95

- In a **weaker class**, work together. Remind students how to form the past participle of regular and irregular verbs.
- In a **stronger class**, students work individually for 30 seconds. Check together.

KEY

to be

Exercise 3 page 95

- Allow 3 minutes to read the instructions and find the examples.
- Answer the questions as a class.

KEY

It is owned by the New York Times Company.
Over 1.3 million copies are printed every day.
It is published online too.

CULTURE NOTE – *THE BIG ISSUE*

The Big Issue has been sold by homeless people in Britain since 1991. The vendors are allowed to keep about half of the money they make from selling it for themselves. The content consists of news about music, films, plays and sport as well as articles about social issues such as homelessness and unemployment. The aim is for homeless people to earn money on the street without begging and to inform people about social issues at the same time. The name of the magazine is a play on words: *Issue* means 'problem' and also 'edition of a newspaper or magazine.'

Exercise 4 page 95

- Students work individually. Allow a minute. Check answers as a class.
- Ask students to read the sentences again and underline vocabulary connected with the press. Explain or elicit the meaning of: e.g. *article, copy, issue, magazine, vendor.* Then check what students have learned about *The Big Issue* by asking: *How often is it published? Who writes some of the articles? Is there a similar magazine in this country?*

KEY

1 is 2 are 3 are 4 is 5 are 6 is 7 is 8 are

For more practice on the present simple passive go to:

Grammar Builder: Student's Book page 122

KEY

1 1 is grown   4 is drunk
   2 are worn   5 is taught
   3 is spoken   6 is eaten

2 1 is contacted   4 are taken
   2 is sent   5 is written
   3 is interviewed   6 is paid

3 1 is grown   5 are sent
   2 are sold   6 are eaten
   3 is spoken   7 is visited
   4 is made

4 1 A lot of paper and cardboard is recycled in Britain.
   2 Books are not sold in this shop.
   3 Camembert cheese is not made in Germany.
   4 Recycled paper is used in newspapers.
   5 Oranges are not grown in Hungary.
   6 Alcohol is not drunk in some Muslim countries.

Exercise 5 page 95 🎧 2.40

- Put the following words on the board and pre-teach them: *tree farm, paper mill, metal sheets, hair dryer, a button, rolls, a lorry.*
- Focus students on the pictures. Can they name any of the things they see?
- Ask students to order the pictures. Allow a moment to think about the task, then play the recording. If necessary, play the recording again. Check as a class.
- Focus students on the sentences. Students work individually for a minute. Check as a class.

KEY

1 Trees are grown on a 'tree farm'. The trees are cut down, then new trees are planted.
2 The wood is taken by lorry to the paper mill where it is cut into very small pieces called 'chips'.
3 The chips are cooked with a lot of water.
4 The mixture is pressed onto large flat metal sheets.
5 The sheets of paper are dried. Then they are put onto big rolls.
6 The rolls of paper are sent to factories where they are made into books, magazines and hundreds of other things.

Transcript 2.40

Owner Hello, and welcome to the tour of this paper mill. I'm going to explain how paper is made. Now, can anyone tell me what paper is made from?

Girl 1 Trees!

Owner That's right. In fact, our company owns a tree farm in Norway. We grow the trees there. When we cut them down, we plant new trees. Anyway, we bring the wood here, to the paper mill. That machine cuts it into very small pieces called 'chips'.

Boy 1 I love chips!

Owner Please, don't touch the machines. They're very dangerous. Hey! Don't touch!

Boy 1 Sorry.

Owner Follow me ... This next machine cooks the chips.

Boy 1 Great!

Owner It cooks them with water. Then the machine over here presses the mixture onto large, flat metal sheets.

Girl 1 How long does it take to dry?

Owner Good question! Not very long at all, because this machine dries it. It's like a giant hair dryer. Please! Don't touch that button ... Step away from that machine!

Boy 1 Sorry.

Owner We put the paper onto enormous rolls. Then we send the rolls to factories where they make books, magazines and hundreds of other things. Right ! Any questions? Yes, you.

Boy 1 I dropped my sandwiches in the machine. Can you get them out?

Exercise 6 page 95

• Allow 5 minutes. Share ideas as a class.
• In a **weaker class**, ask students to note other students' examples, then choose one category and try to memorise all of them. Allow 30 seconds. Ask individual students to say sentences from memory; e.g. *Oranges, grapefruit ... are fruits that aren't grown in this country.* Who can say the longest sentence correctly?
• In a **stronger class**, to make students use the passive, reverse the procedure. Use ideas from the feedback. Name a thing and ask a student to identify the category (1–5), for example:
T: *Cricket*
S: *Cricket is a sport that is not played in this country.*

➡ Lesson outcome

Ask students: *What have you learned today? What can you do now?* and elicit answers: *I can describe the different stages of a process. I have learned to use the passive.*

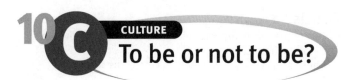

10 C CULTURE
To be or not to be?

LESSON SUMMARY ●●○○○

Reading: an article about Shakespeare; true/false
Vocabulary: types of literature
Listening: interviews; matching
Speaking: talking about writers
Topic: literature

SHORTCUT *To do the lesson in 30 minutes, skip the Lead-in and go through exercise 1 quickly, ask students to do exercises 2 and 3 together in 8 minutes, then check both as a class. Do exercise 7 as a class.*

➡ Lead-in 3–5 minutes

• Inform the class of the lesson objectives.
• Tell students that you want to find out how cultured they are. Dictate and write on the board the questions: *How often do you go to the theatre or watch plays on TV? When did you last read a poem? How many novels do you read a year?* Students note down their answers, then compare in pairs.
• Have a class discussion on the criteria one has to meet to be a cultured person. Does a cultured person see a play once a week/once a year–or is theatre-going not important?

CULTURE NOTE – *TO BE OR NOT TO BE*

To be or not to be: that is the question comes from Hamlet's famous soliloquy (a speech where a character, who is alone on stage, speaks his or her thoughts) in which he contemplates suicide.

Exercise 1 page 96

• Students can work in small groups for 2 minutes noting down all their associations with Shakespeare.
• Share ideas as a class. Ask students to listen carefully and say the things the previous groups did not mention.

Exercise 2 page 96

• Read the instructions and the beginning of the text as a class. Elicit the answer to question 1 (Shakespeare was born in 1564). Explain that some information has to be deduced from the text. Remind students to scan the text quickly, focusing on the task.
• Students work individually, writing/underlining the rest of the sentences.
• Allow 3 minutes. Check as a class.

KEY

1 Shakespeare was born in 1564.
2 At the age of 15 he went to work in his father's business.
3 Anne Hathaway was 26 when he fell in love with her.
4 In 1585 they had twins, Hamnet and Judith.
5 In 1597 he bought a big house in Stratford for his family.
6 Shakespeare wrote 37 plays.

Exercise 3 page 96

- Do not pre-teach any vocabulary. Students work individually for 5–8 minutes.
- Check as a class. Ask students to correct the false sentences.

KEY

1 T 2 T 3 F 4 T 5 T 6 T 7 F 8 T

OPTIONAL ACTIVITY

You can use this idea to occupy **fast finishers** or as a class to make students remember facts from Shakespeare's life. Work with books closed. Put the following numbers on the board: 6, 7, 8, 13, 14, 15, 18, 23, 26, 37, 52, 154, 1564, 1582, 1585, 1592, 1611, 1616. Divide the class into 2–4 groups. Groups take it in turns to choose any number from the board and say what fact it refers to. Keep a fast pace. The group who remember most facts are the winners.

You can play another round using nouns and names; e.g. *John*, *university*, *Susanna*, *London*, *actor*, *house*, *theatre*, etc.

Exercise 4 page 96 🎧 2.41

- Ask students to read the instructions. If necessary, model the pronunciation of the play titles for students to repeat.
- Play the recording once. Check as a class.

KEY

1 c 2 b 3 a

Transcript 2.41

Interviewer	I'm on the streets of Stratford-upon-Avon, where Shakespeare was born and died about 400 years ago. I want to ask some young people what they think of Shakespeare … Hello, excuse me. Can I ask you a couple of questions about Shakespeare?
Andy	Yes, OK.
Interviewer	Have you ever seen a Shakespeare play?
Andy	Yeah, I saw *Hamlet* last year. Our whole class went to see it. We're studying it at school, you see.
Interviewer	What's your opinion of Shakespeare? What do you think of his plays?
Andy	Aw, he's too difficult. I mean, the language is too hard to understand. It's so old-fashioned. I hate it. I just can't understand what it's all about.
Interviewer	OK, thanks for that … Excuse me. Can I ask you, what do you think of Shakespeare? Do you find him very difficult?
Sarah	Well, yes, the language in Shakespeare's plays is difficult, of course, but I have a really good teacher at school who makes it a lot easier. And once you understand the language, you understand how fantastic the stories are. I mean, for example, *Hamlet* is really action-packed and very exciting.
Interviewer	Have you seen any Shakespeare plays?
Sarah	Yes, I've seen *Romeo and Juliet*. We're studying it at school. I've seen *Hamlet* too. You have to see them at the theatre. That's how they should be seen.
Interviewer	OK, thanks very much … Excuse me, I'm just asking young people about Shakespeare. What do you think of Shakespeare? Are his plays interesting?
Mike	Yes, I think so. I mean he writes about important things.
Interviewer	Important things? What, for example?
Mike	Things like love and hate, politics, society, that kind of thing. I also think the people in his plays are interesting. Yeah, the characters are very interesting.
Interviewer	Are you studying any of his plays at school?
Mike	Yes, we're reading *Julius Caesar*. In fact I'm going to see it this evening. That's why I'm in Stratford.
Interviewer	Have you seen any other Shakespeare plays at the theatre?
Mike	Yes, I saw *Romeo and Juliet* and it was set in New York, and the actors' clothes were all modern, and there were gangsters with guns. It was great, because I could understand what was happening. I really began to understand what Shakespeare was trying to say.

Exercise 5 page 96 🎧 2.41

- In a **weaker class**, revise the adjectives used in the recording before the second listening. Ask individual students to give opinions: *Do you think Shakespeare is too difficult? Are his stories fantastic? Are they old-fashioned?* etc.
- Ask students to read through the instructions and the task.
- Play the recording once. Check as a class.
- In a **stronger class**, you can get more feedback by focusing students on the photos and asking them to say what the three teenagers think about Shakespeare. Elicit answers, then ask what the students' own opinions are.

KEY

1 S 2 A 3 S 4 A 5 M 6 M

Exercise 6 page 96

- Allow 30 seconds to fill in the gaps. Read the word *literature* and the sentences out for the students to repeat.
- Check comprehension by asking: *Which types of literature use rhymes? What is the difference between a novel and a short story?*

KEY

1 plays
2 novels, short stories
3 poems

Exercise 7 page 96

- Allow 4 minutes to work in pairs. Get feedback. Encourage students to talk about novelists, playwrights and poets. Are there any books or their authors that students admire?

➡ Lesson outcome

Ask students: *What have you learned today? What can you do now?* and elicit answers: *I can understand information and opinions on Shakespeare. I have learned words for writers and their texts. I have practised reading and listening.*

10D **GRAMMAR**
The passive (other tenses)

LESSON SUMMARY ●●●●○

Grammar: the passive (other tenses)
Reading: short texts about publications

SHORTCUT *To do the lesson in 30 minutes, set exercises 3, 4 and 5 for homework.*

➡ Lead-in 3–5 minutes

- Inform the class of the lesson objectives.
- Ask students in pairs to note down the titles of the five most popular and famous books that have ever been written. Allow a minute. Compare the lists as a class. Why are these books so widely read? What makes a book popular for a long time? Discuss briefly as a class.

Exercise 1 page 97

- Ask students to look at the photo without looking at the text. Elicit guesses about the title of the book.
- In a **stronger class**, ask students to close their books. Read the text out to the class. Check comprehension by asking: *What's the most popular book in the world? How many copies are sold every day? When was it written?*
- In a **weaker class**, ask students to read the text individually. Then check comprehension.

Exercise 2 page 97

- In a **weaker class**, work together. In a **stronger class**, students can work in pairs. Check as a class.

KEY

2 was written	4 has been translated
3 wasn't written	5 have been printed?

For more practice on the passive go to:

> **Grammar Builder 10D:** Student's Book page 122

KEY

5 1 was made
    2 was written
    3 were invented
    4 were performed
    5 was murdered
    6 was discovered

6 1 My camera has been stolen.
    2 The bus stop has been vandalised.
    3 The new DVDs have been taken by shoplifters.
    4 Their house has been burgled.
    5 Three people have been murdered.
    6 Three suspects have been interviewed by the police.

7 1 will be collected
    2 will be cleaned
    3 will be polished
    4 will be taken
    5 will be hoovered
    6 will be returned

Exercise 3 page 97

- Students work individually. Remind them to look at the structures in each sentence and make sure that the pairs use the equivalent tense in the passive or active. Allow 2 minutes. Check as a class.
- In a **stronger class**, students can do some extra practice in pairs. One student in a pair keeps their book closed. The other reads sentences 1–3, elicits the passive from their partner, and checks the answer against sentences a–f. Then they swap – the other student reads sentences 4–6.
- In a **weaker class**, you can read the sentences out, substituting the verb forms with some word; e.g. *Tolkien blob The Lord of the Rings in the 1950s.* Put *blob* on the board. Explain that students must listen to the sentences and note down the phrases which are substituted. Students check their answers individually against the exercise in the book.

KEY

1 e – wrote	4 f – is known
2 d – has been translated	5 c – based
3 a – performed	6 b – was created

Exercise 4 page 97

- It is important that students read the whole text before they start filling in the gaps as knowledge of the context should help them choose the right tenses. Put the following questions on the board: *What are wiki websites?* (Websites written by the people who use them.) *How many people edit Wikipedia?* (20,000) Ask students to read the whole text and find the information. Elicit answers.
- Pre-teach *entry, to add, detailed, to edit, free.*
- Explain that students must use different tenses to complete the task. Remind the class that we use the past simple to talk about a specific occasion in the past and so we usually say when it happened. The present perfect is used with *for* and *since* to say how long the situation has existed. (See lessons 5B and 5D.)
- Students work in pairs for a minute. Check as a class. Elicit what different tenses have been used and why.

KEY

1 is used	4 have been published
2 are written	5 have been added
3 was created	6 is done

Exercise 5 page 97

- In a **weaker class**, ask students in pairs to read the sentences and underline all the time expressions. Allow a minute. Go over the expressions as a class and decide which tense should be used in each case.
- In a **stronger class**, students work individually. Allow 2 minutes. Let them compare answers in pairs before checking as a class.

KEY

1 is banned	5 were chosen
2 is … held	6 was directed
3 was attacked	7 is sold
4 are spoken	8 was … completed

Exercise 6 page 97

- Allow 3–4 minutes. If you are short of time, allocate two randomly chosen questions to each pair. Allow a minute. Check as a class.

KEY

1 hooded tops
2 On the river Thames, in west London.
3 Bethany Hamilton
4 English and Welsh
5 Sean Connery, George Lazenby, Roger Moore, Timothy Dalton, Pierce Brosnan, Daniel Craig
6 any one of the following: *Black Peter, Taking Off, One Flew Over the Cuckoo's Nest, Amadeus*
7 meat
8 1955

OPTIONAL ACTIVITY

Ask students to write eight more questions drawing on information from units 1–10. They can work in class or at home. Collect the questions and play 'The Strongest Link' with the class. The aim of the game is to find the student who remembers most facts. Students play in pairs first. Each round lasts a minute or as long as it takes you to ask each pair two questions. After each round all the players choose the strongest link (the pair whose answers were the most accurate and the fastest) by writing their name on a piece of paper and holding it out for other players to see. You announce who the strongest link is in each round. Play as many rounds as you wish or need to find the winning pair – the pair who won more rounds than any other. Then the two students from the winning pair play against each other. You ask each of them five questions. The one who answers more wins. If there is a draw, play 'sudden death' – the first one to answer one more question than their opponent is the winner.

➡ Lesson outcome

Ask students: *What have you learned today? What can you do now?* and elicit answers: *I can use different forms of the passive. I have learned about the Bible. I have learned about wiki websites.*

Notes for Photocopiable activity 10.1

General knowledge quiz

Pairwork
Language: present and past passive
Materials: one worksheet cut in half per pair of students
(Teacher's Book page 142)

- Divide students into pairs. Give Students A worksheet A, and Students B worksheet B. Give them time to work out the questions, and write them down if necessary.
- In pairs students take it in turns to ask the questions, giving the three possible answers. Explain that the correct answer is shown underneath.
- Students gain a point for each correct answer.

10 E READING
A teenage writer

LESSON SUMMARY ●●●●○

Reading: an interview with an author
Vocabulary: styles of fiction
Listening: a song
Speaking: asking and answering about an author
Topic: literature and entertainment

SHORTCUT *To do the lesson in 30 minutes, do exercises 1 and 8 as a class. Make sure you do not spend more than 10 minutes on the song.*

➡ Lead-in 2–3 minutes

- Inform the class of the lesson objectives.
- Focus students on the pictures. Elicit what they know about the books and their author. Has anybody read either of the books? Did they like it/them?

- If students don't know the author or his books, broaden the topic to fantasy novels generally – do the students like this type of story? Why?/Why not?

Exercise 1 page 98

- Students work individually for 2–3 minutes. Check comprehension by eliciting titles and authors of different styles of fiction.
- Students can share opinions about their most and least favourite styles in pairs. Allow 2–3 minutes. Get feedback.
- If students find it difficult to give reasons, put the following on the board: *the characters, the story, the ending, the dialogues, the atmosphere, the setting,* etc. Explain the words and encourage students to talk about different aspects of styles and particular books.

Exercise 2 page 98

- Read the exam tip as a class. Check comprehension by asking: *If you want to quickly check what is in the interview, which should you read: the questions or the answers?*
- Allow a minute. Check by having a student read the relevant question.

KEY

science fiction and fantasy stories

Exercise 3 page 98

- Pre-teach: *to ban, to prohibit, to fail, ability, mind, to give up.*
- Allow 2 minutes for individual work. Check as a class.
- Ask students what other words are unclear. Put them on the board. Find the words in the interview and elicit or work out the meaning as a class.

KEY

1 b   2 a   3 a   4 b   5 b   6 b   7 a   8 a   9 a

Exercise 4 page 98

- Students work individually. Ask them to go over all the questions filling in the ones they are sure of, then read the questions again and complete the rest of them.
- Let students compare their answers in pairs, then check as a class.

KEY

1 Where	5 Why
2 When	6 Which
3 What	7 How
4 Who	

OPTIONAL ACTIVITY

In a **weaker class**, focus students on what Christopher said about books, feelings and understanding ourselves. Model the pronunciation for students to repeat, then read the sentences together as a class. Ask students to learn them by heart.

In a **stronger class**, discuss the passage with the class. Do the students agree with Christopher? Are books more important than other media, art or the Internet?

Exercise 5 page 99

- Students take it in turns to ask and answer. Allow 2–3 minutes.
- In a **weaker class**, share answers.
- In a **stronger class**, ask more questions to check comprehension.

KEY

1 At home.
2 When he was fifteen.
3 *Eragon*.
4 His parents.
5 Because his first novel became a best-seller.
6 Books.
7 They should write about what excites them the most, be persistent and disciplined, accept criticism and learn all they can about writing.

CULTURE AND LANGUAGE NOTE – *PAPERBACK WRITER*

Paperback writer was written by Paul McCartney and John Lennon and released by the Beatles in 1966. It was the first Beatles song not about love. The song's lyrics are in the form of a letter to a publisher.

a man named Lear – The 'nonsense poet' Edward Lear was one of John Lennon's favourite poets.

The Daily Mail was Lennon's regular newspaper and was often in the studio when they were recording.

the rights – the authority to perform, publish or film a particular work

Exercise 6 page 99 2.42

• Read the instructions as a class. Elicit the meaning of *publisher*. Explain that *to address* means *to talk/write to*.
• Play the recording once. Check as a class.

KEY

1 A writer is addressing a publisher.

Exercise 7 page 99

• Students can work in pairs for 2–3 minutes. Check as a class.

KEY

1 It's a thousand pages, give or take a few.
2 I can make it longer … I can change it round …
3 It's the dirty story of a dirty man. And his clinging wife doesn't understand.
4 It could make a million for you overnight.
5 And I need a job, so I want to be a paperback writer.
6 If you must return it, you can send it here.
7 It took me years to write.

Exercise 8 page 99

• Work as a class. Are there any other expressions students do not understand? Explain or elicit the meaning.

KEY

1 c   2 a   3 b

Exercise 9 page 99

• Brainstorm ideas for both sides as a class.
• Allow students a few minutes to organise their ideas before they do the task in pairs.
• When most people have finished talking, share ideas as a class. Who got their book published? Which of the publishers decided not to publish?

ADDITIONAL SPEAKING ACTIVITY

Explain that students are going to interview each other. They will use the questions from the interview with Christopher Paolini and take the role of a real or imaginary writer.

Read the questions as a class to practise pronunciation and intonation. Discuss whether any will need adapting to suit the new interview (for example, in question 3 they may have to refer to a different type of book or style of fiction). Allow 3 minutes for students to make notes of their answers. If there is no time to switch roles, divide students into As and Bs. While As are making notes, Bs are learning the questions by heart and adding two more.

Put students in pairs to conduct 3–4-minute interviews. If there is time, ask 1–2 pairs to act their interviews out for the class. You can arrange chairs at the front of the class to make it look like a chat show. The rest of the class are the audience.

➡ Lesson outcome

Ask students: *What have you learned today? What can you do now?* and elicit answers: *I can understand an interview with an author. I have learned the words for different styles of fiction. I can understand a Beatles song.*

LESSON SUMMARY ●●●●○○

Functional English: enquiring about and ordering books
Vocabulary: bookshop departments
Listening: dialogues; listening for specific information
Speaking: role-play in a bookshop
Topic: shops and services

SHORTCUT *To do the lesson in 30 minutes, ask students to shorten the preparation in exercise 6 to reading through the chart and then improvise the dialogue out to the class. Put students in pairs across the class so that they have to speak loudly and clearly.*

➡ Lead-in 3–5 minutes

• Inform the class of the lesson objectives.
• Start to draw a mind map on the board with a blank in the middle and three subheadings: *nouns, verbs, adjectives*. Put *novel, to write, boring* on the board in the appropriate categories and elicit what the three have in common (they refer to books). Write *books* in the middle of the mind map. Ask students to copy the map and work in pairs to write more words in the three categories in 2 minutes. Invite students to add words to the mind map on the board. The class correct any spelling mistakes and add new words to their own maps.

Exercise 1 page 100 2.43

• Pre-teach *section, shelf/shelves, in stock, to order, to take (a week)*.
• Play the recording once. Elicit answers.

1 They don't have it in stock/in the bookshop at the moment.
2 In a week or ten days.

LANGUAGE NOTE – POLITENESS
The following language is used by the speakers to sound polite:

I wonder if you could help me. This sentence is often used before a request.

If I/you could (just) + verb. This structure commonly used as a way of making a polite request. The meaning is the same as *'Could I/you ...?'*

Exercise 2 page 100
- Focus students on the vocabulary box. Read it as a class. Work on pronunciation if necessary.
- Check comprehension by eliciting publications available in the departments (see lesson 10A).
- In a **weaker class**, play the recording again. Students listen and read. Pause to correct any pronunciation errors.
- Allow 2–4 minutes to work in pairs.
- In a **stronger class**, ask students to change as many details as possible.

Exercise 3 page 100 🎧 2.44
- Play the recording once. Check answers as a class.
- Elicit any other details that students remember.

KEY
Customer 2

Transcript 2.44
1 **Assistant** Can I help you?
  Customer Yes, I'm looking for a book by Stephen King. I think it's called *Johnny Knockers*.
  Assistant That's *Tommyknockers*.
  Customer Yes, that's it. Have you got it in stock?
  Assistant Let me see. No, I'm afraid we've sold out of that book. But it's already on order. Would you like me to reserve a copy for you when it arrives?
  Customer No thanks. I really need it today. I'll try somewhere else.

2 **Customer** Excuse me. I want to teach myself Hungarian. Can you recommend anything?
  Assistant Try looking under languages. It's at the back of the shop next to the reference section.
  Customer OK, thanks.
  Assistant Did you find anything suitable?
  Customer Yes, I did. *Teach Yourself Hungarian.*
  Assistant That's £9.95 please.
  Customer Can I pay by credit card?
  Assistant Yes, of course.

3 **Customer** Excuse me. Do you know a book called *The Ugly Princess?*
  Assistant No, I don't. Is it for children?
  Customer Yes, it is. But I can't remember the name of the author.
  Assistant Don't worry, I'll look it up on the computer. Ah, here it is. It's by Malcolm Bryant and it costs £5.95 in paperback. But I'm afraid we haven't got it in stock. Shall I order it for you?
  Customer How long will it take?
  Assistant It will be here on Friday.
  Customer OK, that's great.

Assistant Can you write down your name and telephone number? We'll call you when the book arrives.
Customer Yes, sure. Thanks very much.

Exercise 4 page 100
- Students can work in pairs to complete the sentences.

KEY
1 for, by   2 out   3 on   4 under   5 by   6 up   7 on
8 down

Exercise 5 page 100 🎧 2.45
- Play the recording. Students listen and check.

Exercise 6 page 100
- Students choose or invent the title of the book together, then prepare their lines individually. Allow a minute. Remind them to look at the Functions Bank for useful phrases.
- Ask students to rehearse in pairs and make changes if necessary.
- Allow another 2 minutes for students to memorise their roles.

Exercise 7 page 100
- Ask a few pairs to act out their dialogues.
- To involve the whole class, choose one book and ask students in random order to say the next lines of the dialogue. Explain that everybody must listen carefully and follow the scenario from exercise 6.

➡ Lesson outcome
Ask students: *What have you learned today? What can you do now?* and elicit answers: *I can ask for information in a bookshop. I have learned to order books. I have learned to use prepositions.*

10G WRITING
A book review

LESSON SUMMARY ●●●●○○
Reading: a book review
Vocabulary: words for describing books
Writing: a book review
Topic: literature and entertainment

SHORTCUT *To do the lesson in 30 minutes, do exercises 1–4 quickly as a class. Allow 15 minutes for the writing. Collect the letters at the end of the lesson or ask students to finish them at home and bring them to class next time. Give feedback, focusing on positive elements and good use of language as well as on mistakes.*

➡ Lead-in 3–5 minutes
- Inform the class of the lesson objectives.
- Ask students about the books they read for school. Do they like reading them? Why/Why not? Which set book have they just read? Was it good/bad/fantastic/terrible?

Exercise 1 page 101

• Students read the review individually. Elicit answers.

KEY

1 paragraph 3   2 paragraph 2   3 paragraph 1

CULTURE NOTE – *NORTHERN LIGHTS*

Northern Lights is the first in a trilogy called *His Dark Materials*. A film based on the book called *The Golden Compass*, which is the US title of the novel, came out in 2007.

Exercise 2 page 101

• Students work individually. Check as a class.

KEY

1 True   2 False   3 True   4 False   5 True

Exercise 3 page 101

• Go over the phrases in the box as a class. Explain any unfamiliar expressions.
• Students can work in pairs. Check as a class.
• Ask if there are any other expressions in the review which are not in the box and which are useful to talk about books. Elicit: *The author has created …, The story is …, I found it difficult to put down, The characters are …, The book is sometimes compared to …*

KEY

It's a fantasy story set in Oxford.
It's the story of a girl called Lyra.
The ending is very exciting.
I liked the book for a number of reasons.
I identified strongly with Lyra.
I thoroughly recommend it.

Exercise 4 page 101

• Elicit what students know about *The Lord of the Rings* by J.R.R. Tolkien. Who has read the books? Who has seen the films?
• Students work individually. Check as a class.

KEY

1 It was written by	5 In the end,
2 It's set in	6 it was made into a film
3 It's the story of	7 you should read it.
4 The main character is	

Exercise 5 page 101

• Read the instructions as a class. Explain any unknown vocabulary in the section on paragraph 3.
• Allow 3–5 minutes to make notes.

Exercise 6 page 101

• Read the writing tip as a class. Check comprehension by asking: *What tense should you use to tell what happens in the book?*
• Focus students on the second paragraph of the model review. Elicit examples of the present simple used to retell the story.
• Allow 15–20 minutes to write the review. Ask students to follow the model in organisation, layout and length.
• If there is time, ask students to read their reviews out to the class. Write the titles of the books on the board.

ALTERNATIVE WRITING TASK

Write a review (130–150 words) of a textbook that you use at school. Write three paragraphs:

1 General information: title, author, type of book, who it is written for
2 Contents: how the book is organised, some of the topics it covers
3 Your opinion: e.g. is it clear/interesting/up-to-date? Is the information well presented/illustrated? Do you recommend it for students?

➡ Lesson outcome

Ask students: *What have you learned today? What can you do now?* and elicit answers: *I can write a review recommending a book. I have learned expressions to talk about stories.*

Notes on Photocopiable activity 10.2

What's the difference?

Pairwork
Language: vocabulary from units 1–10
Materials: one copy of the cut up worksheet per pair of students (Teacher's Book page 143)

• Divide the class into pairs and give each pair a pile of cut-up cards.
• The cards are placed face down on the table and students take it in turns to explain the difference between the words on the cards.

LANGUAGE REVIEW 9–10

1
1 burglar
2 murder
3 vandal
4 rob
5 drug dealer
6 go

2
1 burglary
2 murder
3 vandalism
4 robbery
5 drug-dealing
6 joyriding

3
1 atlas
2 cookbook
3 play
4 autobiography
5 dictionary
6 manual
7 textbook
8 guidebook

4
1 had finished
2 had left
3 had gone
4 hadn't revised
5 had seen
6 hadn't closed

5
1 didn't like
2 was
3 had seen
4 preferred
5 watched
6 wasn't
7 had watched

6
2 These shoes are worn in Holland.
3 This church was built five hundreds years ago.
4 My bike has been stolen.
5 Pork is not eaten in Iran.
6 Pasta is made in Italy.
7 His first novel wasn't translated.
8 The robbers have been caught.

7 2, 3, 1, 4, 6, 5

8 1 b 2 d 3 a 4 c

SKILLS ROUND-UP 1–10

1 Open answers

2 1 B 2 C 3 A

3
1 How many people were there at the barbecue (at Daniel's yesterday)?
2 Who won the badminton tournament?
3 What was stolen from the house?
4 What did the police say?
5 Why hadn't Joanna bought Daniel a present?

4 Open answers

Transcript 2.46

Narrator	Joanna is in town. She's looking for a birthday present for Daniel.
Joanna	Excuse me. Is there a good bookshop near here?
Man	Yes, there is. There's one in Western Avenue.
Joanna	Can you tell me how to get there?
Man	Let me see … Go straight on and turn left at the traffic lights. Go past the supermarket and turn right into Western Avenue. The bookshop is next to the café.
Joanna	Thanks!
Joanna	Oh, hi. I wonder if you could help me.
Assistant	I'll try.
Joanna	I'm looking for a book for a friend. It's a present.
Assistant	I see. Have you any idea exactly what you're looking for?
Joanna	Well, he really likes sport. So I thought maybe a biography of a famous sportsperson.
Assistant	Oh yes. Is he interested in football?
Joanna	Yes, I think so.
Assistant	There's a very interesting biography of Michael Owen. It's quite new.
Joanna	Have you got it in stock?
Assistant	I'm sorry, we haven't. But I can order it for you.
Joanna	Hmm. No, thanks. I really want to buy it today.
Assistant	There's a good new biography of Tiger Woods.
Joanna	Who's he?
Assistant	He's the most famous golfer in the world.
Joanna	Oh. I don't know if my friend likes golf. Probably not.
Assistant	Well, why don't you go and look in the sport section? It's over there, at the back of the shop. You might get some ideas.
Joanna	OK. Thanks.
Assistant	Have you found something?
Joanna	Yes, I'll have this, please.
Assistant	Sure. That's £8.95.
Joanna	Here you are.
Assistant	Thanks. Here's your book – and your change. Would you like a bag?
Joanna	No, it's OK.
Daniel	Oh, hi! How are you?
Joanna	Fine, thanks. I've got a birthday present for you!
Daniel	But I said you shouldn't buy anything.
Joanna	I know. I wanted to. It isn't much. Here, open it.
Daniel	Thanks. Come in!
Daniel	It's a book!
Joanna	Yes.
Daniel	What's it called? Ah. *Play better badminton*. Very funny!
Joanna	Do you like it?
Daniel	I love it. Thanks, Joanna!

5 A book

6
1 A café
2 It isn't in stock
3 The sports section
4 £8.95
5 A bag, no
6 He loves it.

EXAM For further exam tasks and practice, go to Workbook page 98. Procedural notes, transcripts and keys for the Workbook can be found on the *Solutions* Teacher's Website at www.oup.com/elt/teacher/solutions.

A short introduction to dyslexia

What is dyslexia?[1]

- Dyslexia is one of several distinct learning disabilities.
- It is a specific language-based disorder.
- It's of biological origin (usually genetic).
- Characteristic symptoms are difficulties in single word decoding (reading) usually reflecting insufficient phonological skills. Dyslexia is manifested by varying difficulty with different forms of language. These often include, in addition to problems with reading, a conspicuous problem with acquiring proficiency in writing and spelling.
- These difficulties are often unexpected in relation to age and other intellectual and academic abilities (in some school subjects).
- These difficulties are not the result of a generalised developmental disability (these students have a normal IQ) or sensory impairment (they don't have seeing or hearing problems). Some dyslexic people have very good spatial orientation, visual or auditory memory and technical skills.

What dyslexia isn't (myths about dyslexia)

- Dyslexia is not an illness. However, it appears in two basic medical classifications of diseases: ICD-10 (European) and DSM-IV (American).
- Dyslexia is not a myth. It is a learning difficulty which makes all aspects of dealing with language (especially written language) harder. Most experts today agree that learning to write requires a lot of effort and takes time. It's crucial for dyslexic students to learn how to learn, find out what works for them and consciously develop their own learning strategies. Normally, with time, dyslexic students learn to use their talents and intelligence to cope with their problems.
- Dyslexia is not a lack of intelligence. Students who have been diagnosed as being dyslexic have at least a normal IQ and many of them are highly intelligent.
- Dyslexia is not laziness. However, some dyslexic students may try to use their dyslexia as an excuse for not working. It is important to understand that helping means demanding and motivating, not releasing or absolving from responsibility.
- Dyslexia is not 'no big deal'. People don't grow out of dyslexia. The dyslexic person learns to cope with his/her problems and to use favourable compensation strategies. The earlier help is given, the more effective it is. Constant failure leads to a lack of motivation and/or other negative strategies. These secondary effects are often more difficult to deal with later on. Early encouragement and learner training can therefore make all the difference to a dyslexic student's experience of school and learning.
- Dyslexia is not something rare. The problems associated with dyslexia are roughly similar in some 10% of the population, which means that in an average classroom there are usually a few students with dyslexia.
- Dyslexic students are not all the same. Some of them, having experienced some difficulties in learning their mother tongue, don't have any problems with foreign languages. Some – suffering from severe dyslexia – can hardly learn a foreign language.
- People don't normally grow out of dyslexia. However the symptoms change with time and they are different at different life stages. Their form depends on different educational methods, work input and individual characteristics (intelligence or the nature of deficits). The problems tend to come back after a break in training (e.g. after holidays) and in stressful situations (e.g. an exam).
- Dyslexia is not a reason for failing in life. This is proved by a long list of famous dyslexics (e.g. Hans Christian Andersen, Auguste Rodin, Thomas Alva Edison, Sir Winston Churchill, Albert Einstein). Dyslexic students can succeed at school – they just need the right kind of teaching.

Forms of dyslexia

Most dyslexia researchers distinguish between Developmental Dyslexia in its general meaning as a syndrome of Specific Reading and Writing Difficulties and its forms:

Dyslexia (in its narrow meaning with reference to reading problems only)

Dysortography (spelling problems)

Dysgraphia (handwriting problems)

What is the cause of dyslexia?

Different factors (genetic and environmental) cause biological changes in the central nervous system which leads to certain dysfunctions. As a result the child's psycho-motor development is discordant.

Dyslexic symptoms in school

In most cases weaknesses can be identified in the following areas:

Visual and auditory perception and processing

This can result in difficulties with mastering written and sometimes also oral language:

- learning words/letters/sounds
- spelling: phonic writing (e.g. football/futbol), letters may be reversed, mirrored, replaced by similar ones (p-b-d-g, w-m-n), written in the wrong order (e.g. hlep/help), omitted or added.
- reading (accurate and/or fluent word recognition)
- pronunciation (because this requires good auditory perception and processing)
- expressive writing
- recognising and producing rhymes
- fluency in speech (less common)

Automaticity

- For example, applying even well-known spelling rules or retrieving common words from memory.

Memory

Dyslexic students may encounter problems with:

- short-term memory
- learning sequences such as days of the week and months of the year
- acquiring the knowledge of sounds and words

The technique of writing

- In the case of students with dysgraphia their handwriting can be illegible and the pace of writing slow (because writing requires good fine motor skills).

Spatial orientation

- Students may have trouble differentiating between left and right.
- They may find prepositions difficult (e.g. *under*, *on*, *above*, *below*).

[1] *definition taken from ODS Research Committee and National Institute of Health (1994)*

Concentration

- Dyslexic students may get easily distracted and become mentally tired sooner than their peers.

Organisational skills

Dyslexic students may encounter problems with:

- time management (e.g. often coming late for a lesson, planning their work)
- problems with organisation of materials (e.g. problems with using their Student's Book as a source of useful information, designing the layout of their copybook).

Secondary consequences of dyslexia can be:

- low self-esteem
- low motivation for learning
- being passive (withdrawn)
- becoming aggressive as a form of protest
- becoming a classroom clown
- not enjoying learning/school or even refusing to go to school
- frustration

Dyslexia in the English classroom

Most of the general dyslexia symptoms (listed above) affect students' performance in English lessons. Typical problem areas in English are:

The alphabet

- which results in difficulties with spelling aloud and using dictionaries.

Vocabulary

- because of poor memory and problems with sequences, e.g. learning the 12 months. Dyslexics often experience difficulties with retrieving well-known words from memory.

Grammar

- even applying well-known rules.

All four skills:

- listening: because it requires good concentration span and memory, auditory perception and processing
- reading: because it requires good visual and auditory perception and processing, accurate and/or fluent word recognition
- speaking: (less often) because of problems with automaticity, memory and constructing complex sentences
- expressive writing: because of the semantic, morphological and syntactic aspect of the language. Dyslexics usually have problems with planning their essays. They also tend to write short, simple sentences and over-use high-frequency words.

Spelling

- because it requires good phonological skills, auditory and visual perception and processing, memory and automaticity. Dyslexic students may confuse, leave out, add letters and syllables as well as change their order.

Pronunciation

- For example pronouncing long words (because this requires good short-term memory, auditory perception and processing).

Interference

- The student may mix up all the foreign languages that he/she is learning, especially German and English.

General rules on how to deal with dyslexia

'In my experience, it is the continual sense of failure that makes the whole experience of dyslexia so negative. Obviously, when learning a foreign language in a regular classroom, dyslexic learners experience more problems than their non-dyslexic counterparts, but if you give them sufficient structure, time and practice to acquire the basics on all levels (reading, writing, speaking, comprehension) they can make progress. Mixed with non-dyslexics who learn easily in an intuitive, global way, the dyslexic learner will only experience failure through not receiving enough positive feedback: under this pressure he will start mixing and confusing his words in an effort to keep up.'

(Language Shock – Dyslexia across cultures, 1999).

Psychological aspects

Since students with dyslexia often have low motivation you should:

- Be positive and optimistic. Remember that motivation is the key to self-esteem and to success.
- Encourage the dyslexic student to have a positive attitude towards English. It's important for your dyslexic students to access the culture of English-speaking countries (e.g. listening to English music, getting in touch with native speakers, taking part in a student exchange).

Since students with dyslexia usually have low self-esteem:

- Remember that learners with dyslexia need a lot of positive feedback and praise.
- Help to overcome your dyslexic students' difficulties but not forget about their strengths. It's not a good idea to spend all the time working on their problems!
- Ensure your students with dyslexia achieve some form of success and that they are aware of the fact that they have been successful. Remember it is better to go back a step and give the student a sense of success than to stay on a higher level without success.
- Realise that it's important to reduce the student's stress.

Dyslexic students don't usually believe in themselves, therefore, you should:

- Not be over-protective. Dyslexic students need help but only 'help that leads to self-help'. Your job is to encourage the student to be independent.
- Have high expectations but set reasonable goals.
- Have a positive attitude towards the dyslexic student.

Students with dyslexia may have problems with their classmates. Therefore a teacher should:

- Promote mutual help between students. The dyslexic student takes up a lot of the teacher's time and so it is important that the other students don't miss out.
- Protect dyslexic students from bullying by their classmates. Explain the situation of the dyslexic person, if necessary, in order to increase their peers' understanding.

Organisational matters

- Remember that most parents are experts concerning their children. It is important to get/keep in touch with dyslexic students' parents. Show your willingness to help in co-operation with the parents.
- Study your students' written assessments. They can be an important source of information about your students' strong and weak points. From such documents you can also find out how to work with your dyslexic student.
- Find out about your student's way of learning (especially his/her learning style) and respect it. Every student has individual preferences for visual, auditory, tactile or kinaesthetic processing. In addition some students prefer to work alone and some with others in groups.

General rules on how to teach dyslexic students[2]

> 'If the dyslexic child does not learn the way you teach, can you teach him the way he learns?'
>
> *(H. T. Chasty – consultant in learning abilities and difficulties)*

Remember that dyslexic students can be especially demanding. Therefore:

- Apply an individual approach: what works well for one student may not necessarily work for another.
- Use a variety of activities to revise a topic or structure to keep students' interest.
- Find ways to help your students concentrate. Change the activity regularly and plan lessons including short breaks.
- Don't teach things that are similar one after the other.
- Learn to be well-organised. Dyslexic students need a regular routine to help them stay organised.
- Accentuate the student's abilities and teach through his/her strengths. Difficulties in reading and writing might be compensated by abilities such as a high IQ or visual/technical skills.
- Give exact instructions or explanations of tasks (short and concise).
- Let your students learn by doing. Ask them to prepare vocabulary charts, flashcards, posters, etc.

Use friendly material

- Use large fonts (12–14 point, for example Comic Sans MS).
- A clear layout. The page should be well laid out and not too full.
- Pictograms and graphics to help locate information.
- Picture dictionaries.
- Consistent colour coding.
- Listening material (tape or CD) for use at home.
- A 'window marker' for reading. (See figure 1 below.) It helps dyslexic students with reading. A student should hold it in such a position that the word that is being read appears in the opening (window). This way a student won't get lost while reading.

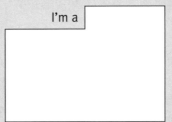

I'm a

figure 1

[2] *'General rules on how to teach dyslexic students' is based on material prepared by D. Sapiejewska (2002)*

1.1 SPOT THE DIFFERENCE

STUDENT A

Describe your picture to Student B. Find eight differences. Put a cross (x) next to each difference.

'My picture is of a bedroom. Two people are sitting on the floor. They are playing a computer game ...'

STUDENT B

Describe your picture to Student A. Find eight differences. Put a cross (x) next to each difference.

'My picture is of a bedroom. Two people are sitting on the floor. They are watching television ...'

1.2 TELL US ABOUT YOU ...

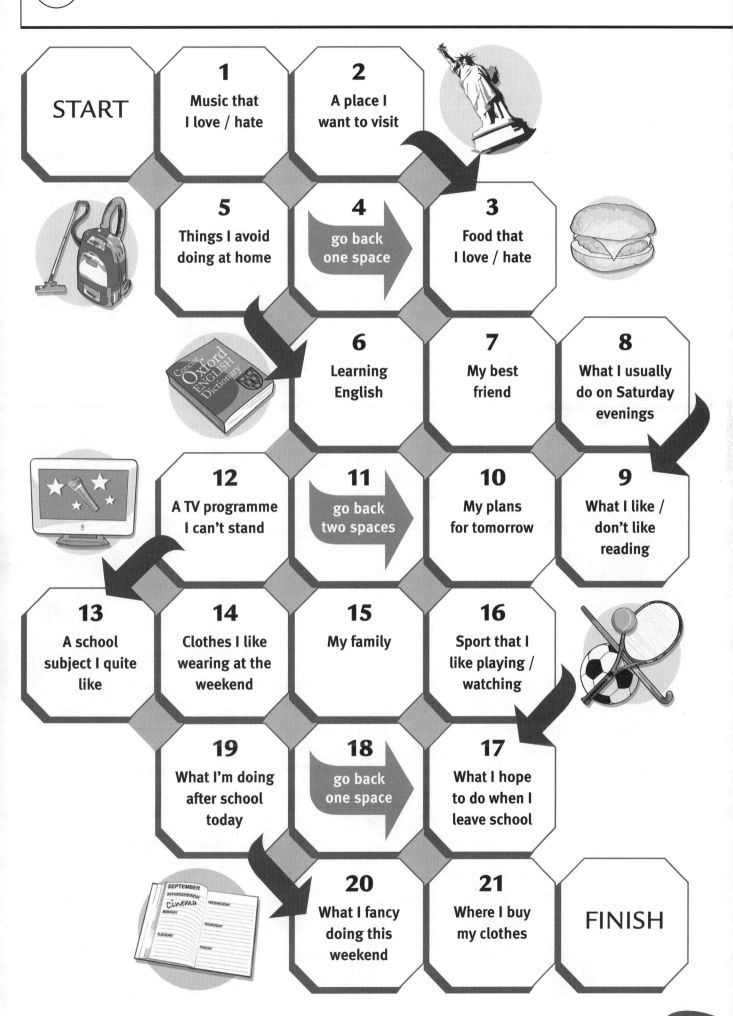

START

1 Music that I love / hate

2 A place I want to visit

3 Food that I love / hate

4 go back one space

5 Things I avoid doing at home

6 Learning English

7 My best friend

8 What I usually do on Saturday evenings

9 What I like / don't like reading

10 My plans for tomorrow

11 go back two spaces

12 A TV programme I can't stand

13 A school subject I quite like

14 Clothes I like wearing at the weekend

15 My family

16 Sport that I like playing / watching

17 What I hope to do when I leave school

18 go back one space

19 What I'm doing after school today

20 What I fancy doing this weekend

21 Where I buy my clothes

FINISH

(2.1) IRREGULAR VERB BINGO

was		brought	
	felt		heard
chose		thought	

flew		felt	
	bought		thought
knew		fell	

was		flew	
	saw		put
left		caught	

ate		threw	
	brought		kept
slept		thought	

left		fell	
	bought		wore
knew		thought	

flew		wore	
	saw		was
ate		caught	

chose		brought	
	fought		heard
put		kept	

ate		threw	
	fought		put
knew		kept	

slept		left	
	caught		fought
saw		fell	

chose		bought	
	wore		felt
slept		heard	

2.2 ROGER FEDERER

STUDENT A (Roger Federer)

Roger Federer was born on ¹_____ in Basel, Switzerland, to Robert and ²_____ Federer. Roger Federer ³_____ at the age of eight. When he was young his idol was Boris Becker. He finished school when he was sixteen years old so that ⁴_____ .

Federer became professional in 1998 when he was ⁵_____ . In the early years he often became very emotional on the tennis court. Nowadays he is much calmer. In 2003 he won Wimbledon for the first time.

Federer's girlfriend is Miroslava Vavrinec, who is also a tennis player. He met her when he was ⁶_____ Sydney in 2000. Miroslava Vavrinec stopped playing tennis

because of a foot injury in 2002.

In 2003 Federer started the ⁷_____ , which supports disadvantaged children, especially in Africa.

Federer speaks three languages. He speaks Swiss German with his girlfriend, ⁸_____ with his trainer and English with his physiotherapist. In his free time he enjoys sitting on the beach and playing cards and computer games.

1 Read the biography of Roger Federer. Complete questions 1–8 to find the missing information.

1 When was _____ ?
2 What is _____ ?
3 What did _____ ?
4 Why did _____ ?
5 How old was _____ ?
6 What was _____ ?
7 What did _____ ?
8 Which language _____ ?

2 Now ask Student B your questions and write the answers in the text.

✂ -

STUDENT B (Roger Federer)

Roger Federer was born on August 8, 1981 in ¹_____ , to ²_____ and Lynette Federer. Roger Federer started playing tennis at the age of eight. When he was young his idol was ³_____ . He finished school when he was sixteen years old so that he could focus on his tennis.

Federer became professional in ⁴_____ when he was 17 years old. In the early years he often became very emotional on the tennis court. Nowadays he is much calmer. In ⁵_____ he won Wimbledon for the first time.

Federer's girlfriend is Miroslava Vavrinec, who is also a tennis player. He met her when he was playing tennis in

the Sydney Olympics in 2000. Miroslava Vavrinec stopped playing tennis because ⁶_____ in 2002.

In 2003 Federer started the Roger Federer Foundation, which supports disadvantaged children, especially in Africa.

Federer speaks three languages. He speaks ⁷_____ with his girlfriend, French with his trainer and English with his physiotherapist. In his free time he enjoys ⁸_____ .

1 Read the biography of Roger Federer. Complete questions 1–8 to find the missing information.

1 Where was _____ ?
2 What is _____ ?
3 Who was _____ ?
4 When did _____ ?
5 When did _____ ?
6 Why did _____ ?
7 Which language _____ ?
8 What does _____ ?

2 Now ask Student A your questions and write the answers in the text.

3.1 DESCRIBE AND DRAW

STUDENT A   Describe this picture to Student B. Use prepositions of place and movement.
Student B will draw what you describe. Do not point at Student B's picture!

Begin like this: 'In the middle of the picture there is a cottage ...'

Listen to Student B and draw the picture below.

in the middle	on the left/right	between	behind	near	next to	opposite
across	over	past	through	along		

✂ -

STUDENT B   Describe this picture to Student A. Use prepositions of place and movement.
Student A will draw what you describe. Do not point at Student A's picture!

Begin like this: 'In the middle of the picture there is a pedestrian crossing ...'

Listen to Student A and draw the picture below.

in the middle	on the left/right	between	behind	near	next to	opposite
across	over	past	through	along		

3.2 GRAMMAR LOTTERY

		CORRECT	INCORRECT	BET	WINNINGS
1	Is there many pollution in Paris?	☐	☐	_____	_____
2	What's weather like here in December?	☐	☐	_____	_____
3	He only speaks a little English.	☐	☐	_____	_____
4	She's looking for the new job.	☐	☐	_____	_____
5	He lives in the village in the north of Spain.	☐	☐	_____	_____
6	There isn't traffic in the city centre.	☐	☐	_____	_____
7	What do you think of American food?	☐	☐	_____	_____
8	She hasn't got a lot friends.	☐	☐	_____	_____
9	Were there many people in the city centre?	☐	☐	_____	_____
10	He walked through the hill to the next village.	☐	☐	_____	_____
11	A lot of people thinks she's very funny.	☐	☐	_____	_____
12	Do you get much pollution in your city?	☐	☐	_____	_____
13	Go over the post box, then turn left.	☐	☐	_____	_____
14	I think your keys are in a kitchen.	☐	☐	_____	_____
15	Do you usually listen to music when you study?	☐	☐	_____	_____

TOTAL [   ]

4.1 TALK ABOUT IT

Which is better?
The Simpsons or *Friends*?
Why?

Which is better?
English grammar or English pronunciation?
Why?

Which is better?
Watching a film at home or watching a film at the cinema?
Why?

Which is better?
Being single or having a boyfriend/girlfriend?
Why?

Which is better?
British pop music or the pop music from your country?
Why?

Which is better?
Reading a newspaper or reading a magazine?
Why?

Which is better?
Travelling by bus or travelling by train?
Why?

Which is better?
American food or the food in your country?
Why?

What's the scariest thing you've ever done?

What's the worst food you've eaten?

Who's the most attractive person in your country?

Who's the laziest person you know?

Where's the hottest place you've been?

Who's the oldest person in your family?

What's the worst TV programme?

Who's the funniest person you know?

4.2 WHAT'S ON?

Scan reading practice: Look at the film guide and see how quickly you can answer the questions.

1 How long is *Charlie and the Chocolate Factory*?
2 Which film is on after *The Matrix*?
3 What kind of film is *Almost Famous*?
4 How many films can you see Keanu Reeves in?
5 Which film should you watch if you like disaster films?
6 What time does the western start?
7 In which film can you hear the voice of Eddie Murphy?
8 On which channel can you see Johnny Depp?
9 Is *Elizabeth* a funny film?
10 Is there a war film on Film Five?
11 Which is the longest film?
12 How many films are about teenagers?

Film Guide   WEDNESDAY 3RD MAY ●

THE MOVIE CHANNEL

5.15pm SHREK 2
One of the funniest animated films of all time. With the voices of Eddie Murphy, Cameron Diaz and many others.

6.45pm ELIZABETH
A historical drama about Queen Elizabeth I of England, with Cate Blanchett.

8.30pm KING KONG
An action film directed by Peter Jackson. Gripping, scary and moving all at the same time.

11.30pm SPELLBOUND
A documentary film about 8 teenagers who are trying to win America's national spelling competition. (ends 12.55)

THE CINEMA CHANNEL

5.00pm HULK
An science fiction action film about a scientist who sometimes changes into a big green monster.

7.15pm MISSION IMPOSSIBLE
A gripping action film about an American agent. Starring Tom Cruise.

9.20pm BILL AND TED'S EXCELLENT ADVENTURE
A comedy with Keanu Reeves and Alex Winter who play the roles of two teenagers who use a time machine to help them with their history lessons.

11.00pm A FISTFUL OF DOLLARS
A 1960s western from Italian director Sergio Leone, starring Clint Eastwood. (ends 12.40)

FILM FIVE

5.20pm CHARLIE AND THE CHOCOLATE FACTORY
An entertaining and funny adventure film about a young boy who wins a tour of the most incredible chocolate factory in the world, starring Johnny Depp.

7.30pm THE MATRIX
A science fiction film about a computer programmer (Keanu Reeves) with a boring life who finds out that his life is virtual, not real.

9.20pm ALMOST FAMOUS
A comedy about a teenage boy who goes on tour with his favourite rock band.

11.20pm THE TOWERING INFERNO
1950s disaster film, starring Steve McQueen, about a fire in the tallest building in the world. (ends 12.55)

5.1 PROVE IT!

1 Complete the sentences with the correct form of the verbs in brackets. Use the present perfect or past simple.

2 Rewrite the sentences to make questions.

3 Ask everyone the questions to find out if the sentences are true about the class.

		ANSWERS
1	Only a few of us _____ (travel) abroad last year.	_____
2	Nobody _____ (eat) frog's legs.	_____
3	Most of us _____ (buy) some clothes last weekend.	_____
4	Some of us _____ (go) to bed after midnight last night.	_____
5	Everybody _____ (have) a job.	_____
6	Nobody _____ (have) the same girlfriend/boyfriend for more than a year.	_____
7	Most of us _____ (see) the *Lord of the Rings* films.	_____
8	Everybody _____ (wash) their hair yesterday.	_____

5.2 REVIEW

START

YOUR FAVOURITE SHOP

Where can you buy a birthday cake?

He bought a _____ of trainers.

VALENTINE'S DAY

The place in the shop where you pay for things.

THE BEST PRESENT YOU'VE EVER GIVEN

THE BEST PRESENT YOU HAVE EVER RECEIVED

!

FINISH

!

Where do you try things on in a shop?

The ticket you get when you buy something in a shop.

Another word for grown-ups is _____.

What _____ are you? Large, small or medium?

!

I haven't seen him _____ 3 years.

SHOPPING ON THE INTERNET

Which do you prefer – small shops or department stores?

A FAMOUS BUILDING

Name 2 things you can buy at a jeweller's.

It doesn't _____. It's too small.

A colloquial word for beautiful is _____.

Where can you buy a newspaper?

THE WORST PRESENT YOU HAVE RECEIVED

YOUR LAST BIRTHDAY

!

I'm looking for a top to go _____ my trousers.

!

A time when you can buy things for less money than usual.

Name 3 things you can buy in an electrical store.

YOUR FAVOURITE CLOTHES SHOP

6.1 TECHNOLOGY CROSSWORD

A

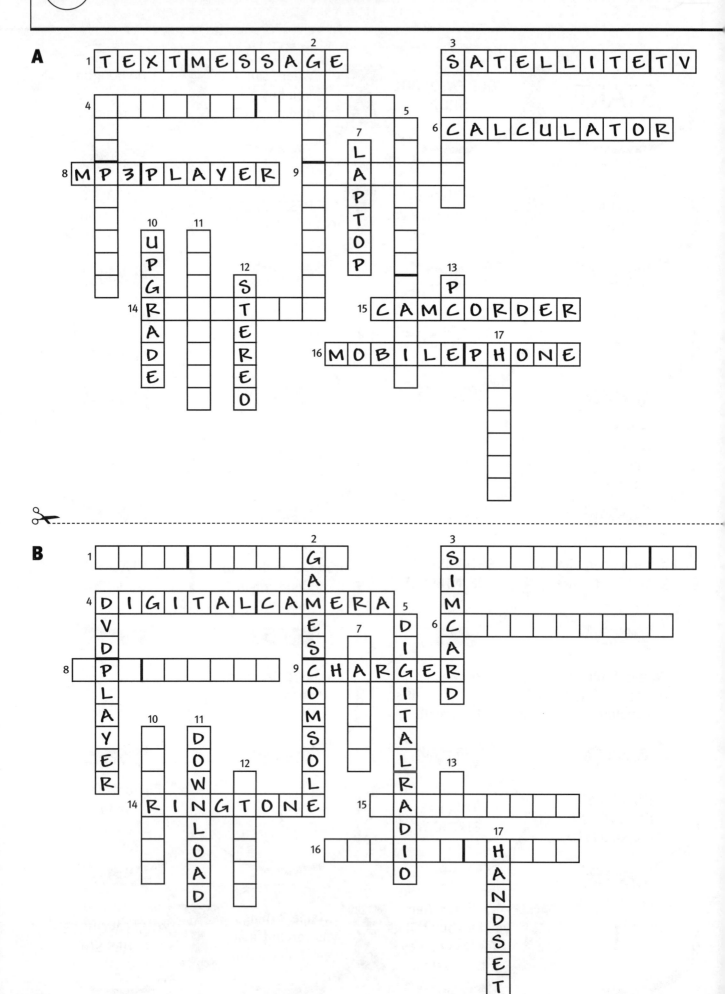

1 TEXTMESSAGE   3 SATELLITETV
6 CALCULATOR
8 MP3PLAYER
7 LAPTOP
15 CAMCORDER
16 MOBILEPHONE

10 UPGRADE
12 STEREO
13 P

B

1   2 GAMESCONSOL   3 SIMCARD
4 DIGITALCAMERA   6 C
8 ...PLAYER   9 CHARGER
5 DIGITALRADIO
14 RINGTONE   15 RADIO
16
11 DOWNLOAD
17 HANDSET

6.2 FIND SOMEBODY WHO...

Find somebody in the class who ...

	NAME	MORE INFORMATION
... thinks they'll go to university in the future.		
... is going to learn to drive soon.		
... might go to the cinema on Saturday night.		
... thinks they'll stay at home tonight.		
... is going to have a lie-in on Saturday.		
... is going to get a part-time job soon.		
... may watch a DVD tonight.		
... might go to a friend's house after this lesson.		
... is going to do some sport today.		
... thinks they'll get married before they're twenty-five.		
... may spend some time living abroad in the future.		
... is going to have a birthday soon.		

7.1 HOW WELL DO YOU KNOW YOUR COUNTRY?

1 Complete the sentences about your country with *must*, *mustn't* or *needn't*.

IN MY COUNTRY

(1) You _____ use a mobile phone while driving a car.

(2) You _____ buy alcohol if you are under eighteen.

(3) You _____ switch off your mobile phone in the theatre.

(4) You _____ go to school or university after the age of eighteen.

(5) You _____ have a licence if you have a dog.

(6) You _____ buy cigarettes if you are under eighteen.

(7) Men _____ get married if they are under twenty-one.

(8) Adults _____ vote in a general election.

(9) You _____ wear a helmet if you ride a motorbike.

(10) You _____ smoke in offices.

(11) You _____ do military service.

(12) You _____ ride in the front of a car if you are under twelve.

2 Which of these rules do you agree with and which do you disagree with? Compare ideas with a partner.

7.2 **INTERNATIONAL BODY LANGUAGE**

STUDENT A   (International Body Language)

1   Read the text and then answer questions 1–6.

Hand gestures are a very important form of communication, especially when people don't speak the same language. Some gestures have the same meaning around the world. But other gestures have a special meaning in a culture that might be different from other cultures. Here are two examples.

 This is called a *thumbs up* sign. We think this sign came from gladiator fights in ancient Rome. The gladiator who won the fight could decide about the future of the gladiator who lost. We now know that the thumbs up sign meant 'kill him' so it didn't have a positive meaning at all.

Nobody really knows where the thumbs up gesture came from but in most parts of the world it means 'everything's OK', except if you are in Sardinia or Greece or the Middle East, where it is very rude.

 This gesture is known as an *eye pull*. In France, when a person points at their eye like this, it means 'I don't believe you'.

In Japan, it is a rude gesture that children sometimes use at the same time as sticking out their tongue at each other. It can also mean 'I'm bored'. In Italy and Spain it means 'Be careful'. It is used as a warning.

2   Now ask Student B questions a–f.

1 What does this mean in most of the world? 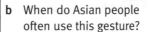	**4** What does this mean in France?	**a** What does this mean in the USA? 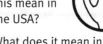	**d** What does this mean in the USA?
2 Is this polite in Greece?	**5** Is this polite in Japan?	**b** When do Asian people often use this gesture?	**e** What does it mean in France?
3 What did thumbs up mean in gladiator fights in ancient Rome?	**6** What does it mean in Spain?	**c** Where can the V sign be rude?	**f** What does it mean in Japan?

 ✂ -

STUDENT B   (International Body Language)

1   Read the text and then answer questions a–f.

Hand gestures are a very important form of communication, especially when people don't speak the same language. Some gestures have the same meaning around the world. But other gestures have a special meaning in a culture that might be different from other cultures. Here are two examples.

 This is called the *V sign*. It was originally a 'Victory' sign but nowadays, especially in the United States, it is a sign for peace. It started to become popular in the 1960s. There is a custom in Asia for people to do the V sign when they are in a photo. This is considered a friendly gesture.

In Britain a V sign with your palm facing you is very rude. Be careful when asking for two things not to make a rude gesture.

If you use this 'OK' sign in the United States and many parts of Europe it means that you like something. But if you do it in France it means 'zero' and gives the opposite message. In Brazil you must be especially careful because it is extremely rude.

In Japan this gesture is a signal for money. If you use it there, people might think you are asking for change in coins.

2   Now ask Student A questions 1–6.

a What does this mean in the USA?	**d** What does this mean in the USA? 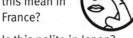	**1** What does this mean in most of the world?	**4** What does this mean in France?
b When do Asian people often use this gesture?	**e** What does it mean in France?	**2** Is this polite in Greece?	**5** Is this polite in Japan?
c Where can the V sign be rude?	**f** What does it mean in Japan?	**3** What did thumbs up mean in gladiator fights in ancient Rome?	**6** What does it mean in Spain?

8.1 MORAL DILEMMAS

If you thought that your boyfriend/ girlfriend was seeing someone else, would you check the text messages on his/her mobile phone?	If your parents went away for the weekend, would you have a party?	If you went to the cinema and somebody behind you was constantly talking during the film, would you tell them to be quiet?	If you saw somebody acting suspiciously on an aeroplane, would you tell the flight attendant?
If there was a piece of steak in your fridge that was two days past its sell-by date, would you eat it?	If you saw your friend's partner holding hands with someone else, would you tell your friend?	If someone gave you a book for your birthday, but you already had that book, would you tell them?	If you were having dinner at your friend's house and you were given a vegetable you didn't like, would you eat it?
If you were in a non-smoking part of a train and somebody lit a cigarette, would you say something to them?	If a shop assistant gave you too much change in a shop, would you give it back?	If your best friend bought a new top that made him/her look awful, would you tell him/her?	If your friend borrowed your camera, damaged it, and offered to pay for the repair, would you accept the money?
If you had missed the last bus home after a party and somebody offered you a lift, and you didn't know them very well, would you accept it?	If you saw a pair of shoes that you loved, but you knew they were made by a company that badly exploits its workers, would you buy them?	If you knew that your ten-year-old brother was smoking cigarettes, would you tell your parents?	If you saw a bird or other small animal that had been injured, would you kill it to 'put it out of its misery'?

8.2 WORD FORMATION – NOUN SUFFIXES

1 Look at these common suffixes that are used to make nouns.

-ment   -ness   -ty   -ion   -ing

Complete the tables below and mark the stress on the words.

Adjective	Noun
happy	
homeless	
ambitious	
similar	
weak	
poor	
rude	
global	
popular	

Verb	Noun
educate	
recycle	
pollute	
govern	
arrange	
spell	
produce	
employ	
improve	

2 Complete the sentences with a word from exercise 1. You will need to change the form of some of the words.

1 There are a lot of people sleeping on the streets. _____ is a big problem in this city.

2 There aren't many _____ between him and his sister. They're completely different.

3 You should always _____ your bottles and newspapers, instead of putting them in the bin.

4 Do you think money brings _____?

5 We made an _____ to meet at the café at 7p.m.

6 The company _____ 600 staff.

7 Do you think there has been an _____ in your English this year?

8 The factory _____ cat food.

9 He is a very _____ politician. He wants to be Prime Minister one day.

10 Can I borrow your dictionary? I want to check the _____ of a word.

11 This tea is very _____ . There's too much water in it.

12 There are so many advantages of travelling by bicycle. It's cheap, it's easy to park and most importantly, it doesn't cause _____ .

9.1 THE O.A.P. SHOPLIFTER

STUDENT A

Mutual dictation

(The O.A.P. shoplifter)

1 Work with Student B and take it in turns to dictate your sentences to each other. You read out a sentence and your partner writes it down. Don't look at Student B's worksheet.

a An eighty-year-old shoplifter tried to escape arrest …

b _____

c Gilles Durand attacked the policeman who …

d _____

e by biting a policeman before he realised that …

f _____

g had tried to bite the police officer several times but …

h _____

i But instead of biting the police officer's arms …

j _____

k he was only able to leave a wet mark from his mouth.

2 Now put the sentences in order to make a true story about a shoplifter.

1 _a_ 2 __ 3 __ 4 __ 5 __ 6 __ 7 __ 8 __ 9 __ 10 __ 11 __

✂ --

STUDENT B

Mutual dictation

(The O.A.P. shoplifter)

1 Work with Student A and take it in turns to dictate your sentences to each other. You read out a sentence and your partner writes it down. Don't look at Student A's worksheet. Student A begins.

a _____

b had stolen a box of CDs.

c _____

d hadn't caused him any harm.

e _____

f Police spokesman Jean-Claude Rousseau said the pensioner …

g _____

h caught the man as he ran out of an electrical shop in Marseilles after he …

i _____

j he had left his false teeth at home.

k _____

2 Now put the sentences in order to make a true story about a shoplifter.

1 _a_ 2 __ 3 __ 4 __ 5 __ 6 __ 7 __ 8 __ 9 __ 10 __ 11 __

(9.2) CRIME QUESTIONNAIRE

1 Tick (✓) the column that describes your opinion.

1 = agree strongly   2 = agree   3 = it depends   4 = disagree   5 = disagree strongly

Your opinion	1	2	3	4	5
Capital punishment is the only solution for some crimes.					
Prison does more damage than good.					
There is more crime nowadays than in the past.					
Parents should never hit their children.					
Violent films and computer games cause violent crime.					
Some people are born bad.					
It should be against the law to throw chewing gum in the street.					
Children who commit crimes should leave their family and live in a special centre for young criminals.					
It should be illegal for companies to sell tobacco.					
Everybody should own a gun for self-defence.					

2 Now compare your answers with your group. Give reasons for your opinions. Write notes to prepare your ideas.

_____

_____

_____

_____

_____

_____

_____

_____

_____

_____

_____

_____

10.1 GENERAL KNOWLEDGE QUIZ

STUDENT A

Make questions using the passive. Then ask your partner.

1 How many people / born / every second?
   a 1   b 3   c 5
   Correct answer: b

2 When / text messaging / invent?
   a 1975   b 1985   c 1995
   Correct answer: c

3 When / Diet Coke / produce / for the first time?
   a 1962   b 1972   c 1982
   Correct answer: c

4 How many cups of tea / drink / per person per day / in the UK?
   a 2   b 3   c 5
   Correct answer: b

5 When penicillin / discover?
   a 1928   b 1935   c 1948
   Correct answer: a

6 When / the first *Harry Potter* book / publish?
   a 1996   b 1997   c 1998
   Correct answer: b

7 In which country / the most chocolate / eat / per person?
   a USA   b Belgium   c Switzerland
   Correct answer: c

8 In which country / chewing gum / ban?
   a Sweden   b Singapore   c Thailand
   Correct answer: b

9 Where / the 1998 World Cup / hold?
   a France   b Brazil   c Japan/South Korea
   Correct answer: a

10 When / the Internet / use / for the first time?
   a 1960   b 1969   c 1975
   Correct answer: b

✂ -

STUDENT B

Make questions using the passive. Then ask your partner.

1 In which city / the 1992 Olympics / hold ?
   a Athens   b Sydney   c Barcelona
   Correct answer: c

2 Where / sandwiches / eat / for the first time ?
   a England   b France   c The USA
   Correct answer: a

3 When / J.F. Kennedy / elect / as President?
   a 1959   b 1960   c 1963
   Correct answer: b

4 How many text messages / send / every year in the UK?
   a 2 billion   b 3 billion   c 6 billion
   Correct answer: b

5 Which language / speak / by most people in the world?
   a English   b Spanish   c Chinese
   Correct answer: c

6 When / the Mona Lisa / steal / from the Louvre?
   a 1911   b 1935   c 1964
   Correct answer: a

7 When / America / discover?
   a 1452   b 1472   c 1492
   Correct answer: c

8 When / Charles Dickens / born?
   a 1812   b 1852   c 1892
   Correct answer: a

9 When / the Eiffel Tower / build?
   a 1817-19   b 1887-9   c 1923-5
   Correct answer: b

10 Where / football / play / for the first time?
   a Britain   b Ancient Rome   c Ancient Greece
   Correct answer: a

10.2 WHAT'S THE DIFFERENCE?

a playwright and a novelist	*to steal* and *to rob*	a best-seller and a paperback	a bakery and a butcher's shop
to wave and *to wink*	*impatient* and *unfriendly*	*can't help* and *don't mind*	*loyal* and *confident*
to cheer and *to cheat*	a field and a hedge	*stressful* and *exciting*	a traffic light and a street lamp
across and *over*	*famine* and *homelessness*	a soap opera and a quiz show	*P.S.* and *R.S.V.P.*
gripping and *scary*	a necklace and earrings	an MP3 player and a portable CD player	*to bow* and *to nod*
terrorism and racism	*to borrow* and *to lend*	a shoplifter and a vandal	*terrific* and *terrified*